TURNING POINTS
2000

Educating Adolescents in the 21st Century

TURNING POINTS
2000

Educating Adolescents in the 21st Century

Anthony W. Jackson and Gayle A. Davis

with
Maud Abeel and Anne Bordonaro

Foreword by David A. Hamburg, M.D.

A REPORT OF CARNEGIE CORPORATION OF NEW YORK

Teachers College
Columbia University
New York and London

Photos were supplied by the National Middle School Association

Published by Teachers College Press, 1234 Amsterdam Avenue, New York, NY 10027

Library of Congress Cataloging-in-Publication Data

Jackson, Anthony (Anthony Wells)
    Turning points 2000 : educating adolescents in the 21st century / Anthony W. Jackson and Gayle A. Davis ; with Maud Abeel and Anne Bordonaro ; foreword by David A. Hamburg.
        p. cm.
    Includes bibliographical references (p.   ) and index.
    ISBN 0-8077-3997-9 (cloth : alk. paper) — ISBN 0-8077-3996-0 (pbk. : alk. paper)
    1. School improvement programs—United States.   2. Middle school students—United States.   3. Teenagers—Education—United States.   I. Title: Turning points two thousand.   II. Davis, Gayle Andrews.   III. Abeel, Maud.   IV. Bordonaro, Anne.   V. Carnegie Council on Adolescent Development. Task Force on Education of Young Adolescents. Turning ponts.   VI. Title.
    LB2822.82 .J23 2000
    373.18'0973—dc21   00-044333

ISBN 0-8077-3996-0 (paper)
ISBN 0-8077-3997-9 (cloth)

Printed on acid-free paper
Manufactured in the United States of America

07   06   05   04   03   02   01   00   8   7   6   5   4   3   2

To

NORWEETA and **SARAH**—AWJ

and

BRYANT and **JACKSON**—GAD

Contents

Foreword

Photo by Bob Durell

GROWING UP IN THE United States includes a landmark event in which the young person moves from a primary, small, intimate environment to a secondary, large, impersonal environment. Children pass this landmark when they make the transition from elementary school to middle grades school—to junior high school or middle school. This usually means a change from a small neighborhood school, where the student spends most of the day in one primary classroom with the same teacher and classmates, to a larger, more impersonal institution, farther from home, with many different classes and teachers. This transition occurs at the same time that most adolescents are experiencing rapid physical, emotional, and cognitive changes.

There is a crucial need to help adolescents at this early age to acquire a durable basis for self-esteem, flexible and inquiring minds, reliable and close human relationships, a sense of belonging in a valued group, and a way of being useful beyond one's self. They need to find constructive expression for their inherent curiosity and exploratory energy, as well as a basis for making informed, deliberate decisions—especially on matters that have large and perhaps lifelong consequences, such as education and health.

Schools and related institutions must provide the building blocks of adolescent development and preparation for adult life. Yet most American middle grades schools have for decades been unable to meet the developmental needs of young adolescents. These institutions have the potential to make a powerfully beneficial impact on the development of their students, yet they were largely ignored as the educational reform movement ignited in the 1980s.

Carnegie Corporation of New York established the Carnegie Council on Adolescent Development in 1986 to place the compelling challenges of the adolescent years higher on the nation's agenda. In 1987, as its first major commitment, the council established a Task Force on Education of Young Adolescents under the chairmanship of David W. Hornbeck, former Maryland superintendent of schools and a nationally recognized leader in education. Members were drawn from leadership positions in education, research, government, health, and other sectors. The task force commissioned research papers and interviewed experts in relevant fields. It met with teachers, principals, health professionals, and leaders of youth-serving community organizations. It examined firsthand promising new approaches to fostering the education and healthy development of young adolescents.

The result was a groundbreaking report, *Turning Points: Preparing American Youth for the 21st Century*. Published in 1989, it strengthened an emerging movement then largely unrecognized by policymakers, building support for educating young adolescents through new relationships among schools, families, and community institutions, including those concerned with health.

Adolescents make choices that have fateful consequences both in the short term and for the rest of their lives—choices affecting their health, their education, and the people they will become. The recommendations of the original *Turning Points* report address this challenge in middle grades schools, while recognizing that the schools cannot do what needs doing in the new century without cooperation from other institutions. Here is a brief overview of the recommendations:

- Large middle grades schools should be divided into smaller communities for learning so each student will receive sustained individual attention.
- Middle grades schools should transmit a core of common, substantial knowledge to all students in ways that foster curiosity, problem solving, and critical thinking.
- Middle grades schools should be organized to ensure success for virtually all students by utilizing cooperative learning and other techniques suitable for this developmental phase.
- Teachers and principals, not distant administrative or political organizations, should have major responsibility and authority to transform middle grades schools.
- Teachers for the middle grades should be specifically prepared to teach young adolescents and be recognized distinctively for this accomplishment.

- Schools should be environments for health promotion, with particular emphasis on the life sciences and their applications; the education and health of young adolescents must be inextricably linked.
- Families should be allied with school staff in a spirit of mutual respect with ample opportunities for joint effort.
- Schools should be partners with various kinds of community organizations in educating young adolescents, including involving them in the experience of carefully considered service learning.

The recommendations in *Turning Points* called for action by people in several main sectors of American society and at all levels of government. The report showed how these groups, working together, could accomplish a fundamental upgrading of education to meet the needs of adolescent development.

In the intervening decade, *Turning Points* has elicited extraordinary nationwide interest and has helped to focus thoughtful attention as never before on the badly neglected subject of early adolescence. The approach taken in this original report and its follow-up activities not only seeks basic improvement of the middle grades school—the pivotal institution of early adolescence—but aims to facilitate the personal development of these young people in and out of school. The reformulation of middle grades schools along the lines recommended in *Turning Points* can improve the life chances of youth from many backgrounds, including those from poor communities.

Dr. Anthony Jackson, who was the principal author of *Turning Points*, led a Carnegie Corporation team in a decade-long follow-up effort, the Middle Grade School State Policy Initiative (MGSSPI), to foster adoption of the recommendations, assess the implementation of these recommendations, and determine the nature and extent of any benefits associated with implementation. Dr. Gayle Davis was the national director of the MGSSPI and worked on the initiative for nearly eight years. *Turning Points 2000* draws on the lessons learned from the MGSSPI and from several other national middle grades improvement efforts and on the latest research. What follows is a brief statement of some essential points of this book.

Turning Points 2000 is an in-depth examination of how to improve middle grades education. The original *Turning Points* provided a valuable framework for middle grades education that resonated deeply with practitioners. *Turning Points 2000* provides much more "flesh on the bone" to guide practitioners in their efforts to implement the model.

The book combines the most up-to-date research with what has been learned from the follow-up Middle Grade School State Policy Initiative and other middle grades school improvement efforts—a blend of wisdom from practice and data from systematic research. The research base on education reform has grown considerably in recent years, and this book incorporates the findings of that research. In drawing heavily on the best available research, *Turning Points 2000* helps to bridge the gap between researchers and practitioners, putting practitioners in touch with research in the framework of a comprehensive and comprehensible model.

Turning Points 2000 places strong emphasis on curriculum, student assessment, and instruction. It shows how changes in school organizational structures (schools-within-schools, teams, and so on), which have been the hallmark of middle grades education reform thus far, are necessary but not sufficient for major improvement in academic achievement. These structural changes must be accompanied by substantial improvement in teaching and learning.

Turning Points rightly drew attention to the need for specialized pre-service (undergraduate and graduate) training to teach young adolescents well, but had less to say about the need for continuous, high-quality professional development of teachers. *Turning Points 2000* adds a section on what constitutes high-quality professional development.

Turning Points 2000 builds on the implicit notion within *Turning Points* that various aspects of middle grades education—like curriculum, instruction, organizational structures, health education and services, and parent involvement—can be usefully thought of as design elements of a system. This new book makes clear that changes in one element of the system influence other elements in the system. Schoolwide improvement ultimately requires considerable change in all these elements.

Finally, *Turning Points 2000* combines an emphasis on developing young adolescents' intellectual capacities with opportunities to meet their emotional and interpersonal needs. This broad, research-based view of middle grades education in the context of adolescent development should be of great use to teachers and all others deeply concerned with the future of our young people.

In short, this book is a milestone on the long road to excellence in education for all adolescents.

David A. Hamburg, M.D.
President Emeritus
Carnegie Corporation of New York

Preface

SOME TEN YEARS AGO, Carnegie Corporation of New York published what was to become a landmark on the road toward reform of the education of young adolescents. The Corporation followed the release of *Turning Points: Preparing American Youth for the 21st Century* with an ambitious decade-long program of grants to states and cities to promote the application of the report's recommendations. Some 225 systemic change schools nationwide implemented Turning Points–based reforms through the Corporation's Middle Grade School State Policy Initiative (MGSSPI), and many other middle grades schools adopted similar and complementary measures.

As experience with the effect of the reforms grew, and as research into middle grades education continued, it became clear to us that the progress made since the publication of the original *Turning Points* warranted examination and analysis. We believed that such an effort would produce a new understanding of what works and what doesn't, an understanding based on actual experience, rather than on theory or anecdote.

With the support of Carnegie Corporation, we set off in 1996 on a journey that has brought us to this book. Along the way, we visited middle grades schools in several states; convened focus groups and conferences; conducted face-to-face or telephone interviews with nearly 200 teachers and principals; consulted with teachers, administrators, students, and parents, as well as with academic experts; undertook an exhaustive literature search; and commissioned background papers when we found the existing literature wanting.

Our goal was to integrate what is known from education research and practice within a coherent approach toward adolescent education that educators can use in their own efforts to transform middle grades schools. Over the past ten years, education research has made enormous strides in documenting "what works" to improve outcomes for students. There are few channels, however, for this information to reach middle grades educators. *Turning Points 2000* attempts to bridge that gap.

The voices of teachers and principals in middle grades schools are the other major source of information for this work. From them we learned first-hand what really makes a difference in the quality of implementation of *Turning Points* recommendations. While most of the examples of practice used throughout this book are drawn from MGSSPI schools, we also gathered information from school- and program-level leaders of several other important school reform initiatives focused wholly or in part on middle schools. Some of these initiatives predate the MGSSPI—for example, the School Development Program founded in 1968 by James Comer at the Yale Child Study Center; the Accelerated Schools Project launched at Stanford University by Henry Levin in 1986; the Middle Grades Improvement Program begun in 1987 in Indiana by the Lilly Endowment under the direction of Joan Lipsitz; and the Edna McConnell Clark Foundation's Program for Student Achievement, which began in 1989 as the Program for Disadvantaged Youth, directed by M. Hayes Mizell.

We also draw on the experience of schools from other key initiatives, including two that began in 1994: the W. K. Kellogg Foundation's Middle Start initiative, directed by Leah Meyer Austin; and the Talent Development Middle School model, directed by Douglas Mac Iver at Johns Hopkins University's Center for Research on the Education of Students Placed At Risk.

Each of these initiatives has its own programmatic goals and areas of emphasis in its approach to middle grades reform. Yet a great deal of overlap provides common ground for extending our knowledge about what is needed to transform today's middle grades schools into tomorrow's high-performance learning environments. These initiatives and new ones to come do not represent "competing" approaches to middle grades reform; rather, they are much-needed alternative approaches that provide schools and districts with choices that will all lead to a critical common goal: vastly improved student performance.

Finally, this book also draws on work in schools of the recently established Turning Points National Design Center at the Center for Collaborative Education (CCE) in Boston. The center, headed by the former director of Massachusetts's MGSSPI initiative, Daniel French, is an approved New American Schools design center.

We describe what *has* happened in the 1990s in order to envision, in considerable detail, what *can* happen in middle grades education in the 21st century. We intend to give both practical guidance and a sustaining vision to middle grades educators as they continue their journey toward high-achieving, equitable, and developmentally responsive schools. Our hope is that *Turning Points 2000* will be helpful to middles grades educators, policymakers, parents, and community members as they pursue change on behalf of young adolescents, no matter what specific pathway to reform they choose to take.

Acknowledgments

W E COULD NOT HAVE written this book without the help of a great many people, and we are grateful to everyone who played a role. We hope that we have not left anyone out, but if we have, we add our apologies to our thanks.

We are grateful for the encouragement and support of our colleagues at Carnegie Corporation of New York. David A. Hamburg, the president of the Corporation from 1984 to 1997, was a constant inspiration; his tireless leadership on behalf of America's children set a standard that we have tried to match, and we thank him for his commitment to this project. His successor as president, Vartan Gregorian, enabled us to complete the *Turning Points 2000* project, and we are grateful for his support. We thank Vivien Stewart, former chair of the Corporation's Education Division, and Michael Levine, deputy chair of the Education Division and senior program officer, who provided critical leadership in guiding this effort to fruition. We also thank Sara K. Wolpert for help in keeping the project on track.

The staff of the Corporation's library went beyond the call of duty to answer our countless questions, search out and acquire the most obscure documents, and clear away the mysteries of bibliographic citation and the World Wide Web. We thank Ron Sexton, supervisor of records/librarian, and Gladys McQueen, records associate, for their invaluable assistance.

Anne McKissick and Loretta Munford, the Corporation's IT gurus, kept our computers running and our files safe. We thank Maude Darucaud-Bates, Jose Rivera, Jared Butt, and Cynthia Centeno, as well.

Throughout the development of this book, the project directors of the Middle Grade School State Policy Initiative (MGSSPI) provided their support, advice, and targeted recommendations of schools and people we should investigate. We extend our thanks to the MGSSPI directors: Danny Barnett of Arkansas; Peggy Burke and Dan French of Boston, Massachusetts; Thaddeus Dumas and Mary Ann Overton of California; Elaine Andrus of Colorado; Richard Lappert of Connecticut; Clifton Hutton of Delaware; Xavier Botana, Deborah Kasak, and Paul Kren of Illinois; Judy Johnson and Ron Klemp of Los Angeles; Antoinette Favazza and Eileen Oickle of Maryland; Dorothy Earle and Priscilla (Pam) Spagnoli of Massachusetts; Walter "Jake" Henderson and Don Kelly of New Mexico; Ken Jewell and David Payton of New York; John Backes, Gaylynn Becker, and Pat Herbel of North Dakota; Andrea Barrientos of Puerto Rico; Diane Devine and Ken Fish of Rhode Island; Ruth Earls, Baron Holmes, and Caroline Lindler of South Carolina; Bob Brundrett, Evelyn Hiatt, and Coila Morrow of Texas; and Tim Flynn of Vermont.

Many individuals contributed to the research, drafting, and reviews that went into this book. We are grateful for the contributions of our consultants: Sandee Brawarsky, Peggy Burke, Karin Chenoweth, Thomas S. Dickinson, Robin Epstein, James Fenwick, Melinda Fine, Matthew Franck, Dan French, Stephanie Hirsh, Joellen P. Killion, Ron Klemp, Richard Lappert, C. Kenneth McEwin, Jennifer O'Neal, Glenda Partee, and Anne Wheelock. We also thank our chapter reviewers Judy Carr, Yolanda Cortez, Bill Eyman, William Kane, Frank Lillo, Douglas Mac Iver, Erlinda Martinez, Jay McTighe, Coila Morrow, Marion Payne, Richard Raiche, and Craig Spilman for their suggestions, corrections, and insights. We especially appreciate the contributions of Joan Lipsitz, Carol Midgley, and Michelle Cahill, who read the entire manuscript and helped us to see things more clearly and make things better; any shortcomings that may remain are our responsibility, not theirs. Kenji Hakuda, Judith Irvin, Margaret J. McLaughlin, and Sam Stringfield responded to our requests for help with vital data and sharply focused expertise, as did Leah Meyer Austin, Steve Mertens, Nancy Flowers, and Peter Mulhall.

We also thank the hundreds of principals, teachers, administrators, and students in middle grades schools across the country who took the time to speak with us as we conducted the research that underlies this book. Without them, this book could not have been written.

We cannot thank Maud Abeel and Anne Bordonaro enough for their major intellectual contribution to this work as primary researchers and contributing authors. If this book flies, they gave it wings. Sue Merritt's research prowess and Reaksia Banks's organizational skills proved indispensable to our efforts to complete the book. Roz Rosenberg's and Beth Monroe's amazing capacity to create order from chaos, and their unflagging optimism, added enormously to the project. We offer our deep appreciation to our editor extraordinaire, Jeannette Aspden, whose skill, dedication, and wisdom are reflected on every page.

Finally, we would like to express our gratitude to our families for sustaining us over the long haul with words of encouragement, gentle humor, and pats on the back when we needed them most. Our special thanks to Norweeta Milburn, Sarah Jackson, and Margaret Jackson; and to Bryant and Jackson Davis, Bob and Nancy Andrews, and the entire Hill family: Jenny, Harold, Silas, and Caris.

1

Turning Points: A Decade Later

T HE MOVEMENT TO ESTABLISH a distinctive form of education for young
adolescents—the middle school movement—reflects the grassroots genius
of American educators. It is the response of visionary and caring teachers,
administrators, and parents to the unique mix of evolving capacities and emerging needs that epitomizes middle grades students.

Over three decades, the movement to develop schools responsive to young
adolescents has made great strides: as Paul S. George told middle grades educators in 1999, "The middle school movement is . . . the most successful grassroots
movement in American educational history" (p. 3). The 1989 publication by
Carnegie Corporation's Council on Adolescent Development of *Turning Points:
Preparing American Youth for the 21st Century* was a milestone in the course of that
movement. It is the thesis of this book, however, that a great deal more is possible, as well as necessary.

In 1986, Carnegie Corporation of New York established the Carnegie
Council on Adolescent Development (CCAD) to "place the compelling chal-

lenges of the adolescent years higher on the nation's agenda" (1989, p. 13). In 1987, the council in turn established the Task Force on Education of Young Adolescents, a distinguished group of educators, researchers, government officials, and media leaders, to examine firsthand the conditions of America's 10- to 15-year-olds and identify promising approaches to improving their education and promoting their healthy development.

In its investigation, the Task Force found early adolescence to be a period of enormous opportunity for intellectual and emotional growth, yet one fraught with vulnerability and risk. The pressures facing young adolescents are indeed formidable, but so, too, is the capacity of many young adolescents to negotiate this period of intense biological, psychological, and interpersonal change successfully. Too often, though, the main educational institution serving young adolescents—the middle grades school—falls far short of meeting the educational and social needs of millions of students. "Middle grade schools—junior high, intermediate, or middle schools—are potentially society's most powerful force to recapture millions of youth adrift. Yet all too often they exacerbate the problems that youth face. A volatile mismatch exists between the organization and curriculum of middle grades schools, and the intellectual, emotional, and interpersonal needs of young adolescents" (CCAD, 1989, p. 32).

In 1989 the Task Force produced its groundbreaking report, *Turning Points: Preparing American Youth for the 21st Century*, which provided a comprehensive approach to educating young adolescents. Drawing on the most effective middle grades practice and the best available research, the report urged a radical transformation of standard educational practices deemed developmentally inappropriate for children just entering the teenage years. *Turning Points* offered eight essential principles for improving middle grades education:

- Large middle grades schools are divided into smaller communities for learning.
- Middle grades schools teach a core of common knowledge to all students.
- Middle grades schools are organized to ensure success for all students.
- Teachers and principals have the major responsibility and power to make decisions about young adolescents' schooling.
- Middle grades schools are staffed by teachers who are experts at teaching young adolescents.
- Schools promote good health; the education and health of young adolescents are inextricably linked.
- Families are allied with school staff through mutual respect, trust, and communication.
- Schools and communities are partners in educating young adolescents.

In Chapter 2, we offer a new set of recommendations, recommendations that grow out of these original Turning Points principles while reflecting lessons learned in the decade since *Turning Points* was published.

Summarizing its intent, the Task Force wrote in *Turning Points* (p. 36):

> The middle grade school proposed here is profoundly different from many schools today. It focuses squarely on the characteristics and needs of young adolescents. It creates a community of adults and young people embedded in networks of support and responsibility that enhance the commitment of students to learning. In partnership with youth-serving and community organizations, it offers multiple sites and multiple methods for fostering the learning and health of adolescents. The combined efforts create a community of shared purpose among those concerned that all young adolescents are prepared for productive adult lives, especially those at risk of being left behind.

In the decade since *Turning Points* was published, nearly 100,000 copies of the full report and over 200,000 copies of the executive summary have been disseminated, and demand for the report continues. Few reports on education reform have been as widely read, and we believe it is instructive to consider why this is so. First, the Task Force itself was highly credible. Chaired by former Maryland superintendent of schools David W. Hornbeck, a nationally recognized leader in education who later became superintendent of schools in Philadelphia, this group of scholars and expert practitioners brought a rigorous, independent perspective to middle grades education.

Turning Points' popularity also reflects its deep resonance with the experience of millions of middle grades educators and others concerned about young adolescents' academic achievement and healthy development. Because it drew heavily on research and best practices, the report gave voice to a long-established community of middle grades scholars and advocates who had not received the national attention that both the importance of their cause and the depth of their insight deserved. In her aptly titled book *Growing Up Forgotten*, Joan Lipsitz (1980, p. xv), a leader in that community, summarized the lack of attention devoted to 10- to 15-year-olds, noting, "We have been startled by the extent to which this age group is underserved."

A third, critically important reason for *Turning Points'* broad dissemination is the content and organization of the report itself. Put simply, *Turning Points* helps make sense of middle grades education. It provides one of the first "whole-school" models of what high-quality education for young adolescents "looks like" in a way that allows reform-minded educators to conduct an orderly analysis of where they are and where they want to go. Much of the value and appeal of *Turning Points* thus lies in its portrayal of the middle grades school as a comprehensible system of interrelated elements, each of which is amenable to improvement. Taken together, these elements offer the promise of vastly more powerful learning environments for young adolescents.

TURNING POINTS AND MIDDLE GRADES SCHOOL REFORM

Has *Turning Points* made good on its promise? Given its broad dissemination, has it changed middle grades teaching and learning? Clearly, the report accelerated a number of trends that were already in the making. For example, although *Turning Points* does not recommend a particular grade configuration for the middle grades school, its support of many accepted middle school concepts and practices has fueled "a meteoric rise of the 'middle school' organizational pattern of 5–8 and 6–8 and the demise of the 7–9 'junior high' pattern." These trends suggest that "middle level education of the nineties is more focused on programs designed to meet the needs of young adolescents" (Valentine & Whitaker, 1997, p. 278).

Shifts in schools' grade configuration have often been accompanied by changes in organizational structures, such as the development of teacher and student teams and the creation of "advisory" programs, practices that were both advocated in *Turning Points.* By the early nineties, most middle-level schools had implemented teacher and student teams, up from 33 percent in 1989 to 57 percent in 1992, and had increased the amount of common planning for teachers, another key *Turning Points* recommendation (Arhar, 1997, p. 50). Overall, a comprehensive review of research on changes in middle-level practice and their impact concluded that "since 1989, *Turning Points* has been the catalyst for development of both components and blueprints for designing and implementing bona fide middle schools throughout the United States" (Hough, 1997, pp. 288–289).

What has happened in individual or groups of middle schools that have attempted comprehensive implementation of *Turning Points* recommendations? Early results from a study of a group of 31 Illinois middle schools conducted by Robert D. Felner and his colleagues at the University of Rhode Island are encouraging. As the schools involved in the study implemented more of *Turning Points'* recommended practices and did so with greater fidelity, their students' scores on standardized tests of mathematics, language arts, and reading achievement increased significantly. Students in the most advanced schools, which had adopted greater curriculum integration and changes in instructional and assessment strategies, achieved mean scores of 298 in mathematics, 315 in language, and 275 in reading, compared to a statewide mean of 250. Felner and his colleagues also found that as schools increase the quality of implementation, student behavioral problems decline and indices of socioemotional adjustment improve (Felner et al., 1997, pp. 543–544).

Similar results were obtained in an evaluation of the 26 Massachusetts schools in the state's Middle Grade Systemic Change Network, which used *Turning Points* as the basis for their reform efforts. The Change Network accounted for most of the middle schools participating in the Education Reform Restructuring Network (ERRN), a larger statewide school reform initiative involving elementary, middle, and high schools. ERRN middle schools had the highest gains on the Massachusetts Educational Assessment Program (MEAP) of all the schools participating in ERRN. "It is particularly encouraging that . . . the improvements that are occurring can be seen at both the low and the high end of the proficiency scales" (DePascale, 1997, p. 14). These schools had increases well above the state norm in the use of effective instructional approaches, including the use of math manipulatives and extended writing assignments, and eighth-grade students were taking algebra at a significantly higher rate than the state average.

Through the W. K. Kellogg Foundation's Middle Start initiative, a group of 20 Michigan schools received grant funds to pursue middle grades improvement efforts. According to data collected by the Center for Prevention Research and Development at the University of Illinois, compared to a group of over 125 Michigan middle grades schools that did not receive support to pursue comprehensive school improvements, grant schools showed dramatic gains in seventh-grade reading scores (+10 percent) and substantial gains in seventh-grade math scores (+6 percent) from 1994–1995 to 1996–1997 on state achievement tests (Mertens, Flowers, & Mulhall, 1998). Nongrant schools improved by 4 percent in both reading and mathematics over the two-year period.

These findings suggest that key elements of middle grades education have proliferated over the past decade and that we have learned a great deal about what affects student outcomes positively. Significant progress has been made in the journey to provide young adolescents with a developmentally responsive education. However, we are only halfway up the mountain, with the most important and perhaps most difficult part of the climb remaining. If the vision of a high-quality middle grades education for all young adolescents is to become a reality, the depth and breadth of change in schools must increase, and that change must extend to schools serving the highest concentrations of low-performing students. The "summit" for middle grades education in the 21st century is excellence in student outcomes and equity in their distribution.

Structural changes in middle grades education—how students and teachers are organized for learning—have been fairly widespread and have produced good results. Research indicates that the adoption of middle grades structures has improved relationships within schools and that students are experiencing a greater sense of emotional well-being (Midgley & Edelin, 1998, p. 195). However, our observations suggest that relatively little has changed at the core of most students' school experience: curriculum, assessment, and instruction.

At the beginning of the next decade, we find that the conclusions reached by researchers in the early 1990s remain true: "Most middle grades classes emphasize passive learning and drill and practice in language arts basic skills, math computation, science facts, and facts of history. Most middle schools infrequently use active and interactive instructional approaches, including writing and editing, student team learning, and other cooperative learning methods, and technology in science and math" (Mac Iver & Epstein, 1993, p. 525). Moreover, recent international comparisons show that U.S. middle grades curriculum is often significantly less coherent, less focused, and less rigorous than the curriculum in other countries (Mac Iver, Mac Iver, Balfanz, Blank, & Ruby, in press, p. 5). Many middle schools are "warmer, happier and more peaceful places for students and adults . . . [yet most schools] have not moved off this plateau and taken the critical next step to develop students who perform well academically, with the intellectual wherewithal to improve their life conditions" (Lipsitz, Mizell, Jackson, & Austin, 1997, p. 535).

It is also clear that changes in middle grades practices have least often occurred where they are needed most: in high-poverty urban and rural communities where unacceptably poor student achievement is rampant. While many of the networks of reforming schools begun by foundations and other groups over the past decade have been concentrated in these areas, and pockets of brilliance have been developed, the middle school movement has much deeper roots in suburban and upper-income areas. The poor quality of middle grades education in America's cities means that up to half the students in our nation's largest cities are unable to make a successful transition to high school (Balfanz & Mac Iver, 2000).

Of course, the implementation of middle grades practices has not always gone smoothly in more affluent areas. In fact, as Jeannie Oakes and her colleagues have found, affluent parents at times mount the most strident resistance to *Turning Points* practices when they are seen as threatening to existing school programs in which their children have thrived (Oakes, Quartz, Ryan, & Lipton, 2000). Still, it is in low-income communities where significant changes in the education of adolescents are needed most.

Clearly, more empirical research is needed on the effect that the kind of practices called for in *Turning Points* have on student achievement and motivation, especially at the national level (Felner et al., 1997, p. 532; Urdan & Klein, 1998, p. 29). Nevertheless, the existing research suggests that when reforms are implemented with integrity, in a manner that leads to authentic change in curriculum, instruction, and assessment and in the organization and climate of the school, dramatic and lasting improvements in student performance can be obtained. When reforms are implemented in a limited or scattershot manner, however, as when changes in grade configuration and teacher and student grouping are not accompanied by substantial changes in teaching practices, improvement in student outcomes is more limited.

Turning Points provided a much-needed framework of principles and related practices that together form a powerful approach to middle grades education. Thousands of schools have used the report to begin their hopeful, arduous journey toward more powerful learning environments for young adolescents. Progress has been made, but there is much, much more ground to cover.

After ten years, we believe it is crucial to gather together and synthesize the lessons learned from these efforts, together with the most current research, to deepen the field's understanding of what it takes to improve young adolescents' academic performance and to foster healthy development. In this work, we seek to provide an in-depth, comprehensive analysis of what it takes to make the *Turning Points* framework applicable to practice, to put a great deal more "flesh on the bone," drawing both on the experiences of middle grades educators over the past decade and on advancements in research. This more detailed picture, we hope, will serve as both a guide and a challenge to middle grades reformers in the 21st century.

EARLY ADOLESCENCE: OPPORTUNITIES AND RISKS

Turning Points drew attention to early adolescence as a fascinating period of rapid physical, intellectual, and social change. It is the time when young people experience puberty, when growth and development is more rapid than during any other developmental stage except that of infancy. Dramatic physical changes are accompanied by the capacity to have sexual relations and to reproduce. It is a time, too, of emotional peaks and valleys, "of trial and error, of vulnerability to emotional hurt and humiliation, of anxiety and uncertainty that are sources of unevenness of emotions and behavior associated with the age" (CCAD, 1989, p. 21). Yet within the trials and tribulations of early adolescence are the opportunities to forge one's own identity, to learn new social roles, and to develop a personal code of ethics to guide one's own behavior.

Early adolescence is a time of discovery, when young people have significantly greater capacity for complex thinking. They are more able to be out in the world, to participate in a wider universe of activities. They are better equipped to make important decisions affecting themselves and others, but their lack of experience leaves them vulnerable. They are better able to fend for themselves, yet they are caught up almost daily in a vortex of new risks.

As it was a decade ago, early adolescence continues to be the time when many young people first experiment with tobacco, alcohol, and illicit drugs. In 1998, 52.5 percent of eighth graders reported having drunk alcohol, and 46 percent reported having smoked cigarettes (Johnston, O'Malley, & Bachman, 1999, Table 6-1d). In some instances, trends for young people's involvement in these risky behaviors have actually worsened during the 1990s. For example, between 1991 and 1998, the percentage of eighth-grade students who had tried any kind of illicit drug, including inhalants, increased from 29 percent to 38 percent (Johnston et al., 1999, Table 1a).

There is some good news in the area of teenage sexual activity and pregnancy. Compared to the early 1990s, fewer teenagers today are reporting having ever had sex: in 1997, 48 percent of teens reported having had sex, compared to 54 percent in 1991 (Centers for Disease Control and Prevention [CDC], n.d.). Among teens who are sexually active, more in 1997 reported using contraception than did similar youth in 1991, and more teens reported being educated about HIV (Alan Guttmacher Institute, 1998; CDC, n.d.). Pregnancy, birth, and abortion rates have all declined among teens since the early 1990s. Nevertheless, the United States still has by far the highest teenage birth rate among developed countries—more than double that of Britain, 6 times higher than Scandinavian countries, and 15 times higher than Japan (Annie E. Casey Foundation, 1998, pp. 10–11).

Besides risking unintended pregnancy, young people who are sexually active also run a grave risk of contracting sexually transmitted diseases. Every year 3 million teenagers—about one quarter of those who are sexually active—become infected with a sexually transmitted disease (Alan Guttmacher Institute, 1998).

Amid the stresses of early adolescence, entry into middle school can itself be troubling. For many young adolescents, the transition from elementary school to a less supportive middle school environment is associated with a decline in self-esteem. Students' sense of their ability to perform well in specific subject areas such as English and mathematics has also been shown to decline after the transition. These changes and other shifts in attitudes about school subjects that can dampen students' motivation to learn reflect a poor "fit" between the learning environment of a typical middle grades school and the intellectual and social needs of young adolescents (Midgley & Edelin, 1998, p. 196).

Clearly, early adolescence is a period of both enormous opportunities and enormous risks. Although many young people reach late adolescence healthy and ready for the challenges of high school and adult life, early adolescence for many others is the beginning of a downward spiral. *Turning Points* describes the dilemma of early adolescence, for the young people and for society, in the following way (CCAD, 1989, p. 20):

> Depending on family circumstances, household income, language, neighborhood, or the color of their skin, some of these young adolescents receive the education and support they need to develop self-respect, an active mind, and a healthy body. They will emerge from their teens as the promising youth who will become the scientists and entrepreneurs, the educators and the health care professionals, and the parents who will renew the nation. These are the thoughtful, responsible, caring, ethical, and robust young people the Task Force envisions. To them, society can entrust the future of the country with confidence.
>
> Under current conditions, however, far too many young people will not make the passage through early adolescence successfully. Their basic human needs—caring relationships with adults, guidance in facing sometimes overwhelming biological and psychological changes, the security of belonging to constructive peer groups, and the perception of future opportunity—go unmet at this critical stage of life. Millions of these young adolescents will never reach their full potential. . . . Early adolescence for these youth is a turning point towards a diminished future.

The trajectory of a young adolescent's life is not wholly determined by social and economic circumstances. The soundness of choices he or she makes and the guidance available to make good decisions are critically important. But many young people have few viable choices because the social institutions that are supposed to provide real and equal opportunities to them are woefully inadequate. Most distressing are the inadequacy of educational opportunities and the pervasiveness of underachievement that virtually guarantee a diminished future for millions of young people.

The National Assessment of Educational Progress (NAEP) measures American students' academic ability in reading, writing, mathematics, and other subjects. Scores on the tests are used to classify students as either below basic, basic, proficient, or advanced. The 1998 NAEP results for reading and writing tell a sad and disturbing story. Across the nation, only one-third of eighth-grade students performed at or above the proficient level in reading (Donahue, Voelkl, Campbell, & Mazzeo, 1999). On the writing test, just over a quarter of all students (27 percent) performed at or above the proficient mark (Greenwald, Persky, Campbell, & Mazzeo, 1999). In mathematics, the most recent NAEP data show that less than a quarter of American eighth graders perform at or above the proficient level, although there has been a significant improvement in performance since 1990 (Reese, Miller, Mazzeo, & Dossey, 1997).

The problems of inadequate academic preparation are greatly compounded for those young adolescents who are poor, members of racial or ethnic minorities, or recent immigrants (see Figure 1.1). These students routinely attend the weakest, most overcrowded, and most segregated schools that offer the fewest high-level courses. Performance is worst in urban schools serving high concentrations of poor students. In these schools, two-thirds or more of students perform below the basic level on national tests, "raising troubling questions about the future of the 11 million children (of all ages) who attend urban public schools" (Edwards, 1998, p. 3).

Comparisons of American middle grades students' academic performance with those of young adolescents across the world provide another equally disturbing perspective on the problem. In 1995, the International Association for the Evaluation of Educational Achievement sponsored the Third International Mathematics and Science Study (TIMSS). The study compared fourth- and eighth-grade students in 41 countries. Although U.S. students scored above the

Figure 1.1 Percentage of eighth graders scoring below basic achievement levels in reading, writing, mathematics, and science, by race and ethnicity

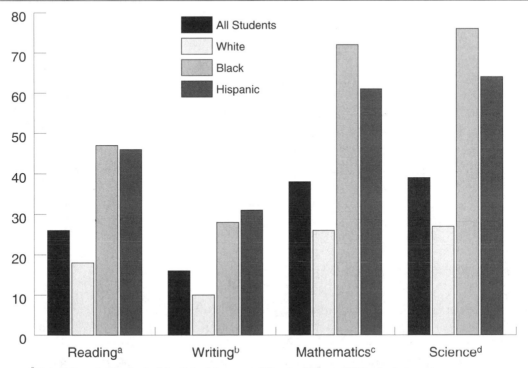

[a] National Center for Education Statistics, National Assessment of Educational Progress, 1998 Reading Assessment
[b] National Center for Education Statistics, National Assessment of Educational Progress, 1998 Writing Assessment
[c] National Center for Education Statistics, National Assessment of Educational Progress, 1996 Mathematics Assessment
[d] National Center for Education Statistics, National Assessment of Educational Progress, 1996 Science Assessment

international average in eighth-grade science, they outperformed just 15 of the other 40 countries. In mathematics, the United States scored below the international average, outperforming just 7 of the other 40 countries (Barton & Coley, 1998, p. 3). U.S. Secretary of Education Richard Riley summarized the findings:

> We don't build a firm foundation for our students in the middle school years. Other nations begin to introduce challenging concepts such as algebra, geometry, probability and statistics. So we shouldn't be surprised that by the twelfth grade, our students have fallen even further behind their counterparts abroad. How can we expect our students to test well in math and science internationally when we do not even ask them to take challenging courses and rigorous tests throughout their middle and high school careers? (National Center for Education Statistics, 1998a)

We may aspire to be a nation prepared for the technological challenges of the 21st century, but these recent NAEP and TIMSS data show that we are still far from that goal. A decade ago, Carnegie's Task Force on Education of Young Adolescents wrote,

> As a nation . . . we face a paradox of our own making. We have created an economy that seeks literate, technically trained, and committed workers, while simultaneously we produce many young men and women who are semi-literate or functionally illiterate, unable to think critically and untrained in technical skills, hampered by high-risk lifestyles, and alienated from the social mainstream. (CCAD, 1989, p. 29)

Today, on the threshold of a new millennium, the challenge has still not been met.

Like its predecessor, *Turning Points 2000* aims to help bridge the gap between current, unacceptable levels of intellectual development and a future in which every middle grades student meets or exceeds high academic standards and other key indicators of a successful school experience. We present a model of middle grades education that we believe has the potential to enable virtually all young adolescents to meet our highest expectations, if we have the will, the energy, and the devotion to equity and fairness required to transform our current institutions.

CORE VALUES OF *TURNING POINTS 2000*

What is the purpose of middle grades education? The question has an almost surreal quality—the purpose of an institution so central in the lives of millions of American adolescents should be obvious. Unfortunately, in the history of middle grades education, the purpose has at times become obscured.

Let us be clear. The main purpose of middle grades education is to promote young adolescents' intellectual development. It is to enable every student to think creatively, to identify and solve meaningful problems, to communicate and work well with others, and to develop the base of factual knowledge and skills that is the essential foundation for these "higher order" capacities. As they develop these capacities, every young adolescent should be able to meet or exceed high academic standards. Closely related goals are to help all students develop the capacity to lead healthful lives, physically and mentally; to become caring, compassionate, and tolerant individuals; and to become active, contributing citizens of the United States and the world. But above all else, and to enable all these other goals to be realized, middle grades schools must be about helping all students learn to use their minds well.

Some would argue that it is unnecessary to assert the primacy of intellectual development in middle grades education. We believe it is necessary. It is necessary because critics of middle grades schools will otherwise continue to assert—wrongly—that middle grades educators do not believe their students are capable of significant intellectual achievement or that they believe it is more important to help students successfully traverse the emotional vicissitudes inherent in this developmental stage.

Along with intellectual development, at the heart of our definition of "middle grades education" is the requirement for equity in outcomes for all groups of students, regardless of their race, ethnicity, gender, family income, or linguistic background. Schools with gaps in the rate at which different groups of students achieve are not successful middle schools. Schools where such gaps are being narrowed can certainly claim to be improving, to be "on the right track," and they should celebrate these critical benchmarks of progress. We do not mean to denigrate the efforts that have been made to improve middle grades education, but we do mean to say that improvement is a benchmark of progress, not the final goal.

Schools grounded in the Turning Points design are dedicated to excellence and equity and to being responsive to the developmental needs of all young adolescents. Where choices must be made about school organization, curriculum, student assessment, instructional methods, student grouping, or any other aspect of middle grades education, the Turning Points approach to middle grades education emphasizes practices that promote the greater good of every student over the enhancement of an elite few. But make no mistake: inherent in this approach is an abhorrence of mediocrity. The greater good of every student requires excellence as a common standard for performance.

The Turning Points values are reflected in the work of the National Forum to Accelerate Middle-Grades Reform, and we endorse the forum's vision (see Box 1.1).

Expectations of Success

Achieving such lofty goals for middle grades education means that educators must have high expectations for all students' success. Currently, such high expectations for all students do not exist among all middle grades teachers, among the parents of all middle grades students, or among all middle grades students themselves. In nearly 80 Michigan middle schools that surveyed students' aca-

Box 1.1 Vision Statement of the National Forum To Accelerate Middle-Grades Reform

The National Forum To Accelerate Middle-Grades Reform represents educators, researchers, professional organizations, and foundations. It works with middle-grades educators, policymakers, leaders in higher education, family and community members, and other stakeholders to identify and replicate successful practices, share resources, and create a coordinated movement for reform of middle grades education. The forum's vision statement is reprinted with permission:

"We, the members of the National Forum to Accelerate Middle-Grades Reform, believe that youth in the middle grades are capable of learning and achieving at high levels. We share a sense of urgency that high-performing schools with middle-grades become the norm, not the exception.

"High-performing schools with middle grades are academically excellent. They challenge all students to use their minds well, providing them with the curriculum, instruction, assessment, support, and time they need to meet rigorous academic standards. They recognize that early adolescence is characterized by dramatic cognitive growth, which enables students to think in more abstract and complex ways. The curriculum and extracurricular programs in such schools are challenging and engaging, tapping young adolescents' boundless energy, interests, and curiosity. Students learn to understand important concepts, develop essential skills, and apply what they learn to real-world problems. Adults in these schools maintain a rich academic environment by working with colleagues in their schools and communities to deepen their own knowledge and improve their practice.

"High-performing schools with middle grades are developmentally responsive. Such schools create small learning communities of adults and students in which stable, close, and mutually respectful relationships support all students' intellectual, ethical, and social growth. They provide comprehensive services to foster healthy physical and emotional development. Students have opportunities for both independent inquiry and learning in cooperation with others. They have time to be reflective and numerous opportunities to make decisions about their learning. Developmentally responsive schools involve families as partners in the education of their children. They welcome families, keep them well informed, help them develop their expectations and skills to support learning, and assure their participation in decision making. These schools are deeply rooted in their communities. Students have opportunities for active citizenship. They use the community as a classroom, and community members provide resources, connections, and active support.

"High-performing schools with middle grades are socially equitable. They seek to keep their students' future options open. They have high expectations for all their students and are committed to helping each child produce work of high quality. These schools make sure that all students are in academically rigorous classes staffed by experienced and expertly prepared teachers. These teachers acknowledge and honor their students' histories and cultures. They work to educate every child well and to overcome systematic variation in resources and outcomes related to race, class, gender and ability. They engage their communities in supporting all students' learning and growth."

demic expectations and their perception of their parents' and teachers' expectations of them, expectations for success were moderate at best across all groups, and students perceived their teachers' expectations of them to be lower than their parents' or their own (Mertens, Flowers, & Mulhall, 1998).

Teachers' expectations of student performance is a thorny issue in American education because of the inevitable overlay of accusations that low expectations for some groups of students reflect racial, ethnic, or class-based prejudice. To be sure, there is racism and class bias within American middle grades schools, and efforts to break down stereotypes through educators' development of greater knowledge about this nation's and the world's cultures are absolutely critical, as are opportunities for educators for candid discussion of issues of prejudice and bias as they affect student performance.

It is dangerously naive to conclude, however, that teachers and administrators (or parents and students) can be "taught" to have high expectations for all students. The hard fact is that many educators believe some groups of students are less able to achieve academically than others because they *see* these groups of students achieving less than others on a daily basis. Teachers of diverse populations of students are faced daily with a moral and a psychological dilemma: How do I account for the fact that some groups of students are generally so unsuccessful academically no matter how hard I try? Put more starkly, is it that some students cannot learn well enough or that I cannot teach well enough? In what is the epitome of a "no-win" position, the vast majority of teachers will conclude that the roots of academic failure lie not within them but within their students.

Enormous differences in the family and social circumstances of America's young adolescents substantially influence their readiness to master rigorous academic content. However, as one principal told us, "We trip over our own hearts when we let these differences become excuses for not expecting that all students can achieve at very high levels." Teachers of students from low-income families do face a greater challenge than teachers of adolescents from middle- and upper-income families, and they need more support.

Innumerable poverty-stricken middle grades students have reached or exceeded high academic expectations. And as educator Ron Edmonds (1979) once said, "How many effective schools would you have to see to be persuaded of the educability of poor children? If your answer is more than one, then I submit that you have reasons of your own for preferring to believe that basic pupil performance derives from family background instead of school response to family background."

What we as a nation must address head-on is the fact that the vast majority of middle grades teachers, like their counterparts in elementary and high schools, do not know how to educate all children to achieve their full intellectual potential. Moreover, it is blatantly hypocritical to expect them to, given the weakness of most teacher preparatory programs and the lack of ongoing professional development opportunities. It follows that an approach toward middle grades education that sets high standards for all students must build in multiple and continuous opportunities for teachers to learn, so that students will learn. Teachers cannot come to expect more of their students until they come to expect more of their own capacity to teach them, and until they have the opportunity to witness their power to elicit dramatically better work from those groups of students who are today failing. Teachers and students need a basis for high expectations grounded in students' real work.

Our bottom line is that you simply cannot get to high academic achievement for every student, or even reasonably expect such high achievement, without high-quality pre- and in-service professional education that is integrated into the daily work of middle grades teachers. This work must include the opportunity for teachers to identify and solve the learning challenges their students face. It is critically important to hold teachers accountable for improving student performance. But to do so without providing the resources for ongoing professional development and collaborative inquiry to improve teaching and learning is a waste of time at best, and a cynical exercise in political self-aggrandizement at worst. Substantial improvement in middle grades students' performance simply will not happen until middle grades teachers are provided with opportunities, regularly and routinely, to improve their ability to teach.

What's at Stake

In the chapters that follow, we describe a way of educating young adolescents that in its structures and practices is designed to enable teachers to learn so that students will learn. To implement this approach fully—that is, to transform existing middle schools to schools grounded in the Turning Points design—is an enormous undertaking. Why bother? As we write this book, the American economy is experiencing one of the longest periods of economic prosperity in the country's history. Unemployment levels, although still uneven among different racial and ethnic groups, are generally much lower than at the beginning of the 1990s. Why should the average American care about middle grades education?

Virtually every book on education reform, the original *Turning Points* included, makes the "economic argument" for improving American schools. It is a compelling argument, no less important for having been made on many occasions. The fact is that the American economy *has* changed from one in which a rudimentary grasp of basic skills enabled one to find employment that would support a family to an economy where having only these skills renders one increasingly unemployable. In relation to other world economies, "the key to both productivity and competitiveness is the skills of our people and our capacity to use highly educated and trained people to maximum advantage in the workplace" (Marshall & Tucker, 1992, p. 82).

As they enter the workplace, virtually all young people will be required to manage an array of sophisticated technologies. As these technologies change, and as new uses for them are found, workers will need to be able to continue learning at high levels throughout their careers. The ability to think abstractly, the ability to solve real, complex problems, and the ability to communicate and work well with others are the skills that will power modern economies for the foreseeable future (Marshall & Tucker, 1992, p. 80). Yet the educational statistics noted earlier make it clear that only a fraction of American middle grades students are developing these skills today. As the American population ages and becomes increasingly dependent on today's youth to ensure its own economic well-being, it is in every adult's self-interest to care deeply that not some but all young adolescents develop the capacity to contribute to the country's economic future.

Another equally compelling argument for "bothering" to take on the huge task of transforming America's middle grades schools resonates even more deeply within the middle grades community and, one hopes, among the American public. It is that every young adolescent truly *deserves* an equal opportunity to achieve at the very highest level. For many middle grades educators, transforming middle grades schools is far more an act of social justice than a means of ensuring a more secure retirement. In a recent study of 16 schools engaged in Turning Points–based reform, researcher Jeannie Oakes and her colleagues (Oakes, Quartz, Ryan, & Lipton, 2000, p. 314) concluded that what motivates the most dedicated teachers and principals is a passion for "betterment" of the school for all students, not for a privileged few:

> We encountered very few who signed up for reform simply as an act of compliance, to keep the mill running, or simply to garner external rewards such as higher test scores, grants, or special designations. Many of the most intensely committed educators intimated that they felt what John Adams may well have meant by a "positive passion for the public good." As one teacher explained, her dedication and long hours are rooted in a "sense of loyalty" and are bolstered by "the sense we get when we know that we've made a difference." Rather than being daunted by their heroic efforts, such educators seemed to thrive. They stayed late after meetings, spent their lunch discussing philosophy, and put themselves on the line to uphold their beliefs.

The average American should care about the quality of middle grades education, about every child succeeding, for the same reasons middle grades educators do: as a matter of social justice and national economic self-interest. It is dangerous economically and unjust morally to educate millions of American youth poorly when we have the knowledge and the means to educate them well. If we can find the will to care about every young adolescent, in the 21st century we will move closer to realizing our cherished ideals of lasting, shared prosperity with equal opportunity for all.

TURNING POINTS 2000: PURPOSE, PROCESS, AND PLAN

As noted, the purpose of this book is to provide an in-depth analysis of the Turning Points model of middle grades education based on the most current research and the experience of hundreds of middle grades schools that are attempting to improve results for young adolescent students. Its primary purpose is to provide information useful to teachers, principals, district officials, parents, community members, and others in and close to middle grades schools who seek to transform inadequate schools into schools that enable all students to use their minds well and to meet or exceed high academic standards. The book should also be useful to advocates and decision makers working to establish policies at the local, state, and federal level to improve the education and development of America's young adolescents.

In the tradition of the original report, we have attempted to blend information from research and practice to provide a comprehensive view of middle grades education. We draw extensively on our observations of what practitioners have found to work well in the implementation of *Turning Points* recommendations, but we have not undertaken a case study of the lessons learned from those efforts. Several such analyses of the process of implementing reforms have been done in the 1990s that we highly recommend (see, for example, Ames & Miller, 1994; Lewis, 1991, 1993, 1995, 1999; and Oakes et al., 2000).

Our intent here is to describe what *has* happened in the 1990s in order to envision, in considerable detail, what *can* happen in middle grades education in the 21st century. Our hope is to give both practical guidance and a sustaining vision to middle grades educators as they continue their journey toward developmentally responsive, equitable, and high-achieving schools.

Also in keeping with the *Turning Points* tradition, we aspire to bridge the gap between academic research and classroom practice. Over the past ten years, education research has made enormous strides in documenting "what works" to improve outcomes for students. There are few channels, however, for this information to reach middle grades educators. This work attempts to bridge that gap in a manner that will inform the efforts of practitioners, parents, and community members to improve middle grades education.

We further seek to dispel the belief that has gained some currency at the end of the 1990s that middle grades education has "failed." There is, in fact, a kind of backlash against the kinds of practices recommended in *Turning Points* in some communities because dramatic gains in academic achievement are not yet evident in schools attempting to implement changes. If we have learned anything over the past ten years, it is that gains in student achievement and other positive outcomes for students require comprehensive implementation of reforms over an extended period of time. Moreover, comprehensive reform is difficult work, fraught with unanticipated barriers, to say nothing of organized resistance. Nevertheless, there is mounting evidence that when educators stay the course of comprehensive reform, student outcomes do improve. And as we learn more about what comprehensive reform requires, especially regarding the kind of professional development and curricular materials needed, improvements in student performance can be achieved quicker than thought possible in the past, even in schools serving very low-income students (Balfanz & Mac Iver, 2000). Far from having failed, middle grades education is ripe for a great leap forward. Our hope is that this book will help middle grades educators maintain their courage and commitment as they continue their journey up the mountain.

Sources of Information

Our mission is to integrate what is known from education research and practice within a coherent approach toward adolescent education that educators can use in their own efforts to transform middle grades schools. Much excellent research in education supports these efforts, but a huge need remains for more in-depth studies of ways to improve the education of all children, young adolescents included. We have chosen to focus on those studies that provide solid, practical information about what works and, equally important, about *why* educational practices have the intended or unintended effects that they do.

The voices of teachers and principals in middle grades schools are the other major source of information for this work. Through face-to-face and telephone interviews with nearly 200 principals and teachers, we learned firsthand what really makes a difference in the quality of implementation of *Turning Points* recommendations.

The vast majority of these teachers and principals are in schools that were part of Carnegie Corporation's Middle Grade School State Policy Initiative (MGSSPI). Begun in 1990, a year after the release of *Turning Points*, the MGSSPI was a national program of grants designed to stimulate statewide changes in the policy and practice of middle grades education. The Carnegie initiative had two main goals:

- To promote widespread implementation of the *Turning Points* reform principles through changes in state policies that encourage local schools to adopt promising practices
- To stimulate the development of schools serving those most in need— youth from low-income families—to produce high-achieving, healthy young adolescents

The MGSSPI initially provided $60,000 planning grants on a competitive basis to each of 27 states. From 1991 through the end of the program in 1999, the initiative focused its support, through a series of two-year grants ranging from $50,000 to $360,000, on 15 of these states: Arkansas, California, Colorado, Connecticut, Delaware, Illinois, Maryland, Massachusetts, New Mexico, New York, North Dakota, Rhode Island, South Carolina, Texas, and Vermont. Under the MGSSPI umbrella, Carnegie Corporation also supported *Turning Points*–based initiatives in Boston, Los Angeles, New York City, and Puerto Rico.

In the early years of the MGSSPI, 1990–1993, the program emphasized the development within states of a broad awareness of middle grades students' needs and of the kinds of promising practices described in *Turning Points* to meet them, as a basis for developing state policies supporting middle grades reform. Over the course of the initiative, most of the 15 states developed or affirmed comprehensive middle grades policy statements reflecting the *Turning Points* recommendations. Several states established or accelerated specific middle grades teacher certification and licensure requirements. In all states, awareness of the inadequacy of most middle grades schools to meet their students' intellectual and developmental needs was raised substantially.

In 1993, MGSSPI states were encouraged to become more directly involved in supporting the implementation of *Turning Points* reforms by establishing networks of "systemic change schools." During the course of the initiative, over 225 schools were involved in these networks across the MGSSPI sites. Across all the schools, about 50 percent of all students received free or reduced-price meals because of low family income. States supported these networks of schools in a myriad of ways, including intensive professional development, coaching, opportunities to exchange knowledge and solve common problems, support for data-based self-assessment, and leadership training.

Besides grant funds, the states and schools received expert assistance from three technical assistance providers. The Council of Chief State School Officers provided or brokered on-site consultation and convened numerous conferences, meetings, and training sessions to support change in both middle grades policy and practice. The Center for Prevention Research and Development at the University of Illinois and, later, the National Center for Public Education and Social Policy at the University of Rhode Island coordinated states' and schools' efforts to collect and use detailed data on progress in implementing *Turning Points* reforms as a way of stimulating systematic change.

While most of the examples of practice used throughout this book are drawn from MGSSPI schools, we also gathered information from school- and program-level leaders of several other important school reform initiatives focused wholly or in part on middle schools. Some of these initiatives predate the MGSSPI—for example, the School Development Program founded in 1968 by James Comer at the Yale Child Study Center; the Accelerated Schools Project launched at Stanford University by Henry Levin in 1986; the Middle Grades Improvement Program begun in 1987 in Indiana by the Lilly Endowment under the direction of Joan Lipsitz; and the Edna McConnell Clark Foundation's Program for Student Achievement, which began in 1989 as the Program for Disadvantaged Youth and which is directed by M. Hayes Mizell.

The book also draws on the experience of schools from other key initiatives, including two that began in 1994: the W. K. Kellogg Foundation's Middle Start initiative, directed by Leah Meyer Austin; and the Talent Development Middle School model, directed by Douglas Mac Iver at Johns Hopkins University's Center for Research on the Education of Students Placed At Risk.

Each of these initiatives has its own programmatic goals and areas of emphasis in its approach to middle grades reform. Yet a great deal of overlap provides common ground for extending our knowledge about what is needed to transform today's middle grades schools into tomorrow's high-performance learning environments. These initiatives and new ones to come do not represent "competing" approaches to middle grades reform; rather, they are much-needed alternative approaches that provide schools and districts with choices that will all lead to a critical common goal: vastly improved student performance.

Finally, this book also draws on work in schools of the recently established Turning Points National Design Center at the Center for Collaborative Education (CCE) in Boston. The center, headed by the former director of Massachusetts' MGSSPI initiative, Daniel French, is an approved New American Schools design center. As the name implies, the center's approach to middle grades reform and the *Turning Points*–based practices described in this book are highly congruent. Our hope is that *Turning Points 2000* will be helpful to middles grades educators pursuing change on behalf of young adolescents, no matter what specific pathway to reform is taken.

Plan of the Book

The nine remaining chapters of *Turning Points 2000* closely parallel the major chapters of the original *Turning Points*, although each chapter in this book goes into considerably greater depth than the original work. The order of the chapters has been changed somewhat, reflecting our sense of how they logically relate to each other within the book and also emphasizing where we believe middle grades educators need to concentrate their attention: improvement in curriculum, assessment, and instruction. The order of the chapters should certainly not be taken as a preferred sequence for the implementation of the practices they describe. In fact, an essential aspect of the Turning Points model of adolescent education is that there are no linear relationships between elements of the approach that imply (or dictate) a rigid sequence of actions, as if the elements were steps on a ladder. Instead, Turning Points is a *system* of interacting elements, where change in one element both requires change in other elements to be fully implemented and, in turn, causes change in other elements of the model that enable still other changes to occur. The *Turning Points 2000* recommendations and the dynamic character of the Turning Points model are explored in Chapter 2, Turning Points 2000: A Design for Improving Middle Grades Education.

Chapter 3, Curriculum and Assessment to Improve Teaching and Learning, argues that all students must have access to a rigorous, standards-based curriculum. Furthermore, we make the case that the content and method of student assessment must actually precede and guide choices regarding instruction, the opposite of much current practice. The chapter presents a process of "backward design" that middle grades teachers are successfully using to align standards, curriculum, and assessment in a way that promotes interdisciplinary construction of knowledge and "learning with understanding."

Chapter 4, Designing Instruction to Improve Teaching and Learning, builds on the previous chapter by showing how choices regarding instructional methods necessarily reflect choices regarding curriculum content and assessment methods. We try to show how well-crafted assessments are essential in making high expectations practically meaningful, or "transparent," to students and, as such, are a *first* step toward their mastery of rigorous content material. The chapter explores effective teaching strategies that engage students actively in learning within schools where they are grouped heterogeneously with regard to learning needs and past performance.

Chapter 5, Expert Teachers for Middle Grades Schools: Pre-service Preparation and Professional Development, addresses the continuum of educational experiences that teachers of young adolescents must have if their students are to achieve at high levels. The chapter argues that training specific to middle grades education is required if teachers are to meet young adolescents' needs as learners. Moreover, high-quality middle grades education programs will not be widely available unless teachers in middle grades schools are required to be certified and licensed as middle-level educators. Once in the classroom, teachers initially require opportunities to hone their craft under the guidance of a skilled mentor, and throughout their careers they must have professional development opportunities that are primarily collaborative in nature, embedded in their daily work, and always focused on improving outcomes for students.

Chapter 6, Organizing Relationships for Learning, focuses on the importance of relationships as the conduit of learning. It explores the ways in which organizational structures affect relationships among the adults and young people in the school and the way that relationships can either enhance or impede student learning and healthy development. Chapter 7, Democratic Governance to Improve Student Learning, then builds on these findings to demonstrate that through solid relationships between faculty members and students comes greater understanding of how each young person can be educated well. We argue that teachers and administrators in the school are in the best position to make choices about the kind of content, instructional practices, and methods of assessment that will enable each student to learn at high levels. The chapter presents structures and methods for involving all faculty members in making informed choices, in a context where it is clear that those making critical educational choices will be held accountable for their impact on student learning. We examine the principal's key leadership role as a facilitator of systematic change. The local district's role in fostering high-quality decision making is also explored, as is the way an accountability system can support school improvement efforts.

To be fully engaged in school and focused on learning, young adolescents need help in negotiating the myriad social, physical, and psychological changes they are experiencing. Chapter 8, A Safe and Healthy School Environment, describes how schools can enhance middle grades students' capacity to avoid risky behaviors and can take advantage of their increased maturity to develop the attitudes and skills that will enable them to lead healthful, productive lives. Ways of successfully linking middle grades schools and community health agencies are addressed.

Schools' connection to people and organizations within the community are explored further in Chapter 9, Involving Parents and Communities. This chapter examines the critical role that parents play within the school, as decision makers, as volunteers, and in other roles; as well as at home, by working with teachers to engage their children in their schoolwork. How schools can continue to meet the needs of young adolescents and their families during nonschool hours is also described, and we look at the (re)emerging concept of "community schools."

The concluding chapter, Taking Action: Challenges and Opportunities, revisits some of the key themes of the book and examines some common trends in the experiences of educators as they have attempted to implement *Turning Points* recommendations. We examine the kinds of challenges educators have faced in attempting to create excellent, equitable middle grades schools, as well as potential responses to these challenges.

When we refer to the "Turning Points model" and the "Turning Points design" in subsequent chapters, we mean the model and design described in this book, which we see as the current version of the Turning Points model. This model is an extension or outgrowth of the original. We have attempted to provide as much evidence from research as possible to support our assertions about the way middle grades education "ought to be." Much of what is here, however, represents the distilled wisdom of the middle grades educators that we have had the great fortune to know over the past ten years. Our "voice" in this book echoes the voices that we have heard and from whom we have learned so much. In our attempt to analyze and synthesize all that we have learned from middle school educators from Compton to Cambridge, from El Paso to Montpelier, we hope we do justice to their enormous wisdom and to their devotion to improving the lives of young adolescents.

2 Turning Points 2000: A Design for Improving Middle Grades Education

Photo by Doug Martin

THE ORIGINAL *TURNING POINTS* report envisioned a 15-year-old who had been well served during the middle years of schooling (Carnegie Council on Adolescent Development, 1989, p. 15). Demonstrating five characteristics of effective human beings, that 15-year-old would be

- An intellectually reflective person
- A person en route to a lifetime of meaningful work
- A good citizen
- A caring and ethical individual
- A healthy person

This vision of a 15-year-old reflects the philosophy behind *Turning Points* and *Turning Points 2000*; it includes every student in the middle grades, even English language learners and those who may have substantial disabilities or who receive special education services. Middle grades schools should serve the oft-cited "whole child," challenging students to think critically, to work industriously, to contribute to their communities, to care about others, and to care about their own physical and mental health. Those "whole" children become adults whose beliefs, attitudes, and behaviors contribute to the success of our democratic society, a society concerned about its own and the world's citizens.

We define success as achieving the Turning Points vision outlined above. One overarching goal, ensuring success for every student, drives the Turning Points model of adolescent education. This goal is the central focus of every effort to improve schools for young adolescents, just as a ship's navigator plots a course based on the North Star, or a mountain climber keeps the peak of Mount Everest in sight, at least figuratively, during the trek to the top. Every maneuver, every adjustment somehow affects progress relative to that point, either toward it or away from it.

THE *TURNING POINTS 2000* RECOMMENDATIONS

The original *Turning Points* report offered eight principles, or recommendations, for improving middle grades schools (see Chapter 1); those recommendations were intended to ensure success for every student. In *Turning Points 2000,* although we continue to rely on the premises underlying those original eight recommendations, our new recommendations reflect what we have learned in the decade since the first report's publication. We now call for middle grades schools that

- *Teach a curriculum grounded in rigorous, public academic standards for what students should know and be able to do, relevant to the concerns of adolescents and based on how students learn best.* Considerations of both excellence and equity should guide every decision regarding what will be taught. Curriculum should be based on content standards and organized around concepts and principles. A mix of assessment methods should allow students to demonstrate what they know and what they can do.
- *Use instructional methods designed to prepare all students to achieve higher standards and become lifelong learners.* To be effective, instruction should mesh with three other aspects of teaching and learning: the standards and resulting curriculum outlining what students should learn; the assessments students will use to demonstrate their knowledge and skills; and the needs, interests, and learning styles of the students themselves. Classes should include students of diverse needs, achievement levels, interests, and learning styles, and instruction should be differentiated to take advantage of the diversity, not ignore it.
- *Staff middle grades schools with teachers who are expert at teaching young adolescents, and engage teachers in ongoing, targeted professional development opportunities.* Schools should hire staff specifically trained for the middle grades and should provide mentors and "induction" to teachers new to the profession or the school. Schools should also engage teachers in ongoing professional devel-

opment—driven by results, based on standards, and embedded in their daily work—that yields improvements in student learning. A facilitator, either full- or part-time, should coordinate professional development opportunities.

- *Organize relationships for learning to create a climate of intellectual development and a caring community of shared educational purpose.* Large schools should be divided into smaller learning communities, with teams of teachers and students as the underlying organizational structure. To ensure strong teams, schools must pay attention to the nature and quality of interactions among teacher and student team members, ensuring that teams continually concentrate their efforts on achieving high standards for both teaching and learning. Schools should also attend to critical elements affecting team success, such as team size, composition, time for planning, and continuity.

- *Govern democratically, through direct or representative participation by all school staff members, the adults who know the students best.* All decisions should focus relentlessly on attaining the goal of success for every student and should be based on data drawn from various sources. Schools should be proactive, not reactive, in their efforts to ensure every student's success, using a "living" school improvement plan to direct actions in both the short and the long term.

- *Provide a safe and healthy school environment as part of improving academic performance and developing caring and ethical citizens.* Healthy lifestyles and academic success are tightly interwoven—improvement in one leads to improvement in the other, both directly and indirectly. Positive intergroup relations are essential to a safe and healthy school. Middle grades schools, in partnership with the community, should support physical and mental health and fitness by providing a safe, caring, and healthy environment, health education, and access to health services.

- *Involve parents and communities in supporting student learning and healthy development.* Schools and families must collaborate to establish continuity (for example, similarly high expectations) and communication between home and school; to monitor and support students' schoolwork and academic progress; to create opportunities outside the school for safe, engaging exploration; and to improve the school itself through parent and community involvement on site. Schools and communities should forge connections to provide needed services to students, offer career exploration opportunities, expand learning beyond regular school hours and outside school walls, and advocate for the school improvements critical to ensuring success for every student.

Readers familiar with the eight recommendations from *Turning Points* will notice a few changes in comparing those eight to the seven *Turning Points 2000* recommendations. Five of those changes are crucial to understanding the *Turning Points 2000* design. First, we have recognized that ensuring success for every student is the overall goal of the *Turning Points 2000* design, not a recommendation or means to attaining that goal on a par with the others, as it appeared in the original report. Every recommendation has an impact on ensuring student success in attaining the Turning Points vision (see Figure 2.1).

Figure 2.1 The *Turning Points 2000* design

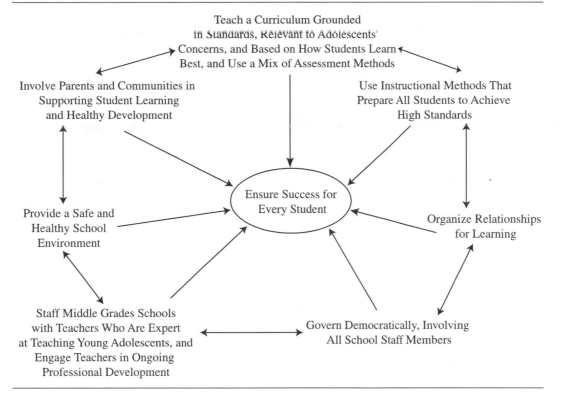

Teach a Curriculum Grounded
in Standards, Relevant to Adolescents'
Concerns, and Based on How Students Learn
Best, and Use a Mix of Assessment Methods

Involve Parents and Communities in
Supporting Student Learning
and Healthy Development

Use Instructional Methods That
Prepare All Students to Achieve
High Standards

Ensure Success for
Every Student

Provide a Safe and
Healthy School
Environment

Organize Relationships
for Learning

Staff Middle Grades Schools
with Teachers Who Are Expert
at Teaching Young Adolescents, and
Engage Teachers in Ongoing
Professional Development

Govern Democratically, Involving
All School Staff Members

Second, we have reordered the list of recommendations, and the chapters that follow, to reflect the centrality of teaching and learning to ensuring every student's success. The focus on teaching and learning should drive changes in organization, governance, teacher preparation and professional development, culture and environment, and connections to parents and community. However, we repeat a caution stated in Chapter 1: The order of the recommendations and the chapters is not meant to imply an order for implementing the design.

To clarify this further, we see the recommendations as "design elements." How these design elements should be organized into a whole depends on many factors unique to individual schools, including what progress schools have already made in becoming high-performance learning communities. Schools are not blank slates on which this design or any other can be drawn without restriction or concern for the unique nature and status of the school itself. The *Turning Points 2000* design, like instruction for students, should meet schools where they are and help take them where they need to go to ensure success.

Third, we have changed the terminology that describes what should be taught. The original report called for "teaching a core of common knowledge." In recommending a core of common knowledge, *Turning Points* actually foreshadowed the standards movement with its emphasis on defining what knowledge and skills all students should master. However, we have since come to believe that the original report's description of a "core" does not appropriately or fully

- Reflect the ever-expanding nature of important knowledge
- Address the skills and habits of mind that young adolescents should acquire
- Account for the changing concerns of young adolescents
- Incorporate the growing understanding of how students learn best

Instead, as described in the original report, a core of common knowledge seems to imply an inflexible, prescribed body of knowledge that is too limiting for both students and teachers.

In *Turning Points 2000*, we call for teaching a curriculum grounded in, though not strictly limited to, rigorous, public standards for what students should know and be able to do, recognizing that standards should be flexible to reflect changes in society. We also recommend that the curriculum be tied to adolescents' concerns, in a call for relevance missing from the original notion of a core. And we urge that curricula reflect the latest findings about how students learn best, so students can become the critical, reflective thinkers and problem solvers we would like them to be.

Fourth, we have turned one original recommendation—to teach a core of common knowledge—into two recommendations: teach a curriculum grounded in standards, in the concerns of young adolescents, and in how students learn best; and use instruction designed to prepare all students to achieve higher standards. The addition of a recommendation focused on instruction reinforces the prominence of teaching and learning in the *Turning Points 2000* design. Moreover, separating out instruction highlights how vital it is to the success of any effort to affect what happens inside classrooms.

Like our reordering of the recommendations, though, this change also comes with a caution. Curriculum, assessment, and instruction are intertwined, each inevitably affecting the other two. Any effort to change curriculum and assessment without changing instruction, or to change instruction without considering curriculum and assessment, will fail. The backward-design process for developing curriculum, assessment, and instruction, described in Chapters 3 and 4, demonstrates vividly the relationships between and among these three elements of teaching and learning.

Finally, we have combined two of the original report's recommendations—reengaging families and connecting schools to communities—into one recommendation. This fifth and final major difference between our recommendations and those of the original Turning Points task force follows on from what we have learned about the inseparable connections between families and the communities in which they live. Families do not succeed without community support, and communities do not succeed without support from families. For example, consider the importance of high expectations for student learning. Many things can affect expectations, including the socioeconomic and demographic characteristics of the community, families' education levels, and the availability of community resources such as libraries and recreational facilities, which, in turn, affect families' capacity to support student learning. These tightly woven bonds between families and community make it impossible to separate out a school's responsibility to involve one or the other. Both must be engaged if students are to succeed.

We have made other changes in our recommendation list, though none so vital as the five outlined above. We made each change purposefully, after considering what we have learned to do, and not to do, in the decade since *Turning Points* was published. To be absolutely clear about our intentions, all the changes do not in any way diminish or divert our dedication to the vision of a 15-year-old who has experienced a high-performing middle grades school. That vision will become reality when students and adults operate within an active learning community, engaging the world and each other in an ongoing quest to attain the knowledge and skills embedded in high standards for teaching and learning.

THE DESIGN SYSTEM

Together, the seven recommendations form a *system,* an interacting and interdependent group of practices that form a unified whole. Each recommendation, or element, within this system influences the expression and reinforces the impact of other elements. As is true of all systems, the *Turning Points 2000* design system cannot be separated into self-contained components, where each can be addressed independently of the others. Instead, the design system we describe, composed of the seven *Turning Points 2000* recommendations for improving middle grades schools, must be dealt with holistically, systemically, to ensure success.

It's easy enough to draw a diagram of a system, like the one in Figure 2.1, and include arrows between various components, arrows that naturally go in both directions. "See," the diagram seems to say, "all this stuff affects all this other stuff." However, improvement efforts based on such diagrams are often disappointing because the interrelatedness of the elements is never seriously considered. How design elements interact is noted on paper but forgotten in practice.

Although a great deal of energy has gone into understanding each recommendation in the original *Turning Points* report, very little has been devoted to figuring out how the recommendations interact with each other. One generalization about systems is that they follow rules. If we want to improve a middle grades school, we must devote attention to discerning the unique rules and norms that will determine how the Turning Points design elements affect, and are affected by, each other in an individual school.

How will a change in governance, for example, affect teaching and learning? How will a change in parent involvement strategies affect student health? Recall that in our description of ensuring success for every student, we pointed out that each maneuver and adjustment affects the school's position relative to the goal of every student fulfilling the Turning Points vision of a 15-year-old. A change in governance structures, for instance, can move a school toward this goal, away from it, or even around it, like a climber circling a mountain without moving closer to the peak.

Another generalization about systems is that they interact with other systems. The design system we advocate will interact with a particular school as a system, with the district system within which that school resides, with the state educational system, and with the national educational system. Talk about complexity! The only guarantee is that there are no guarantees about what will happen when these complicated systems meet, or perhaps more accurately, collide. In the face of such complexity, a school needs a clear plan or theory of action to achieve its goals. Such a plan, described in Chapter 7, enables the school to maintain its integrity and purpose in the face of other influences, while allowing the school faculty to learn from and respond to these influences intelligently.

Peter Senge, organizational guru and author of *The Fifth Discipline*, recommends identifying points of high leverage in a system (Senge, Kleiner, Roberts, Ross, & Smith, 1994, p. 347). Dennis Sparks (1994), executive director of the National Staff Development Council, compares leverage points to a ship's rudder, in that minor adjustments in the rudder have major implications for the ship's direction over time. Attending to leverage can allow members of a learning community, singly and together, to move mountains, not just scale them.

To summarize, as Newton observed, a body at rest tends to stay at rest, and a body in motion tends to stay in motion. We obviously advocate getting into motion toward the goal of ensuring success for every student, recognizing the interactions within our design system of recommendations, and identifying the leverage points that engage the school in an upward spiral of continuous improvement.

CAUTION: NO HALF MEASURES

Motion for motion's sake will not necessarily be helpful in the quest to ensure that all students achieve high standards. Sarason (1990, p. 8) explains the confusion between change and progress:

> To confuse change with progress is to confuse means with ends. Keeping those ends in mind, informing as they should the means in the most pervasive ways, is a responsibility that too often fades into the background in the turmoil of change. The means become ends in themselves and, therefore, the more things change the more they remain the same, or worse. It is the rare revolution that has been true to its initial vision.

All the Turning Points recommendations are means to the end of ensuring success for every student. For example, many middle grades schools have made tremendous changes in educational structures—forming teams of teachers and students, establishing site-based decision making, devising more flexible schedules, and so on. Such changes in structure are vital to attaining the goal of ensuring success for every student and should be celebrated.

However, as we have learned over the past ten years, it can be difficult for schools to maintain their momentum for improvement as they get closer to the heart of schooling—classroom practice. Some schools change structures but go no further. In a study of middle schools with excellent reputations, Jeannie Oakes found that, beneath an attractive surface of structural changes, classroom practices and climates had scarcely changed at all (Slavin, 1999, p. 3). Lipsitz, Mizell, Jackson, and Austin (1997, p. 535) recognized middle grades schools' success in making crucial structural changes, but also argued that it is time for schools to stop being merely "poised" for curricular and instructional change and to get on with the job. Without improvements in classroom practice, the goal of ensuring success for every student will remain out of reach.

Richard Elmore (1995, p. 24) offers three main reasons that reformers like to change structures. First, changing structures, like forming teacher teams or altering the schedule, is a very visible manifestation of the desire to change the school. Symbolically, structural changes signal the seriousness of the intent to reform. Second, transforming structures, as difficult as it may be, is easier than the possible alternatives, like significantly altering teacher attitudes or dismissing teachers and administrators who do not support improvements. Finally, structures are appealing targets for modification because changing them will make things obviously different, so it feels as if progress has been made. However, altering structures does not necessarily lead to improved teaching and learning. For example, creating a school leadership team may seem significant, but a leadership team may not actually have an impact on teaching practices in classrooms. School governance will be different, but the classroom remains the same.

Fred Newmann (1993, p. 4) contends, "Structure without substantive purpose leads nowhere in particular." We agree. Admirable as intentions may be, such structural modifications as dividing teachers and students into teams, modifying schedules, or creating decision-making teams have limited impact without a purposeful, laserlike focus on how these structural changes will enable improved student learning.

As Sam Stringfield and his colleagues (Johns Hopkins University & Abt Associates, Inc., 1997, pp. 11–13) pointed out in a longitudinal study of "high magnitude" reform efforts with complex guiding principles, "Acceptance of only a limited number of those principles diminishes the power of the strategy." The danger with complex reform strategies, like the Turning Points design, is that schools can "blunt or downsize" the improvement effort (Huberman & Miles, 1984). In downsizing an improvement effort, a school would tackle only one or a few of the guiding principles, while ignoring the rest. Such well-intended efforts can lead to disaster. Stringfield (Johns Hopkins University & Abt Associates, Inc., 1997, pp. 11–17) provides hypothetical examples of how half measures can lead to an individual school's failure, using the Coalition of Essential Schools (CES) model and James Comer's School Development Program:

> For example, a school that is part of CES can organize in teams and adopt exhibitions of mastery, but without acceptance and implementation of the inquiry method exemplified by essential questions or creative application of "student as worker," little curriculum or instruction may actually change. Similarly, Comer schools may implement the structure of the School Plan-

ning and Management Team and the Mental Health Team, but without substantial change in interactions between staff, community, parents, and students, the goal of community support for children may not happen.

Preliminary results from a study of Turning Points–based reform efforts, in contrast, point to the power of a systemic approach. According to early results from this research, the Turning Points model, when implemented comprehensively and with fidelity, results in significant improvements in student achievement. The further along a school is in implementing the principles holistically, apparently the greater the impact on achievement (Felner et al., 1997, pp. 528–550).

ENSURING SUCCESS FOR EVERY STUDENT

David Hornbeck, former superintendent of schools in Philadelphia and chair of the task force that produced the original *Turning Points* report, often speaks of ensuring success for all students. He has taken to turning to his audiences and asking, "What is it about the word 'all' that you do not understand?" His question reflects both the pervasiveness of the stated sentiment that all children can learn and the equally pervasive lack of action based on the sentiment.

Perhaps the lack of action can be attributed to a common misconception that "all" really translates into "most." Readers familiar with the original *Turning Points* will have noted a small, but important, change in the language we have been using to describe our goal. Instead of the phrase used in the original report, "ensuring success for all students," we now say "ensuring success for every student."

Margaret McLaughlin, a professor and special education expert at the University of Maryland, suggested the change. She said that special educators tend to use "each" or "every" student instead of "all" because people have become accustomed to automatically assuming that "all" is a synonym for "most," excluding students with disabilities (personal communication, January 15, 2000). Because we really do mean *every* student, we chose to alter the wording of our goal statement to avoid any confusion.

To reiterate, our goal is to ensure that every student fulfills the Turning Points vision of becoming an intellectually reflective person, a person en route to a lifetime of meaningful work, a good citizen, a caring and ethical individual, and a healthy person. The *Turning Points 2000* design system is intended to put middle grades schools in motion toward that goal. The design system is grounded in the original Turning Points model and blends the wisdom of both the latest research and the best practice. The following chapters describe each of the recommendations that together make up the design.

3 Curriculum and Assessment to Improve Teaching and Learning

Photo by Greg Beckel

TO PREPARE ALL STUDENTS to think critically, lead healthful lives, and behave ethically and as responsible citizens, the original *Turning Points* recommended that middle grades schools teach a core of common knowledge. Since the report's 1989 publication, educators have learned a great deal about how to define, assess, and teach the core of common knowledge. All of what has been learned affirms an essential truth about education: Improvement in student performance across all groups requires a relentless focus on the heart of schooling—that is, on teaching and learning.

As noted in Chapter 2, we have moved away from the term "core of common knowledge" because it implies a prescribed, fixed universe of knowledge, a concept inappropriate for the information age. It also ignores the skills and habits of mind that students should also acquire, the changing concerns of young adolescents, and the growing understanding of how students learn best. We now recommend teaching a curriculum grounded in rigorous, public academic standards, relevant to the concerns of adolescents, and based on how students learn best.

Content or academic standards, which spell out what students should know and be able to do, form the basis for the curriculum we recommend. Academic standards provide the link between excellence and equity by setting consistently high, public expectations for *every* student. As a reflection of the school's broader goal of enabling young adolescents to reach their full intellectual potential, the effort to support every student, including special education and English language learners, in meeting or exceeding high academic standards should drive all other aspects of school improvement. By holding limited-English-proficient (LEP) students to the same standards as other students, we have a much greater chance of achieving educational equity.

A discussion of teaching and learning based on standards must address three aspects of day-to-day life in a classroom: curriculum, assessment, and instruction. Backward design—an approach that weaves together curriculum, assessment, and instruction in developing rigorous units of study—undergirds the organization of this chapter and the next. In backward design, developing a unit of study begins with identifying the relevant standards and developing the curriculum based on them. Educators then decide what assessment methods will best allow students to demonstrate what they have learned, and, finally, they determine how to prepare students, through diverse instructional methods, to do well on the assessments. The name "backward" design is an acknowledgment that, traditionally, educators have often begun their planning with instruction, targeting favorite activities, then matched the activities to curriculum, often as defined by a textbook, before considering assessment (Mitchell, Willis & the Chicago Teachers Union Quest Center, 1995, p. 5; Wiggins & McTighe, 1998, p. 8).

This chapter focuses on two elements of backward design, using standards as the basis for curriculum and developing assessments that embody the standards. The next chapter highlights the third element, designing instruction that will engage students deeply in learning and prepare them to do well on the assessments. These two chapters on teaching and learning are critical to everything that follows. For example, the organizational structures described in subsequent chapters—teaming, flexible scheduling, democratic governance—should all be established in response to a curriculum that is substantive, significant, and relevant to the concerns of young adolescents.

STANDARDS AND CURRICULUM: THE STARTING POINTS OF BACKWARD DESIGN

To develop curriculum, teachers must begin with academic standards, the agreed-upon statements of what students should know and be able to do. Performance standards, which define how good is good enough, can also be used as a foundation for curriculum. Performance standards are not as widely used or as developed as academic standards, however, so our discussion will focus on academic standards as the basis for curriculum.

Standards: Excellence and Equity

Why should the middle grades curriculum, as well as assessment and instruction, be based upon academic standards? Because standards support the twin towers of an education that ensures success for every student: excellence and equity.

To promote excellence, high standards demand a thorough understanding of essential knowledge, require critical thinking and problem-solving skills, and encourage habits of mind that can be applied across disciplines. Habits of mind (see Box 3.1) include self-discipline, flexibility, reflectiveness, dependability, and perseverance (Harris & Carr, 1996, p. 5; Marzano & Pickering, 1997, p. 262; Wiggins & McTighe, 1998, p. 171).

To support equity, standards set the expectation that *all* students can meet or exceed high standards. To make sure that "all" really means all, every student must have the support and time required to take him or her from where he or she is to where the standards say he or she should go. Ensuring that support means providing access to high-quality teaching, resources, and materials in an atmosphere of high expectations for all students. But, as educator and author Anne Wheelock (1998, p. 4) acknowledges, "[T]he process of moving from the simple statement 'all children can learn' to results that match that expectation involves hard work." (The Individuals with Disabilities Education Act [1997] requires that all students, including those with disabilities, have access to the curriculum and that these students must participate in accountability measures, like statewide performance-based or standardized tests. Though a

Box 3.1 Examples of Habits of Mind

Educators at Central Park East Secondary School in New York City believe that habits of mind should be evident in both teacher and student work and relationships (Wheelock, 1998, p. 51). They post key questions reflecting the habits of mind they particularly value in every classroom:

- *Looking for evidence:* How do we know what we think we know? What's our evidence? How credible is that evidence?
- *Identifying viewpoint:* Whose perspective are we reading, hearing, and seeing? What other perspectives might exist if we changed our position?
- *Making connections:* How is one thing connected to another? Is there a pattern in evidence?
- *Considering alternatives:* How else might it have been? What if . . . ? Suppose that . . . ?
- *Assessing importance:* What difference does it make? Who cares?

few students with disabilities may have a slightly different curriculum, emphasizing different facts and skills, every student should progress to much higher
standards through mastering the same critical concepts and processes that under-
lie the standards.)

Academic and performance standards are worth the effort because they
define excellence, making the aims of education clear, and they define expectations, so that educators expect, or at least should act as if they expect, that all
students will achieve that excellence. The latter point reflects the fact that social psychologists and other scholars have shown through research that it is initially easier to change behavior than to change attitudes. If educators doggedly
pursue instructional approaches to help each child meet high standards "as if"
all children are capable of doing so, then the educators' own attitudes and expectations will change as students respond positively to the instruction.

Even without clear, public standards, some students have learned through
the private discourse of family and community life what it takes to succeed in
school and why it is important to do so in preparation for adult life. Large numbers of others, however, especially low-income and minority students, have only
the faintest clues to what excellence "looks like" and cannot readily observe
within their struggling families and in their distressed communities the difference that acquiring a good education can make. Lost in a maze, with few clear
notions of the meaning and value of "good work," many of these young people
decide not to play at all in a game in which they are not expected to compete,
much less win. Setting standards is not enough: it is a beginning, not an end.
The game of teaching and learning without standards, however, is inherently
unfair, destined to leave many children marginalized in a society where, more
than ever, knowledge is power.

Selecting and Adapting Standards. For many schools, the idea of selecting academic standards may seem nonsensical. Schools do not select standards—
standards are imposed by the state education department or the local district.

Clearly, nearly all American schools will need to address mandated state
and/or local standards, if they are not doing so already. Forty-nine of the 50
states (all except Iowa) have developed some version of standards (American
Federation of Teachers, 1999). Yet a school runs a grave risk in merely accepting
such standards as the revealed wisdom of some all-knowing higher authority!
Instead, each middle grades school, as a distinct learning community, must
analyze its state and local standards to determine if they provide an adequate,
high-quality basis for developing a coherent, engaging curriculum. Where the
standards do not measure up, by the kind of criteria discussed below, a school
will need to adapt and augment state and local standards to prepare students
to do well on assessments and, more importantly, to be truly able to use their
minds well.

To ensure the use of rigorous standards that will promote both excellence
and equity, schools should use demanding criteria to analyze state and local
standards, and, if necessary, select additional standards from the myriad of
sources available. Almost inevitably, educators will need to supplement and

modify standards to encompass fully what a particular school community believes its students should know and be able to do. Setting the standards for a school is "more a matter of selection than creation" (Mitchell, 1996, p. 16). The following criteria for identifying excellent academic standards reflect a synthesis of the recommendations from different organizations, each on the leading edge of reform based on standards: the Education Trust, the National Education Goals Panel (NEGP), and the National Center on Education and the Economy. Academic standards should be

- *Concerned with the essential ideas.* That is, with the important concepts of the disciplines (Mitchell, 1996, p. 22; National Education Goals Panel [NEGP], 1993, p. 13; Tucker & Codding, 1998, p. 57). Concepts and principles are the foundation for any unit of study. A concept is a single word or phrase that serves as a label for a class or category of things with shared attributes. Concepts are organizing ideas that can be divided into two major categories: generic or universal concepts that cut across disciplines (e.g., power, systems, change); and content-specific concepts that are critical to a narrower band of disciplines (e.g., individual rights in the study of governments, tempo in the study of music, evolution in biology) (Texas Education Agency, 1999; Tomlinson, 1998, p. 5). Principles or generalizations are rules that generally govern how concepts function. For example, if "change" is the concept, then one generalization would be that change has both a cause and an effect (Tomlinson, 1998, p. 5). (See Box 3.2 for more examples of concepts and generalizations.)
- *Useful and clear.* Standards should address what students will need to know and be able to do in the real world of work, citizenship, higher education, and lifelong learning. They should be specific enough to form the basis of the curriculum. The standards should be written so that teachers, students, parents, and community members can easily understand them (Mitchell, 1996, p. 22; NEGP, 1993, p. 13; Tucker & Codding, 1998, p. 57).
- *Rigorous, accurate, and sound.* Standards should be challenging, focusing on depth over breadth; encouraging habits of mind supportive of sustained effort (e.g., reflection, persistence, creativity); reflecting sound scholarship in the disciplines; and representing the best, cutting-edge knowledge about what is essential to know and to be able to do within and across disciplines (Mitchell, 1996, p. 22; NEGP, 1993, pp. 12, 18).
- *Brief.* If each standard requires too many words to describe it, the standard itself will not be memorable. In the case of standards, flowery ("jargony") language can lead to weeds, not blossoms (Mitchell, 1996, p. 22; NEGP, 1993, pp. 13–14; Tucker & Codding, 1998, p. 57).
- *Feasible, taken together.* The standards should be cumulatively feasible for a school and its students (Mitchell, 1996, p. 22; NEGP, 1993, pp. 13–14; Tucker & Codding, 1998, p. 57). When analyzing all the standards, across disciplines, the school has to decide if it is possible for the students to achieve all the standards within the time frame (semester, school year) being considered. Too often, American schools try to cover too much ground. The Third Interna-

Box 3.2 Some Sample Concepts and Generalizations

Change
One change leads to another.
Change may be positive or negative.
Change is inevitable.
Change may be planned or spontaneous.

Patterns
Patterns are everywhere.
Patterns allow for predictions.
Patterns are subject to change.
Patterns have segments that are
    repeated.

Order
Order may be natural or artificial.
Order comes out of chaos.
The order of things provides information.

Relationships
Relationships may bring about change.
Relationships may be simple or complex.
Relationships may be natural, forced,
    or chosen.
Relationships are connections.

Systems
Systems may be natural or artificial.
Systems interact.
Systems follow rules.
Systems are made of parts that work
    together.

Power
Power takes many forms.
Power may be used to facilitate,
    dominate, or maintain.
Power may be used or abused.
Power may be internal or external.

Source: Adapted from Texas Education Agency (1999).

tional Mathematics and Science Study (TIMMS) yielded a valuable lesson: quantity and quality are not equivalent. U.S. math and science textbooks include many more topics than German and Japanese textbooks, but the TIMMS revealed that German and Japanese students significantly outperform U.S. students in both subjects. U.S. mathematics texts cover 175 more topics than German and 350 more than Japanese texts; U.S. science texts address 930 more topics than German and 433 more than Japanese (Schmidt, McKnight, & Raizen, 1997; Schmoker & Marzano, 1999, p. 19).

- *Assessable.* Each standard should include a verb indicating an action that can be assessed—for example, "analyze," "compare," "exhibit," "compose," "apply," "solve," "connect," "demonstrate," "criticize," "decide" (Bloom, 1956, pp. 201–207; Mitchell, 1996, p. 22). Verbs like "understand" and "appreciate" are not assessable. If a standard is assessable, then (Mitchell, 1996, pp. 22–23; NEGP, 1993, pp. 14–15)

    Teachers can use the standard to teach and to evaluate student progress toward meeting the standard.

Students can use the standard to self-assess their own learning.

Parents can make sense of the standard in light of their children's work.

Employers and universities can connect the knowledge, skills, and habits embodied in the standards to their business and higher education needs.

- *Developmental.* Standards should be appropriate to the developmental capacity of students as they age, with the knowledge and skills that standards require growing in sophistication to match students' increase in capacity. Repeating the same topics across several grade levels, so often the case in American education, does little to advance expectations for students (Mitchell, 1996, p. 23, NEGP, 1993, pp. 15–16).

- *Selected and modified or supplemented by consensus.* The people who will use the standards should be involved in selecting and modifying or supplementing the standards. Those who will use the standards include teachers, administrators, students, parents, and representatives of higher education, businesses, and the community (Mitchell, 1996, pp. 19, 22; NEGP, 1993, p. 13; Tucker & Codding, 1998, p. 57). So far, the standards-setting process has been an extraordinarily middle-class-driven phenomenon. In fact, the process of setting standards should reflect the diversity of society. It should involve, for example, teachers, parents, and community members who understand students with disabilities, students from low-income communities, and students from homes where English is a second language. The discussions among these various constituencies about what is essential, clear, useful, balanced, and so on, can prove enlightening, even transforming, for the participants. Indeed, standards cannot serve as the driving force behind all efforts to improve a school if all these groups do not feel that their voices have been heard and considered during the standard-setting process.

- *Adaptable and flexible.* Standards should be flexible enough to allow for differences across localities. They should be adaptable to varying regional, state, and cultural concerns and interests. The standards should not give any specific advantage to students from any particular backgrounds (NEGP, 1993, p. 15; Tucker & Codding, 1998, p. 57). Though essential concepts and principles may not vary by locality, the most vivid manifestations of those concepts will vary, and standards should be flexible enough to allow for multiple avenues of study.

"Place-based" curriculum exemplifies the notion of embedding work in a local setting, connecting the community to other related contexts, and adding value to others in the school and in the community. Students can strengthen their connections to the community—its people, economy, cultural and social history, natural resources, flora and fauna—and can view themselves and be viewed by others as making essential contributions to their communities (Haas & Nachtigal, 1998). For instance, in science, the study of the subject-specific concept "ecology" may focus on industrial water pollution in communities on the Mississippi River and industrial air pollution in the Northeast. Such a place-based curriculum could thus relate to local resources and needs, leading students to genuine expertise in an important issue and even public presentation of findings and recommendations.

Tailoring Mandated Standards. Some states and districts have developed academic standards that meet all the criteria. Unfortunately, however, state and district standards that do not meet the criteria are not uncommon. What should a school do when faced with unwieldy or downright poor state or district standards? What the school should not do is ignore the twin towers of excellence and equity. The following are ideas that should be useful in addressing two common complaints about mandated standards.

One common complaint is that the standards are not focused on the big ideas within or across subject areas. Even a poorly designed standard, such as one based on a list of facts, can be transformed into a useful guideline if teachers incorporate those discrete facts into a system that addresses the essential concepts, the big ideas that such standards do not explicitly state. For example, a standard might indicate that students should know the dates for the major battles of the American Civil War. Learning to this "standard" is a memorization task, not an exercise in conceptual understanding. However, if the Civil War were studied as part of analyzing the concept "patterns," a connection could be made to a generalization about patterns, for example, that patterns allow for predictions. With that concept and principle in mind, the list of dates no longer stands in isolation, but becomes part of a larger understanding that the dates tie into a pattern of engagement determined by such factors as weather, road conditions, supply lines, and military tactics. This pattern allows for predicting not just approximate dates of battles in the Civil War but, with modifications, patterns of military engagement generally, providing students with an opportunity to understand contemporary conflicts such as the crisis in Kosovo in 1999.

A second common complaint is that the sheer number of standards makes it impossible for a school to attend to every one of them. Taken together, mandated standards in the disciplines, or even within a single discipline, may require more time for teaching, learning, and assessment than any school could ever hope to provide. Teachers' and administrators' concerns about "covering" everything that the standards apparently demand often ties directly to their concern (or fear) about being held accountable for "a little bit about everything." Coverage means touching on many topics or facts, in a shallow fashion (to wit, the American textbook). Coverage may also be defined as hiding or obscuring from view or knowledge. The irony is that superficial coverage often subverts understanding, and without understanding, students do not succeed on the very measures for which schools are held accountable (Ashton & Webb, 1986; Tye, 1985, p. 141; Wiggins & McTighe, 1998, p. 3). On a test covering a myriad of topics, students are hard pressed to recall facts presented in isolation, devoid of meaning or connection, and teachers are held accountable for the inevitably highly variable performance.

To direct teaching and learning toward understanding will require *uncovering* the absolutely essential concepts and ideas embedded in lengthy standards and developing a curriculum that reflects these essential concepts, both subject-specific and generic, thus revealing connections within and across content areas. With concepts as the framework for learning, the topics and facts can be hooked into a structure, within which those seemingly disconnected scraps become part of a coherent whole. To be sure, this is no small task, but it is a necessary one if poorly conceived state and local standards are to make sense as the basis for educating young adolescents.

In her systematic examination of how standards, assessments, and accountability were affecting classroom practices in elementary and middle schools, Margaret McLaughlin (2000, p. 24) describes the sense of urgency driving the teachers:

> Perhaps the most overriding concern expressed by teachers across all four districts was how to deliver these standards and meet the new expectations with *all* students. Indeed, the need for strategies for the students who were struggling dominated the conversations with teachers about standards and assessments. . . . [T]eachers considered that new curricular reforms, e.g., standards, were clashing with the available instructional time. Teachers reported having to teach more concepts, skills, and processes during a semester or school year. The result [was] an ever-increasing pace of instruction that left little time for reteaching or catching up slower students.

McLaughlin says that teachers can become caught up in a "treadmill effect," going faster and faster to cover more and more, and leaving students behind as they rush to deal with all the standards. She recommends that educators instead prioritize what to teach by envisioning a continuum from most vital to least vital. All the knowledge, skills, and habits of minds that every student should learn are on one end of the continuum, and farther along the continuum are some things that could fall by the wayside.

Comparing and Selecting Standards. As a way of assessing the quality of state and local standards and in order to adapt these standards to meet the specific needs of a particular school community, schools can obtain copies of standards documents from the professional organizations and the 49 state education agencies that have developed standards. However, the stack of documents that would result from requests to all these organizations and states would prove very unwieldy, both literally and figuratively. The standards documents vary on every criterion outlined in the preceding section, so that making comparisons and selections across them, by hand and without a road map, would be a daunting task. Instead, educators can turn to two sources for quicker and easier access to the multiple standards documents: Achieve, Inc., and the Mid-Continent Regional Education Laboratory.

Achieve, Inc., is an organization created at the 1996 Second National Education Summit to track each state's progress toward raising expectations for all students. Achieve offers an interactive clearinghouse for standards on its website, www.achieve.org, through which users can access a searchable database to compare standards, assessments, or workplace skill needs across states, and even across countries. The clearinghouse also provides samples of assessment questions, student work, and lesson plans that are linked to state standards (Achieve, Inc., 1998).

The Mid-Continent Regional Education Laboratory (McRel), a nonprofit education organization that specializes in "applied educational research and development" (Marzano & Kendall, 1996, p. 28), has developed a database that presents the available standards in a common, accessible format. Partly funded by the federal Office of Educational Research and Improvement, the database is available on the World Wide Web at www.mcrel.org/standards-benchmarks/.

McRel analyzed all the standards and related documents, across various disciplines, from professional organizations, states, and privately funded projects. It then constructed standards and benchmarks derived from 85 sets of standards documents. Each benchmark has a "citation log" that shows which documents the standard appears in, either explicitly or implicitly (Marzano & Kendall, 1996, pp. 28–29, 31). For each standard, McRel provides benchmarks at four levels: primary, upper elementary, middle grades, and high school. Benchmarks, as defined by McRel, "describe the specific developmental components of the general subject-area knowledge identified by the standard" (Marzano & Kendall, 1996, p. 25). For example, one standard for mathematics reads, "Uses a variety of strategies in the problem-solving process." The middle grades benchmark would break that standard down into components appropriate for middle grades students—for example, "understands how to break a complex problem into simpler parts or use a similar problem type to solve a problem." One of the high school benchmarks for the same standard asks that students "construct algorithms for multi-step and non-routine problems."

Developing Curriculum Based on Standards

Curriculum Development Using Backward Design. Curriculum defines the specifics of *what* students should learn: the concepts and generalizations, the related topics and facts, and the skills and habits of mind that will enable learning. Curriculum based on standards defines in exact terms what students should know and be able to do.

In backward design, educators start with the academic standards that define what students should know and be able to do, then decide on the assessments that will allow students to demonstrate their mastery of the knowledge and skills, and finally develop the instructional experiences that will prepare students to show what they have learned. The next sections describe the basic components of developing curriculum based on standards, although the actual process is variable and continuous. As teachers design a unit, both assessment and instructional methods can have implications for curriculum, making the design process iterative, and creative, at every juncture (see Box 3.3).

Selecting standards for a unit of study. The process of curriculum development for a unit of study begins with an analysis of what students should learn during the unit, as outlined in academic standards. To be eminently practical, schools could *begin* by designing curriculum grounded in the standards that they know will be assessed in current state norm-referenced or criterion-referenced

Box 3.3 Backward Design

Five years ago, Salem, Massachusetts, merged its two middle schools into one. Today, despite having more than 100 teachers and 1,100 students—half of them poor and a third of them Dominican immigrants whose first language is Spanish—Collins Middle School is a thriving learning community.

Teacher collaboration makes possible Collins's schoolwide emphasis on a purposeful form of curriculum planning often called backward design. Employing this method, teachers start by studying standards and then setting goals for students based on those standards. They then conceive of projects that will give students—who have a variety of learning needs—opportunities to demonstrate that they have gained the requisite understandings and skills. Then teachers choose instructional activities that support their overall intent.

As Collins teachers create curriculum, revisiting and fine-tuning their plans every year, they always begin by asking the question: What is it we want students to know and be able to do? The standards Collins teachers consult to answer that question are the seven Massachusetts Curriculum Frameworks: Arts, English/Language Arts, Health, Mathematics, Science and Technology, Social Studies, and World Languages.

For each framework, the Salem school district has a team that includes teachers from kindergarten through the 12th grade, parents, community leaders, and experts such as staff from local museums. They decide which part of each framework will be done at each grade level. With the information from the district framework teams in hand, Collins teachers meet as grade-level subject area teams and hammer out what units they'll do.

Nancy Jennings Pelletier, a seventh-grade science/math teacher at Collins, and her team chose three units for the year: the characteristics of life, which included cell biology, classification, and one-celled organisms; the human body; and biomes.

The team made sure that these units addressed the state standards. For example, the science framework states that children should be able to describe the idea that in complex multicellular organisms, cells have specialized functions, communicate with each other, and are mutually dependent. Two of the seventh-grade units—the characteristics of life and the human body—helped students achieve mastery of that standard.

As they develop units, Collins teachers often use the Atlas template, a tool developed by the Cambridge-based Education Development Center to guide schools in developing curriculum. The Atlas template requires teams to fill in blanks describing the theme of each unit, the questions that will drive their exploration and the essential understandings—the most important concepts, generalizations, and issues—they want students to grasp.

The science teachers also delineated the skills students would practice and develop during the unit and the habits of mind that will be stressed throughout. They

BOX 3.3 CONTINUED

divided the skills into those needed for science, reading and writing, research and technology, and critical thinking. And they said that students would learn to ask questions that could be answered by experiments, to measure accurately, to make predictions, to write lab reports, to find reference materials, to develop graphs, and to recognize cause and effect.

Then, the science teachers planned how they would address and assess understandings and skills. They decided on key products—called benchmark performances—that students would develop. They had to think about what kinds of practice and instruction students would need as they develop their products and what kind of feedback would help students understand the criteria for high-quality work.

After the team signed off on the units and the major understandings and skills, Pelletier paired off with another science teacher to work out the nitty-gritty of how her unit would proceed. Teachers at Collins often pair off this way, Pelletier says. "The work is so involved, it's difficult to do it alone," she adds. "Kids could write questions about micro- and macro-organisms till the end of time, but we needed to focus them on developing questions they could investigate and research. They had to come up with a plan for an experiment and show me it would work."

Pelletier made a rubric for all the components of her unit, which included quizzes, tests, speeches, and writing journals, as well as the final exhibition. The criteria she established for the final exhibition meant that students would be assessed on how well they understood and used the scientific method, cited research, and drew on a variety of resources.

Pelletier introduced the students to the scientific method and took them to a local pond, where they collected protists and fungi. She worked with small groups of students, pushing them to hone their questions in ways that would lead them to the essential understandings she knew they had to get out of the unit.

The kids also discussed what makes a good question, and critiqued each other's ideas. One student wanted to ask: What is athlete's foot and why do people get it? The student was going to scrape fungus between kids' toes, Linda Darisse, the math/science curriculum coordinator, says. "The kids decided that was the grossest thing they ever heard. 'Redesign your experiment,' they said." The student decided to do a survey instead.

The three-fold storyboards students presented at the unit's finale had to show the scientific process. They had to include their original hypothesis and how it changed, data, illustrations, a conclusion, and a description of new questions raised by their experiment. "They were masterpieces," Pelletier says, calling the unit "the most rewarding thing" she's ever done. "It wasn't just about curriculum. We're teaching them how to be independent learners."

Darisse points out that Pelletier's unit worked well both for the kids who in other schools might be tracked into gifted-and-talented programs and for those who might be tracked into so-called remedial programs. "If you individualize, everyone works at their own level," says Darisse. (The classes at Collins are heterogeneously grouped, though the district has alternative placements outside Collins for the very few children—seven of more than 1,100—whose behavior problems make them disruptive in the classroom.) "Some of the exhibits were sophisticated and others were plain and ordinary, but all the students learned about scientific methods."

"This kind of curriculum planning is as much circular as it is backward because you keep going back," says Darisse. Laura Chesson, director of math and science programs at the Center for Collaborative Education (CCE) in Boston, coaches in Collins classrooms and attends the school's curriculum meetings. On a regular basis, Collins teachers reflect on whether they've met their goals. Chesson explains, "You plan the curriculum, teach it, assess the students, and then look at the student work and review the assessment to see if you need to make changes to your curriculum and instruction in order to help your students better meet standards."

assessments (Schmoker & Marzano, 1999, p. 20). By this we mean focusing on the essential concepts and principles within the standards that will be assessed, not on isolated facts or discrete skills with no broader conceptual understanding. Starting with the standards that are incorporated within state tests can help educators avoid the energy-sapping effort of trying to address every single mandated standard, even though many of them may turn out to be irrelevant or unassessable. To be clear, however, young adolescents need a much richer curriculum than could be captured on a state test. Reviewing what standards are assessed at the state level is only a beginning point in developing middle grades curriculum.

Concepts and essential questions. Most efforts to learn begin with questions. As Grant Wiggins (1998, p. 209), a respected expert on assessment, points out, "'Why are we doing this?' and 'What is its value?' are questions that any curriculum should explicitly address, and a student should rarely need to ask. The answers should be evident."

To answer these questions, curriculum writing should be grounded in three strategies. First, the entire curriculum—including what is addressed, how it is addressed, and in what sequence—should be organized around important concepts and questions. "Essential" concepts and questions, drawn from the standards, provide the rationale for inclusion, or exclusion, of particular content (Mitchell, Willis, & the Chicago Teachers Union Quest Center, 1995, pp. 4–5; Pate, Homestead, & McGinnis, 1997, pp. 34–35; Wiggins, 1998, p. 209). Second, the curriculum should reflect the concerns of young adolescents. Third, the work should be oriented toward the assessments, the tasks students will undertake to demonstrate their knowledge and skills.

Concepts frame the big ideas a curriculum will address. Concepts can be "generic" in that they cross several disciplines, like "relationships" or "order." They can also be integral to the understanding of a discipline—that is, "subject-specific," like perspective in art, hubris in literature, or justice in ethics (Tomlinson, 1998, p. 5). Concepts may stand alone, or they may be embedded within essential questions, which should "demand answers . . . inspire and energize student learning" (Mitchell et al., 1995, p. 5).

Research has revealed that experts in various fields rely on extensive knowledge of the subject matter (Chase & Simon, 1973, pp. 33–81; Chi, Feltovich, & Glaser, 1981, pp. 121–152). Their knowledge, however, cannot be depicted as a list of distinct facts. Instead, "expert" knowledge is connected and organized around important concepts, like Newton's second law of motion (Bransford, Brown, & Cocking, 1999, p. 9). If experts' knowledge is structured around concepts (the organizing or big ideas), then curriculum should be structured in the same way in order to foster conceptual understanding. However, "many approaches to curriculum design make it difficult for students to organize knowledge meaningfully. Often there is only superficial coverage of facts before moving on to the next topic; there is little time to develop important, organizing ideas" (Bransford et al., 1999, p. 30).

In an example of the power of concepts, researchers asked expert physicists and competent beginners how they would go about solving particular physics problems. Experts usually mentioned the major principle(s) or law(s) that were applicable to the problem, together with a rationale for why those laws applied to the problem and how one could apply them. In contrast, competent beginners rarely referred to the major principles and laws in physics; instead, they typically described which equations they would use and how those equations would be manipulated (Chi et al., 1981, pp. 121–152; Larkin, 1981, pp. 311–334; Larkin, 1983, pp. 75–98).

Essential questions, concepts, and generalizations help students remember facts and topics, because these overarching notions help organize the seemingly trivial into meaningful patterns (Erickson, 1998, p. viii; Tomlinson, 1998, p. 5). Young adolescents are ready to seek out patterns, to make connections, to try to figure out the world around them and their place in it as part of their journey toward adulthood. With the big ideas guiding their learning in school, they can see how historical precedents could affect their own futures, how mathematics can help them make sense of the seemingly random, and how literature provides insight into the state of humanity.

Concepts and essential questions focus on the big ideas that reveal patterns while deeply engaging students in the process of making sense of the world around them. Essential questions should incorporate concepts and provide opportunities and incentive for students to discover or construct meaning out of the seemingly random swirl of facts. Like concepts, essential questions can be generic, cross-disciplinary, or subject-specific (see Box 3.4).

Concepts and essential questions will effectively drive a unit of study if they

Box 3.4 Examples of Essential Questions

Is our history a history of progress?

Can novels reveal inner life without falsifying it?

Do statistics lie?

"War is diplomacy by other means." Is this true? Is it immoral if we believe it?

Are some aspects of language and culture not understandable by people from other cultures?

Is terrorism wrong? Do revolutionaries differ from terrorists? Or from criminals? Were our country's founders terrorists?

Is gravity a fact or a theory?

Do mathematical models conceal as much as they reveal?

In what ways are animals human? In what ways are humans animals?

Is biology destiny?

What does it mean to be free in a democratic society?

What natural disasters are most likely to occur in your area, and how should the community prepare?

What would happen if all bacteria and fungi were eliminated from earth?

Is there life in outer space?

Does history repeat itself?

If the sale of tobacco in the United States were banned, what types of replacement crops could be used to maintain the economy?

Do the United States or the United Nations have the right or the responsibility to interfere in the internal affairs of foreign countries?

Do the federal government or state governments have a responsibility to give financial assistance to people who have suffered losses due to major catastrophes (such as floods, hurricanes, and tornadoes)?

Is it possible to sustain the projected world population with present food production methods?

Source: Adapted from Wiggins (1998) and Mitchell et al. (1995).

- Highlight a major understanding, problem, issue, or idea at the heart of the discipline or disciplines (Harris & Carr, 1996, p. 16; Wiggins, 1998, p. 214).
- Encompass several standards and focus the unit of study (Harris & Carr, 1996, p. 16).
- Connect with all students' lives—their experiences, understandings, and interests—by being culturally relevant to diverse populations (Harris & Carr, 1996, p. 16; Tomlinson, 1998, p. 6).

- Provoke and sustain student interest. For example, "It's one thing to ask 'Did Gorbachev fulfill or undermine the promise of the Russian Revolution?' It is another to ask 'Who blew it?' The latter question clearly works better for working with adolescents than the former, even if their purpose is the same" (Wiggins, 1998, p. 215).
- Relate to the world outside the school (Harris & Carr, 1996, p. 16), particularly to the local community. Making the bridge is particularly important for English language learners, whose home and school lives may be quite disparate.
- Foster creative, critical, and higher-order thinking (Tomlinson, 1998, p. 6; Wiggins, 1998, p. 215).
- Demonstrate patterns critical to the area(s) studied and to all students' lives (Tomlinson, 1998, p. 5).
- Yield no single obvious right answer and require both skills and content to answer them, in the case of essential questions (Mitchell et al., 1995, p. 50; Wiggins, 1998, p. 214).
- Relate to other concepts and questions. Essential concepts and questions can be seen as the parents of a family of related concepts and questions that anchor a unit. Student questions that arise during the unit can clarify the overarching question or concept (Wiggins, 1998, p. 215).

To improve the selection of an organizing concept or question, whether for disciplinary or integrated study, teachers should critically ask the following questions (Texas Education Agency, 1999, p. 13):

- What do students need to know about _____ to face compelling challenges in the future?
- How will the study of _____ help students become collaborative, cooperative citizens?
- What do students need to know about _____ in order to be self-directed, lifelong learners?

Concepts and essential questions should be grounded in the standards, but generating them does not have to rely solely on looking at standards documents. Student and teacher questions and concerns, community concerns and resources, source materials, and the like can all be used as sources of concepts and questions to be explored. The trick is ensuring that standards are embedded in the concepts and questions that emerge from these other sources.

Connecting to the concerns of young adolescents. Beane (1997) argues that the most powerful sources for concepts and questions are "the concerns of young people and social issues." He points out that personal and social concerns are likely to frame the way young people already organize their knowledge and experiences, making "'integration' all the more probable and meaningful" (p. 15). The connection between student concerns and learning also makes it all the more essential to develop a curriculum that is accessible and culturally relevant to today's diverse student populations, regardless of their socioeconomic or language background. For example, a strong curriculum should integrate multiracial and multiethnic materials and activities, such as plays, music, and role playing. All students should be presented with multiple perspectives and have the opportunity to link the new concepts being taught to their own experiences. In creating such a curriculum, the students' cultural and language diversity adds to the classroom environment, forming an instructional setting that encompasses rather than alienates students outside the "mainstream."

If students can discover the connections between disciplines and themselves, the current world, and the future that awaits them, the curriculum we have been trying so hard to "cover" may at last be uncovered as meaningful, relevant to their own lives, and motivating.

Linking skills to content and capability. Once the concepts have been identified, teachers must make decisions about which skills should be incorporated in the unit. To the extent possible, units of study should encompass critical or higher-order thinking, problem solving, research, communication, social and affective skills, and habits of mind (Pate et al., 1997, p. 35). To determine which skills to include in a unit of study, teachers and students can draw from two main sources: the content (that is, the standards, concepts, and questions to be incorporated into the unit) and the gaps that need to be filled in students' existing skills.

As part of meeting the criteria of "assessability," standards reveal, sometimes quite explicitly, which skills will be required for success. Concepts can also imply the skills students will need to acquire understanding. For example, to understand the concept of "perspective" in a visual arts unit, a student will likely need to research and analyze paintings, critique the use of perspective in various works of art, and perhaps use creative thinking skills to draft his or her own piece of artwork that incorporates perspective.

Essential questions may imply that students will need to use certain skills to answer the queries. Requisite skills (such as to compare, contrast, synthesize, and criticize) are implied in finding answers to questions such as the following: What is the nature of addiction, and what systems in the body are affected by it? What are the implications, both social and political, of research on addiction and addicts' control over their behavior? How does the generalization, "systems interact," play out in analyzing the connections between the muscular system and the nervous system? Where and why do the connections break down?

Once they have identified the skills required by the content that students will address, teachers and students should work together to determine which skills and habits the students already have and which ones they need to develop or strengthen (Pate et al., 1997, p. 35; Texas Education Agency, 1999, p. 39). Do they need to learn how to justify their problem-solving strategies, target their research, or analyze the truth of competing arguments? Could they use practice in social skills, like collaborating on projects, listening actively, or persisting through difficulties? How should communication skills be incorporated— for example, strengthening their capacity to write for different purposes and audiences and to speak with passion, persuasiveness, and accuracy?

Disciplinary and Integrated Curriculum. Academic standards are typically organized by discipline or subject—standards for language arts, standards for science, standards for math, and so on. The original *Turning Points* report calls for integrating subject matter across disciplines, a seemingly problematic suggestion in light of discipline-based standards (CCAD, 1989, pp. 47–48). However, we do not subscribe to the notion that curriculum must be either discipline-based or integrated, a notion that Heidi Hayes Jacobs (1989, p. 13) calls the "polarity issue." Instead, curriculum should encompass both sides of the polarity. Concepts and essential questions, unlike most standards, can function both within disciplines *and* across them.

Although disciplines and departments have reigned in schools for decades, few would contend that these structures have led most students to deep understandings of the various subjects. For example, as the TIMSS results revealed so dramatically, American students lag behind their peers in other industrialized nations in the two key disciplines the study considered—science and math (Schmidt, McKnight, & Raizen, 1997, pp. 116–120).

Clearly, something else needs to happen if students are to meet or exceed high academic standards. We can start by recognizing that schools, as learning organizations, likely learn the way individuals do: "learners use their current knowledge to construct new knowledge and . . . what they know and believe at the moment affects how they interpret new information. Sometimes learners' current knowledge supports new learning, sometimes it hampers learning. . . ." (Bransford et al., 1999, p. 141). If we want to improve teaching and learning in schools, reformers must start with where the schools are, just as teachers must discover what their students understand, and misunderstand, in order to target curriculum, instruction, and assessment appropriately.

The disciplinary approach. If schools and the educators within them start from a discipline-based viewpoint, then improvement can begin by focusing on teaching and learning in the disciplines. Greeno (1991, p. 175) compared learning a discipline thoroughly to "learning the landscape": "learning your way around, learning what resources are available, and learning how to use those resources in conducting your activities productively and enjoyably." Each discipline presents an incredibly complex landscape, requiring extensive knowledge and skills. To teach effectively, teachers must master both content knowledge and instructional skills tied specifically to the content (McDonald & Naso, 1986, p. 8); they must also tailor both content and instruction to facilitate learning by nonnative English speakers. More than just knowing the map of the discipline's landscape, which roads connect and which just lead to dead ends, expert teachers can anticipate where their students may get lost—that is, they are aware of common misunderstandings—and draw on effective instructional strategies to help the students reach their learning destinations. Cooperative learning, for example, can be a successful technique both to teach content to and raise self-esteem among all students, particularly those whose native language is not English.

Going deeper in each discipline will address the "mile wide and inch deep" criticism of American curriculum in the TIMSS report (Schmidt et al., 1997).

Too much of traditional curriculum is fragmented and fragmenting, essentially fostering students who cannot see the forest for the trees. Subject-specific concepts and essential questions can reveal the connections, providing a bird's-eye view of the forest and motivating learners to plunge into the woods with compass in hand.

The integrated approach. For schools that understand the power of the big ideas for deepening curriculum within disciplines, using that power to show connections across disciplines is a logical step. Broad-based generic concepts, generalizations, and questions that go across disciplines are the driving force of integrated curriculum design (Jacobs, 1989, pp. 16–17; Texas Education Agency, 1999, p. 7; Tomlinson, 1998, pp. 4–6). We will use the term "integrated" rather than "interdisciplinary" because we believe that it better captures the coherence in curriculum design that we advocate. However, practitioners often use these terms interchangeably to describe any effort to make curriculum connections across disciplines, and though some researchers (e.g., Powell & Faircloth, 1997, pp. 209–219) argue that the terms should not be used interchangeably, for our purposes, interdisciplinary and integrated mean the same thing. (For more on how we define different curriculum designs, see Box 3.5).

The integrated approach requires each teacher on a team to rank the standards and the resulting key concepts and essential questions within his or her own discipline, "selectively abandoning" content and skills from the traditional, often packed, curriculum. The teachers then bring their discipline-based priorities to a team effort to discover overlaps in the concepts, questions, skills, and habits of mind that undergird their disciplines. Standards are used as rich sources of ideas for revealing the connections across disciplines. As the commonalities emerge from their discussions, the teachers can identify the overarching ideas and processes they will integrate across subjects (Fogarty, 1991, pp. 76–80). Teams should begin by developing pilot integrated units of three to four weeks' duration, since integration of this complexity will require time, energy, and a willingness to reflect on one's practice.

Within this model, for example, the concept of "systems" and the generalization "systems are made up of parts that work together" could guide the study of societies in social studies, systems in the body in science, features of a story in language arts, and rules of algebra in mathematics. In a seventh-grade team using the key concepts of systems, interdependence, and change in an integrated unit,

> One student told [his math teacher] it helped him to understand equations better to think about them like changes in the lives of people. Another student wrote that she liked history better when she could think of it like an equation, where things on one side of the equal sign change when things on the other side change. . . . Teachers of the [team] find that they can connect subjects easily within their own domains by inviting students to talk about concept- and principle-based connections they are seeing. . . . Most satisfying to both the [students] and their teachers is the high relevance that subject matter takes on when organized around concepts and

BOX 3.5 Definitions and Examples of Curriculum Designs

Integrated Design

Use a broad-based concept, theme, or essential question that goes across all the disciplines as the driving force of curriculum. We offer two examples of integrated design. The first is oriented around a student-generated question; the second around a teacher-generated concept.

Example: Student-generated questions; concepts, skills, and generalizations are all taught in a context authentic to the questions.

Question: What will the future be like?

Social Studies: How will our government operate? Investigate the current political system, its advantages and disadvantages, and make predictions about how democracy will evolve.

Math: How long will we live? Investigate insurance actuarial calculations, looking at the variables considered, the potential factors influencing those variables, and use accepted formulas to make predictions about longevity.

Science: What will the environment look like? Analyze current protections for the environment and the current status of certain ecosystems, and make predictions about what will happen if nothing changes and what could happen if laws and regulations were made more environment-friendly.

Language Arts: What important themes will dominate literature? How will technology affect communication—in particular, writing? Look at modern literature to analyze connections between typical themes and plot devices and current events, then make predictions about how those themes may change.

(Based on an example in Schumacher, 1995, p. 76).

Example: Teacher generated concept and generalization; all related content and skills are taught and learned in relation to the broad-based concept and generalization.

Broad-based concept: Patterns

Generalization: Patterns allow for prediction.

Social Studies: Analyze wars over 100 years to determine patterns of cause and effects. Predict what can be expected for the next 100 years.

Math: Examine patterns of division of numbers and prime numbers. Predict other prime numbers.

Science: Analyze plate tectonic theories and their patterns for prediction of the earth's movement.

Language Arts: Examine patterns of change due to conflict in characters' actions and attitudes and predict future development

(Example adapted from Texas Education Agency, 1999).

Multidisciplinary or Parallel Design

Lessons or units developed across many disciplines with a common organizing topic.

> *Example:* Teacher-generated topic
> *Topic:* Rainforest
> *Science:* Forest biomes
> *Social Studies:* Geography and history of tropical regions
> *Language Arts:* Read *The Emerald Forest*
> *Math:* Charts and graphs of rainfall and deforestation
> *Fine Arts:* Build a simulated rain forest.

(Example adapted from Texas Education Agency, 1999).

For more on levels of curriculum integration and how some researchers distinguish between "integrated" and "interdisciplinary" curriculum, we recommend:

Schumacher, D. H. (1995). Five levels of curriculum integration defined, refined, and described. *Research in Middle Level Education, 18*(3), 73–94.

principles. Both teachers and students continue to make comparisons between systems, interdependence, and change in their own lives, the school, news, movies, music, and so on. . . ." (Tomlinson, 1998, pp. 4–5)

The weaknesses of the multidisciplinary approach. Contrast the integrated approach described above with the far more common multidisciplinary, or topic-based, approach. In a multidisciplinary approach, units are developed across several disciplines with a common topic, sometimes called a "theme," as the organizer. The topics are often drawn from what Beane (1997, p. 14) calls "appealing topics," like "oceans," "dinosaurs," or even "apples."

Though such topics may generate interesting activities and projects, they share a few common weaknesses. The topics themselves do not seem to warrant the time invested in them (Edelsky, Altmeyer, & Flores, 1991, pp. 64–68). Topic-based units can fall prey to the "cool" factor, meaning that they may be fun to do and may lead up to showy culminating tasks, but they may not connect to standards and vital concepts in any meaningful way. Coila Morrow (1999), an expert on standards-based professional development in Texas, bemoans the classrooms full of "sugar cube Alamos" and detailed cardboard castles. These concrete projects do require "hands-on" work, given the glue and construction materials required, but they too often have little to do with fundamental, relevant, or substantive concepts. These topic-based studies also tend to focus on facts and information instead of ideas and principles, promote coverage rather than understanding, demonstrate little relevance to students' lives, and have little potential for transfer to new contexts (Tomlinson, 1998, p. 6).

To be clear, the important question is what organizing ideas drive the unit's focus on a topic. Sugar cube Alamos may be fine, for example, if their construction requires students to think critically, applying important historical and mathematical concepts, analyzing proportion to make design decisions, and the like. If the critical thinking required is limited to where to find sugar cubes in an age of powdered artificial sweeteners, however, then the unit is just showy, not substantive.

Finally, topic-based multidisciplinary units can feel "forced," with some subjects fitting the topic well and others fitting like square pegs in round holes. A math teacher (Ray, 1999) expresses her concern with this particular problem:

> Four years ago, I became very frustrated. Each time integrated/thematic instruction came up, there was generally at least one non-math content teacher who tried to bring in math through statistics. It seemed like every time a new idea came up, the statistics thing came up again. Keeping statistics of Civil War battles . . . keeping statistics on pollution . . . keeping statistics on the number of times a person did so and so . . . keeping statistics etc. . . . On and on with the statistics. Connections are what is most important. Sometimes, the connections come from within a particular content area; in other words, connecting what is being taught now with prior learning of something that seemed to be totally different, such as probability and Pascal's triangle.

Resources to Support Curriculum. To support curriculum based on standards, teachers will need access to rich, engaging resources. Once a school has identified the standards and curriculum to be taught and learned, teachers will need to begin gathering materials to support instruction, and that process will continue when the instructional methods have been planned in detail. The textbook industry thrives because educators do not have time to produce their own resources. However, today's textbooks typically will not mesh precisely with the standards, concepts, and questions to be addressed. Though the ideal might be to have teachers create their own curriculum materials, the reality does not allow enough time or support for that to happen. What should educators do in the real world of limits, without sacrificing quality?

First, educators can audit the curriculum materials currently available to them, including textbooks. In a curriculum audit, educators analyze these materials to discover how well aligned the resources are with the standards, concepts, and questions outlined in the curriculum. They will almost certainly identify gaps, places where the currently available materials fall short of supporting the learning outlined in the standards (Tucker & Codding, 1998, pp. 89–91). We recommend the work of Fenwick English (1992) for more information on effective auditing of curriculum.

To fill the gaps, educators may need to do two things: find commercially available materials that will align much more closely with the curriculum, or develop or pull together their own resources to bridge the gaps. Any commercial materials a school considers purchasing should first be audited in relation to the standards, concepts, and questions, just as the school's currently available materials were scrutinized. Educators should apply the same examination process to materials available from the various national reform initiatives. (See Box 3.6 for examples of questions to ask when evaluating curriculum programs.) Although an abundance of materials are available, nothing will plug all the holes. When teachers create or gather their own resources, again, the test of effectively supporting the standards must be met (Tucker & Codding, 1998, pp. 89–91).

Box 3.6 **Assessing Curriculum Packages: Some Questions To Ask**

Will this curriculum engage students in the "big ideas" of a discipline or disciplines?

Will this curriculum allow students some choice over the work they do to learn content in depth and some control over the resources they will use to understand those big ideas?

Will this curriculum involve students in in-depth discussions in heterogeneous groups?

Will this curriculum require students to develop critical thinking skills by gathering information, posing questions, synthesizing data and ideas, solving problems, and communicating?

Will this curriculum involve students in creating products much as real scientists, historians, social scientists, mathematicians, and authors create a product?

Will this curriculum allow students opportunities to see themselves in their learning?

Will this curriculum encourage students to seek feedback on, reflect on, and refine their thinking and their work?

Will those in the world outside the school use or value the products students create through this curriculum?

Will this curriculum encourage teachers' own development as learners?

Source: Adapted from Wheelock (1998).

ASSESSMENT: THE MIDPOINT OF BACKWARD DESIGN

Assessment should be designed to provide ongoing, useful feedback, to both students and teachers, on what students have learned. This feedback should be used to improve teaching and learning progressively, not just to audit student performance (Wiggins, 1998, pp. xi, xiii). Effective assessment should connect directly to curriculum and instruction. Simply put, assessments should be perfectly meshed with what we want students to learn.

Content standards outline what all students should know and be able to do, thus providing the foundation for teaching and learning. Essential concepts, principles, and questions are the frame built on that foundation, the walls and beams that organize knowledge and skills into coherence. In this metaphor, the carpenters (students) demonstrate their mastery of knowledge and skills when the structure they have built meets the relevant building codes, passing inspection and proving ready to support lifelong learning.

Assessment's Connection to Curriculum Based on Standards

Curriculum based on standards can be divided into three categories: knowledge and skills worth "enduring understanding" (Wiggins & McTighe, 1998, p. 10), those that require mastery (prerequisites), and those that require just simple familiarity. These categories have direct implications for prioritizing what a unit of study will include and deciding how to determine whether students have learned the requisite knowledge and skills.

For all students to be successful, to meet or exceed the "building codes" (performance standards), they must have a thorough understanding of the standards that form the foundation and the concepts and questions that form the frame. Wiggins and McTighe use the term "enduring understandings" to describe those things that anchor a unit of study. These are the things we want students to remember after they have forgotten the details.

Students also should master significant knowledge and skills that lie on the continuum between enduring understandings and simple familiarity. Such knowledge and skills are the "prerequisite(s) . . . needed by students for them to successfully accomplish key performances" (Wiggins & McTighe, 1998, p. 10).

We do not expect students to develop enduring understanding of everything they learn. At a rudimentary level, some things are just "worth being familiar with" (Wiggins & McTighe, 1998, p. 9). For example, in a science class, students would need an enduring understanding of plate tectonics, mastery of important knowledge like the connection between tectonics and volcanoes, and familiarity with the location of volcanoes in the Pacific's "ring of fire." Unfortunately, all too often much time and effort has been devoted to knowledge and skills that warrant only familiarity, like memorizing lists of facts, with the result that students do not gain the skills and enduring understandings they need to acquire and manipulate knowledge.

Using a Variety of Assessment Methods

Even though some 90 percent of evaluation takes place in the classroom, teacher preparation programs incorporate very little training in conducting meaningful evaluations (Mitchell, 1992, p. 3). To decide what assessments will reveal evidence of familiarity, mastery, and enduring understanding, teachers must consider a range of assessment methods that allow for ongoing and cumulative feedback, otherwise known as formative and summative assessment.

A curriculum should incorporate a variety of assessment methods, ranging from informal to formal, in the same way a court of law accepts evidence ranging from circumstantial to concrete. The range of assessment methods includes

- *Informal checks for understanding,* the kinds of activities, like oral questions, observations, and class discussions, that occur every day (Wiggins & McTighe, 1998, p. 12). Both students' responses to teachers' questions and students' questions for teachers serve as gauges of learning progress. This type of assessment is particularly useful for English language learners.
- *Traditional quizzes and tests,* typically made up of multiple-choice, true/false, fill-in-the-blank, and short essay questions (Wiggins & McTighe, 1998, p. 12). Weekly quizzes, for example, can provide a snapshot of students' grasp of factual information.
- *Interviews, questionnaires, and conferences,* all of which gather evidence from students by asking them for it. Interviews and conferences can provide valuable one-on-one time and immediate feedback. Regular interviews and conferences can also help students get better at self-assessment, as teachers indicate how students should prepare and what materials they should bring to a discussion of their progress (Stowell & McDaniel, 1997, p. 141).
- *Performance tasks and projects,* which are both examples of authentic or alternative assessment, so named because it provides an alternative to traditional tests and quizzes. Authentic assessment allows students to provide evidence of their learning in contexts and on tasks that draw on real life and real situations (Wiggins & McTighe, 1998, p. 12; Stowell & McDaniel, 1997, p. 141). Performance tasks "require students to actively accomplish complex and significant tasks, while bringing to bear prior knowledge, recent learning, and relevant skills to solve realistic problems" (Stowell & McDaniel, 1997, p. 142).

To focus a unit of study on enduring understanding, performance tasks or projects should be cornerstones of the unit's assessments. Such tasks give students the chance to demonstrate the depth and complexity of their knowledge and skills, while also allowing them to show that they can use those capacities in context. Performance tasks assess students' enduring understandings and their mastery of important knowledge and skills.

More traditional modes of assessment, like tests and quizzes, should be used to assess knowledge and skills that will contribute to success on performance tasks, including those things that students should just be familiar with and the prerequisites they will need to master (Wiggins & McTighe, 1998, pp. 13–15). Interviews and conferences can round out the assessment repertoire for a unit of study, providing "gut checks" in all three categories of content to be learned: the enduring understandings, the prerequisites, and the simply familiar. (See Box 3.7 for an example of multiple forms of assessment in practice.)

To assess students' work meaningfully, teachers must answer two basic questions: where should we look to find evidence of learning, and what should we look for to distinguish degrees of understanding? Wiggins and McTighe (1998, pp. 65, 67) encourage teachers to think of students "like juries think of the accused: innocent (of understanding) until proven guilty by a preponderance of the evidence."

Taken together, the assessment methods should be sensitive to small gains, should consistently monitor learning—daily is best—and should lead to corrections in instruction (Margaret McLaughlin, personal communication, January 15, 2000).

Focus on Authentic Assessment

In putting together a variety of assessment methods for the curriculum, teachers typically have little trouble incorporating the traditional methods like quizzes and tests. However, authentic assessment methods represent new territory for many educators, worthy of a closer look.

Authentic assessment methods concentrate on complex tasks, allow students to demonstrate what they can do in much the same way that adults do in settings outside the school, and require students to produce solutions or other products that demonstrate their learning (Darling-Hammond, Ancess, & Falk, 1995, p. 2). These methods engage students in learning by enabling them to make connections between themselves and the world outside. Put differently, they make learning interesting to students and relevant to their concerns.

Authentic assessments help students develop the skills to assess their own progress and products, to reflect on what they are, and are not, understanding. That reflection can motivate students to seek out the information and capacities that will fill in the holes they discover in the fabric of their learning. Such intrinsic motivation holds much more promise for their futures as lifelong learners than the extrinsic motivators of grades and adult demands (Mitchell, 1992, p. 19).

Preparing for an authentic assessment is, in itself, a learning activity (Fischer & King, 1995, pp. 52–53). To meet what Wiggins (1998, p. 217) calls the "work requirements," students must continually investigate and enrich their own understanding, think critically, solve problems, make decisions, and, in many such tasks, collaborate effectively with their peers.

Authentic assessments should also push students to apply and transfer their knowledge and skills in different contexts. Application and transfer are key indications of enduring understanding. Experts, in addition to organizing their knowledge around concepts, can identify other contexts in which their

Box 3.7   Multiple Forms of Assessment at Camels Hump

About 12 years ago, Susie Girardin thought it would be neat to do a unit on flight with her fifth graders at Camels Hump Middle School in Richmond, Vermont. She poured her considerable verve into making the unit exciting for her students. They heard from a visiting stunt pilot; they made wind socks; they studied wings at a bird museum. Yet looking back, Girardin doubts the children carried any enduring knowledge about flight with them into adulthood. If she ran into her former students today, she says, the only thing they probably would remember is that the wind socks resembled giant condoms fluttering outside the school.

Part of the problem, says Girardin, is that the unit wasn't tied to any standards. Lacking a specific purpose for teaching what she taught, she didn't have deliberate goals for what students should know or be able to do as a result of the unit. It was just so much "activity land," she says, a contrivance that's rampant among well-meaning teachers. Moreover, because she didn't use multiple forms of assessment throughout the unit in order to give kids different ways to show their learning, she didn't know what they really got out of it.

Today Girardin ties all of the teaching in her multi-age fifth- and sixth-grade classroom to standards. And she infuses her practice with a wide variety of assessment methods, allowing plenty of opportunity for students with diverse learning needs and styles to demonstrate that they have met the multilayered expectations embodied in those standards. Girardin and her teammate of ten years, Kerry Young, teach in a double-sized room that includes some children who come to school hungry and others who have their own horses.

Girardin and Young have not abandoned traditional assessments, such as multiple-choice quizzes, which capture student mastery of discrete facts. But they have made what are known as "authentic," "alternative," or "performance" assessments a prominent part of their teaching. These methods—which include journals, skits and plays, videos, surveys, posters, newspapers, labeled models, timelines, and debates—give Girardin detailed information about her students' learning lives, she says. Lacking that kind of information early in her teaching career, Girardin didn't know why she wasn't able to reach some of her students. The array of assessment tools now in her quiver ensures that she can help all children meet the standards.

"I have 53 students, and they all learn and show their knowledge in a multitude of ways," Girardin remarks. "I can't just trust my instincts. I need proof." Using a variety of assessment methods makes teachers reflective, she contends. When kids don't do well, instead of blaming the students or themselves, Girardin says teachers can look at the assessment and ask themselves questions such as, "Was the concept important enough that I need to go back?" "Was it the assessment tool itself, and they know the information but I didn't ask for it right?"

Her students often help select and design the assessment tools by which they are evaluated. Sometimes Girardin and her students review sample rubrics she has

BOX 3.7 CONTINUED

collected. Students discuss what is expected of them and put the rubrics in their own words. Girardin also shows students benchmarks, giving them a firsthand look at what constitutes excellent work, as well as adequate and inadequate efforts.

Because Girardin engages students in developing the criteria by which their products and performances are judged, they're better able to assess their own work, says Peggy Burke, Turning Points' program director for the New England region at the Center for Collaborative Education in Boston.

Whereas traditional assessment methods demand that students select a response from offerings presented by their teacher, authentic methods require that students construct a response based on their independent work. The latter can be hard at first on students who excel at absorbing and spitting back out the main points in a textbook chapter, Girardin says. With alternative assessments, they have to make meaning out of their new knowledge. And, paralleling the demands of the grown-up world, they have to put their new skills into action. "They're used to getting A's, and all of a sudden to get a 4 or 100 or an A they have to show me what they can do with the information."

Nontraditional assessment methods not only stretch the kids who ace tests; they give those who don't a chance to shine. Girardin herself isn't great at memorization and recitation, she says. She sings professionally on the side, but after performing at weddings promptly forgets the words and melodies of the songs she sang. "I don't hold information like that," she says. "Let me write about what I learned, talk about it, dramatize it. Just don't make me take a test."

Her commitment to using multiple forms of assessment influences Girardin's instructional choices. She makes sure, for example, that the culminating activities with which she concludes standards-based interdisciplinary studies enable students to demonstrate what they know and can do. Her kids have presented town officials with suggestions for solving municipal problems. One student who had served as class president attended a town meeting as part of an independent research project on governance. His culminating project was writing a booklet geared to future student office holders on the decision-making powers of the class president.

While making sure to assess students at every step of the way and to use a variety of methods over the course of each unit, Girardin guides students to choose assessment tools based on the depth of learning she's after, which she conceives of as three concentric circles of knowledge. Girardin explains:

> The first circle is information it's nice for everyone to know, such as how many farmers there are in Vermont. It's extraneous. You could travel into adulthood without it and know where to access it. For that, I give a true-and-false or multiple-choice test.
>
> The second circle is what I think all kids should have. So for farming in Vermont, that would be information about why farms have declined over the past ten years. It's more thought-provoking. There's no single answer. You can't

just say "sheep," or "the stock market." The answer is more mazelike and in-depth. For that, I assess the kids on products and performances. I might have them go out and interview people, do a group project, have guest speakers and write editorials.

The third and innermost circle is enduring knowledge. It's the hardest to assess. It's "How does this affect you as a 12- or 13-year-old in my class?" It's "What decisions do you think our legislature should be making?" It's "What do you know and feel when you see a farm tumbling down or a farm property subdivided into a big box store or a trailer park?" As an assessor for this circle, I'm not looking for regurgitation. I'm looking for that child's particular way of framing the information. I might have them come up with a journal or do an inquiry or have them design an individual research plan about something they're unsure of and go out and find out what they can.

Girardin admits that when she first embraced standards-based teaching and new assessment methods she thought textbooks and tests were to be avoided entirely. "But like all things I've learned since hitting my 40s, you don't throw the babies out with the bath water. You really need to have a good healthy assortment," says Girardin, adding that for some of the information they need—like multiplication tables—tests and traditional homework assignments make the most sense.

However, she says, to base the whole assessment of a child on quizzes and worksheets just checks for one kind of understanding. "It doesn't tell me as an assessor what that kid can do. It doesn't tell me how that child assimilates information or deduces information."

knowledge is applicable and then apply their knowledge appropriately in those contexts (Bransford, Brown, & Cocking, 1999, p. 9). The ability to identify other contexts in which their knowledge is applicable will allow students to know "when, where, and why to use the knowledge [and skills] they are learning" (Bransford et al., 1999, p. 31). For example, students can memorize mathematical formulas and concepts, but if they cannot transfer this knowledge to a variety of situations, they may not know which of those formulas to apply when designing a house.

The standards, concepts, and essential questions within the curriculum should be the first sources for ideas about authentic assessment. Teachers and students can brainstorm together, then refine and adapt their ideas to fit the standards, "revealing real-world connections that mirror the natural connections in [the] standards" (Mitchell et al., 1995, p. 52).

Examples of authentic assessment methods include simulations, formal debates, exhibitions, position papers, scientific experiments, individual and group research projects, and portfolios. Whatever the form, to be successful on a performance task in a unit of study based on critical concepts and essential questions, students must learn the substantive content and applicable skills necessary to do well. Wiggins (1998, pp. 216–217) offers these examples of performance tasks from a global studies course:

- Design a tour of the world's most holy sites.
- Write an International Bill of Rights.
- Write and research a position paper for your school administration on how to handle the diversity of viewpoints on the proper celebration and recognition of religious holidays in the school.

Every performance task must be customized to accommodate the standards to be addressed and the interests, needs, backgrounds, and learning styles of students (see Chapter 4 for more information on learning styles).

Though much has been written about particular authentic assessment methods, the purpose of this section is to outline the benefits and characteristics of these methods as a whole, not to describe particular strategies in detail. However, since rubrics and portfolios are both popular manifestations of authentic assessment, we will describe them briefly.

Rubrics. A rubric outlines a set of criteria, usually on a four- or six-point scale, with performance descriptions that define the range of performance on an authentic assessment task (Stowell & McDaniel, 1997, p. 142). Like performance standards that detail how good is good enough, rubrics describe exceptional, acceptable, and unacceptable work. For a specific performance task, teachers, often with the help of students, craft a rubric by first describing the high end of the scale, the exceptional work, then progressing through the other categories. At every point on the rubric's scale, its creators must decide what specific evidence they should see of the understandings and skills the assessment is to incorporate. Even-numbered rubrics work better than odd-numbered ones. Scorers will too often choose the middle score in an odd-numbered rubric.

Ideally, for each performance task teachers and students have a rubric *and* examples of student work that have received each score on the rubric's scale. The rubric itself should include enough detail to guide the students' efforts to succeed on the task, but the samples of student work are much richer sources of guidance.

Portfolios. A portfolio is a selection of a student's work, designed to demonstrate progress toward a predetermined goal (Mitchell et al., 1995, p. 105). The key word in this definition is "selection." Not merely a collection of everything a student has done, a portfolio contains pieces the student or the teacher decides are representative of the student's efforts, understanding, and skills. Especially when students decide on the contents, the construction of the portfolio is instructive in itself, as the students must be reflective in assessing their own progress and products. Portfolios reveal the students' growth over time, often across disciplines, and allow students to demonstrate their talents in fields outside a specific subject area, even including interests beyond academic work (Stowell & McDaniel, 1997, p. 144).

Although portfolios may contain as many as 50 "artifacts" of student work, 10 to 15 is more common. Student portfolios typically contain the following kinds of artifacts (Stowell & McDaniel, 1997, p. 144):

- Showcase pieces
- Work in progress
- Work the student has learned from
- Work that shows growth
- Goal statements
- Collaborative work
- Explanations of work
- Things from outside the school

Students typically include a cover letter that explains each piece and why it is in the portfolio, a letter that also requires the students to reflect on their improvement over time. As teachers and students become more comfortable with using portfolios, the students take on more responsibility for the quality of the work in their portfolios, and the teachers rely more on the students' detailed account of their progress toward achieving the standards that the collections demonstrate (Lamme & Hysmith, 1991, pp. 620–629). For example, portfolios can be useful as the basis for discussions in student-led conferences, parent–teacher conferences that are planned and conducted almost entirely by students (see Box 9.1 for more on student-led conferences).

Mitchell et al. (1995, p. 131) contends that "portfolios are the most flexible form of performance assessment. . . . They can be adapted to whatever purpose seems important, provided that the purpose is clear at the outset. And the amount of information they can provide about teaching and learning approaches infinity." However, she cautions that their very flexibility may be cause for concern. For example, if portfolios are used for accountability, of students or their teachers, portfolio contents must be standardized, and their readers must be reliable. Like anything else, portfolios cannot be all things to all people, although that tantalizing illusion is part of their allure.

CONCLUSION

Because academic standards outline what every student should know and be able to do, they also define excellence and equity. A curriculum based on standards should focus on the big ideas, encompass critical skills, and foster habits of mind that will produce lifelong learners. Assessment should tie in directly to curriculum based on standards, delineating how students will demonstrate that they understand the big ideas and can put their skills into practice.

In backward design, teachers plan a unit of study by deciding what standards the unit will address; developing a culturally relevant curriculum based on those standards that is applicable to all students, including English language learners; and determining how students will provide evidence of their learning through a variety of assessment methods. The remaining element of backward design is planning instruction—figuring out how to enable students to demonstrate what they know and can do. The next chapter describes instruction and its intertwined relationships with standards, curriculum, assessments, and the needs, interests, and learning styles of students.

4 Designing Instruction to Improve Teaching and Learning

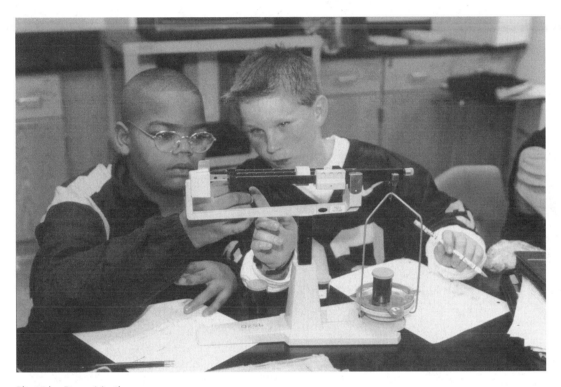

Photo by Doug Martin

ALL THE TURNING POINTS principles, taken together, lead toward a single goal: ensuring that every student achieves success. We define success as the Turning Points vision of a 15-year-old who, after a successful experience in the middle grades, is intellectually reflective, caring, ethical, healthy, a good citizen, and en route to a lifetime of meaningful work. To reach that goal, middle grades educators must substantially strengthen the heart of schooling—teaching and learning. The rhythms of teaching and learning are driven by what students should know and be able to do, as defined by the curriculum; what evidence will demonstrate their knowledge and skills, as outlined by assessment methods; and how they will be prepared to meet those standards, through instruction.

Instruction is the daily bread of classroom life, composed of the tools, strategies, lessons, and activities teachers and students use to learn. As described in the previous chapter, planning instruction is a critical element of backward design (see Box 3.3). Backward design (Mitchell et al., 1995, p. 5; Wiggins & McTighe, 1998, p. 8) entails

- Identifying what students should know and be able to do by the end of the unit, as outlined in content standards
- Developing a detailed curriculum based on those standards
- Deciding what assessments will allow students to demonstrate that they have achieved the standards
- Designing instruction to prepare students to do well on the assessments, as part of an overall effort to prepare them to think critically, lead healthful lives, and behave as caring, ethical, and responsible citizens en route to a lifetime of meaningful work

This chapter is based on what we have learned about teaching and learning over the past ten years, blending the wisdom of research and the best classroom practice. In it, we outline instruction's key connections and describe three useful models for organizing instruction; we then offer our own recommendations. We note the role that technology may play in instruction, and we also look at the particular needs of language minority students. Finally, we highlight the special case of teaching reading in the middle grades.

INSTRUCTION'S KEY CONNECTIONS

To be effective, instruction must mesh with three other aspects of teaching and learning:

- The *curriculum*, which is based on agreed-upon standards outlining what students should know and be able to do, the concerns of young adolescents, and how students learn best
- The *assessments* students will use to demonstrate their knowledge and skills
- The needs, interests, and concerns of *students* themselves

Standards form the basis for curriculum, supporting both excellence and equity by setting public, high expectations for *every* student. To prepare students to achieve the standards, teachers must themselves become students of their academic discipline(s). Each discipline represents a complicated landscape, through which teachers must help their students learn to maneuver with ease (Greeno, 1991).

Beyond mastering content knowledge, teachers must also become proficient in using effective instructional skills. Disciplinary knowledge and instructional knowledge *interact*, contradicting the common misconceptions "that teaching consists only of a general set of methods, that a good teacher can teach any subject, or that content knowledge alone is sufficient" (Bransford et al., 1999, pp. 143–144). Teachers should know both the written and unwritten instructional rules of the road that will help their students avoid common obstacles, take advantage of straightforward connections, and find their way to the enduring learning that will support their achievement of high standards.

Ongoing assessment, both formal and informal, should be used as a diagnostic tool, revealing what students have learned and pointing out gaps in their understanding and skills that need to be filled (Angelo & Cross, 1993, pp. 3–7; Wiggins & McTighe, 1998, pp. 12–13). Instruction should be organized to enable students to demonstrate what they have learned on the assessments, and it should be modified or extended based on the gaps in understanding and skill that students exhibit on those assessments.

To ensure the success of every student, instructional practice must address learners with diverse levels of readiness, rates of learning, preferred means of learning (learning styles), experiences, interests, and cultural backgrounds. To work effectively with such diversity, teachers must also become "students of their students" (Tomlinson, 1999, p. 2), adding a new dimension to the idea of a learning community.

EQUITY AND EXCELLENCE

Chapter 3 described how academic standards support both equity and excellence by setting high, public expectations for all students. To enable all students to achieve those high standards, teachers must use equitable and excellent instructional methods that meet students where they are and get the students where the standards say they should go, preparing them to succeed on assessments that reveal the students' knowledge and skills.

Organizing instruction appropriately for students who vary on multiple dimensions has taken many different guises. By far the most common method middle grades schools have used is tracking (Epstein & Mac Iver, 1990; Lounsbury & Clark, 1990, p. 138; Valentine, Clark, Irvin, Keefe, & Melton, 1993, p. 57), or placing students in distinct classes or groups based on actual or perceived evidence of capacity to learn (Braddock & Slavin, 1992, p. 1; Wheelock, 1992, p. 6).

Tracking may appear to be a rational way for a complex organization to deal with diverse "raw materials," in this case the students. In hopes of more efficiently accomplishing the goal of teaching all students, schools break up a large heterogeneous group into smaller, homogeneous groups (Gamoran, Nystrand, Berends, & LePorte, 1995, p. 688; Thompson, 1967, p. 70). Schools then establish a structure in which teachers deal with each small group separately, in much the same way that factory managers would send steel through one machine for processing and rubber through another. Since each small homogeneous group has different needs, the structure allows educators to target, at least theoretically, instructional practice appropriately for each group.

However, schools are not factories, and three critical characteristics of the real world get in the way of tracking's purported efficiency. First, grouping students is not a neutral act: research has demonstrated repeatedly that minority and economically disadvantaged students are overrepresented in the lower tracks (Braddock, 1989; Oakes, 1995, p. 60; Oakes, Gamoran, & Page, 1992, pp. 570–608). Though apparently objective, the measures used to divide students into groups by perceived ability reflect the culture and society within which the school operates. Grading practices, access to challenging curriculum and instruction, even allegedly "scientific" standardized tests all reflect a pattern of discriminatory practices buried deep in the psyche of American schools. As Gamoran et al. (1995, p. 689) point out, "the allocation of status within schools tends to coincide with social status outside schools."

Second, tracking reinforces inaccurate, and ultimately damaging, assumptions about intelligence. A bell-curve view of the distribution of human intellectual capacity says that intelligence is fixed, immutable, so that some children are capable of learning to high levels and some others simply are not. Those seen as relegated to the lower end of the bell curve are not expected to have, and are not given the opportunity to demonstrate, the capabilities of those on the upper end (Tucker & Codding, 1998, pp. 32–33).

Far from being fixed, however, intelligence and capacity can grow throughout life (Gelb, 1998, pp. 3–4), with experience playing a vital role in building and modifying the mind's structures (Bransford, Brown, & Cocking, 1999, p. xvi). In a review of more than 200 studies of the nature of intelligence, Bernard Devlin (1997, p. 468) found that heredity accounted for no more than 48 percent of IQ, leaving the other 52 percent to be determined by environment, education, and prenatal care.

Third, the technology of schools, instruction, is complex, not well understood, and ultimately dependent on human interaction. Unlike the gleaming machines of an automobile factory that stamp each piece of steel with the same imprint, teachers do not "merely apply treatment to objects. Instead, teachers interact with students, who are not inert raw material, but sentient, intentional subjects" (Gamoran et al., 1995, p. 689).

Instruction in tracked classes thus falls short on measures of both equity and excellence. Tracking affects students unequally, both by grouping minority and economically disadvantaged students in lower tracks and by providing unequal educational opportunities to students. Instruction in lower-track classes is typically far from excellent, often depending on rote memorization and recall, isolated facts, worksheets, and a slow pace (Oakes, 1985, pp. 61–112; Page, 1991, pp. 233–252). In contrast, higher-track students more often have the chance to use critical thinking and problem-solving skills and move at a faster pace (Oakes, 1985, pp. 61–112). Tracking language minority students also perpetuates their segregation from "mainstream" students and makes it difficult to foster a sense of school community.

The least experienced or least successful teachers frequently teach lower-track classes, with veteran teachers given higher-track classes like a reward for surviving the battle (Finley, 1984; Oakes, 1990; Oakes et al., 1992, p. 583). Similarly, highly trained veteran teachers are less likely to teach in high-poverty schools, where many language minority students are enrolled. The students who most need high-quality instruction are regularly the least likely to have access to it.

The gap in achievement between lower-track students and their higher-track peers widens, even after factoring out initial differences between the two groups (Gamoran & Mare, 1989). In short, the educational and occupational prospects of lower-track students worsen, instead of improve, despite the rhetoric about tracking's efficiency for teaching all students (Wheelock, 1992, p. xi).

An example shows how tracking works against both equity and excellence, leading to changes in everyone's expectations for students and a downturn in student achievement, even among very bright adolescents:

> [A] high school . . . , after adding an "honors" calculus class to its math program, found that student performance declined overall. With the establishment of a "top track," students and teachers alike came to assume that *only* students ranked at the top could achieve at the highest levels, and all involved expected less than before of those in the regular class. In this way, tracking institutionalizes the perception of intelligence as a fixed characteristic that some students have "more" of, while others have "less." (Wheelock, 1992, p. 91)

Despite mounting evidence of its inherent inequity and ineffectiveness (see, for example, Braddock & Slavin, 1992, pp. 1–16; Gamoran et al., 1995; Oakes, Gamoran, & Page, 1992; Wheelock, 1992, pp. 6–12), both educators and parents have been reluctant to move to classes containing students of diverse ability and achievement levels (Lynn & Wheelock, 1997b; Wells & Serna, 1996). One significant source of that reluctance has been a lack of knowledge about what equitable and excellent instruction looks like in a classroom with students of diverse abilities (Wheelock, 1992, p. xi).

Parents of the students designated as "gifted" often fear their children's education will be held back in untracked classes. When confronted with resistance from such parents, Sue Galletti, then principal of a middle school in Washington state, invited those parents to participate in the process of placing students into tracks.

> I gave them the data on 200 6th graders, with no names attached. . . . I explained the process we used to select students for the [gifted] program, and I said, "Now it's your turn." They started messing with the data and started to see things they didn't like. They saw a student with good test scores who wasn't going to get in because he had an IQ of 129 (the cutoff was 130). They saw another student who had an IQ of 149 who was out because he didn't have high enough test scores. They started to get very uncomfortable. And then I told them, "What I want you to realize is that a number of you in this room won't be able to get your children into the gifted program because of the exercise you're going through right now." It had a real impact on them. They hadn't realized how unfair it was to select 25 kids for a special class when there were so many talented kids in the school." (Lynn & Wheelock, 1997a, p. 2)

The parents at first proposed running two gifted classes, to expand the number of students served. Gradually, the conversation moved from eliminating tracking to expanding the gifted program to all students. Research from Joan Cone, Richard Marsh, and Mary Anne Raywid reveals that students of all ability levels can prosper in heterogeneous classes (Cone, 1993; Marsh & Raywid, 1994). Even the top 3 percent of students perform better in heterogeneous classes, if the curriculum and instruction are engaging (Wheelock, 1992, p. 76).

To ensure excellence and equity, schools should not track students. Fortunately, good instruction crosses the tracks. The engaging, rich strategies successful for those students considered to be of high ability also work well for those considered to be of low ability. The next section describes three sets of guiding principles for organizing instruction to improve the performance of all students.

THREE MODELS FOR ORGANIZING INSTRUCTION

Effective instructional methods must connect to the curriculum, to the assessments that will allow students to show what they have learned, and to the students themselves. Instruction is complex because those three connectors—curriculum, assessments, and students—vary from classroom to classroom, and sometimes vary from day to day.

Even after extensive review of the literature, interviews with practitioners, and ten years' worth of formal and informal observations, we could not identify a single existing model that pulls together everything that we believe to be important in making decisions about instruction. Instead, in the sections below we describe three useful models for organizing instruction—authentic instruction, WHERE, and differentiated instruction—each of which attempts to organize instruction systematically, based on the current state-of-the-art knowledge about how people learn. All three models contain elements that seem vital to successful instruction, though they emphasize different things and offer a range of specificity, from most general (authentic instruction) to most specific (differentiated instruction). After describing the models, we offer our own recommendations for organizing instruction, drawing on the key shared traits of the three models and adding a few ideas that appear either in only one model or not at all.

Authentic Instruction

According to Fred Newmann and his colleagues at the Center on Organization and Restructuring of Schools, authentic instruction is grounded in "authentic achievement," which they deem to be the ultimate goal of schooling. Authentic achievement represents "intellectual accomplishments that are worthwhile, significant, and meaningful, such as those undertaken by successful adults: scientists, musicians, business entrepreneurs. . . . With children, we are concerned with a more restricted conception of achievement, one that can be accomplished in schools" (Wehlage, Newmann, & Secada, 1996, pp. 23–24).

Criteria. To be authentic, achievement must reflect three overarching criteria (Newmann, Marks, & Gamoran, 1995, p. 3; Wehlage et al., 1996, pp. 24–26):

- *Construction of knowledge:* Students should construct or produce knowledge, instead of just reproducing or identifying understandings that others have created.
- *Disciplined inquiry:* Students should engage in cognitive work that requires them to rely on a field of knowledge, search for understanding, and communicate, in "elaborate forms," their ideas and findings.
- *Value beyond school:* Students' accomplishments should have value—either aesthetic, utilitarian, or personal—beyond just documenting their competence.

For each of the three authentic achievement criteria, Newmann and his colleagues have outlined standards for "authentic instruction" that will support authentic achievement.

The first criterion for authentic achievement, construction of knowledge, reflects the ideas of constructivism and the most current research on how people learn. Specifically, people construct new knowledge and understandings based on what they already believe and understand (Bransford et al., 1999, p. 10; Brooks & Brooks, 1993, p. 4). In describing constructivism as one of the best practices for learning, Zemelman, Daniels, and Hyde (1998, p. 8) argue, "Children do not just receive content; in a very real sense, they re-create and reinvent every cognitive system they encounter, including language, literacy, and mathematics."

As a corollary, teachers must pay attention to the nature of a student's understanding, since a student's beliefs could be limited, naïve, or entirely false. Building on an inaccurate base of knowledge only leads to more inaccuracy. For example, as Bransford et al. (1999, p. 10) write:

> Consider the challenge of working with children who believe that the earth is flat and attempting to help them understand that it is spherical. When told it is round, children picture the earth as a pancake rather than like a sphere. If they are then told it is round like a sphere, they interpret the new information about a spherical earth within their flat-earth view by picturing a pancake-like flat surface inside or on top of a sphere, with humans standing on top of the pancake. The children's construction of their new understandings has been guided by a model of the earth that helped them explain how they could stand or walk upon its surface, and a spherical earth did not fit their mental model.

Authentic instruction that addresses the construction of knowledge requires students to engage in higher-order thinking, that is, "manipulating information and ideas by synthesizing, generalizing, explaining, hypothesizing, or arriving at conclusions that produce new meanings and understandings" (Newmann, Secada, & Wehlage, 1995, p. 29). Instruction that pushes students to engage in these more complex thinking skills provides opportunities for them to construct knowledge.

The second criterion for authentic achievement requires that knowledge be constructed through disciplined inquiry, in which students use a prior knowledge base, seek in-depth understanding, and communicate their conclusions in an "elaborated" fashion (Newmann et al., 1995, p. 9). In drawing upon a prior knowledge base, students must go beyond parroting back information they've been given. Instead, they must use the existing concepts, facts, vocabulary, and conventions within a discipline or topic to develop their own critiques, questions, and even new paradigms.

To pose new questions and ideas, students must strive for in-depth understanding, for what Wiggins & McTighe (1998, p. 10) would call "enduring understandings," the big ideas that undergird the knowledge base. Authentic instruction based on disciplined inquiry also requires engaging students in substantive conversations with the teacher and their peers. These conversations build "an improved and shared understanding of ideas or topics" (Newmann et al., 1995, p. 35). To demonstrate their understanding, students should be asked to use elaborated communication—symbols, visuals, and verbal and written language—in ways that express both the big ideas and the nuances. In contrast, schools often ask students to convey what they have learned only through short responses—multiple choice, fill-in-the-blank, or brief sentences (Wehlage et al., 1996, p. 26).

The final criterion for authentic achievement requires that students engage in cognitive work with value beyond school. Most traditional student work, like spelling tests and multiple-choice quizzes, is contrived to document competence as defined by schools. In contrast, adults' work is intended to yield a product, an idea, or to have "an impact on others beyond the simple demonstration that they are competent" (Newmann et al., 1995, p. 11). For example, adults might write a letter to the county council, build a bookcase for a child's room, or help their community generate ideas for handling neighborhood traffic congestion. To support value beyond school, authentic instruction links to the world beyond the classroom, so that students can "make connections between substantive knowledge and either public problems or personal experiences" (Newmann et al., 1995, p. 40).

Not all classroom activities will meet all the criteria for authentic achievement all the time. "For example, repetitive practice, retrieving information, and memorization of facts or rules may be necessary to build knowledge and skills as foundations for authentic performance. . . . The point is not to abandon all unauthentic work in school, but to keep authentic achievement clearly in view as the ideal valued end" (Newmann & Associates, 1996, p. 27).

Brief Analysis. Authentic instruction is one part of a model to promote authentic achievement in schools. Newmann and his colleagues also discuss authentic assessment tasks and authentic student performance, outlining standards for both within the three broad criteria for intellectual quality: construction of knowledge, disciplined inquiry, and value beyond school (Newmann & Associates, 1996; Newmann et al., 1995).

Newmann's recent research generally confirms the value of authentic learning. In a study of 24 public schools, when teaching was consistent with the standards for authentic instruction, assessment, and performance, students achieved at high levels, regardless of social background (Newmann & Associates, 1996, p. 14). Moreover, the researchers found that authentic instruction and assessment could be provided reasonably equitably and that the effect on student achievement was also equitable (Newmann & Associates, 1996, p. 70). Another research study showed that students taught with methods focused on understanding and connections to the outside world outperformed their peers from more traditional classrooms in their use of advanced skills and did as well or better on traditional tests (Knapp, Shields, & Turnbull, 1992, pp. 19–28). Studies of eighth-grade students reveal better performance among those from more authentic instructional settings (Silver & Lane, 1995).

The authentic achievement model is deliberately silent on many aspects of classroom life, such as following directions, contributing to group work, and use of individual learning time. The silence connotes the importance of the model's focus on intellectual quality, not its dismissal of these other areas of student performance, which the authors acknowledge could justifiably be weighed in assessing progress (Newmann et al., 1995b, p. 63).

The model is silent on other aspects of teaching and learning as well, like the nature of the content to be taught, the specific instructional tools to be used, the allocation of grades to students, school accountability, and teacher evaluation (Newmann et al., 1995, pp. 63–66). Again, the silence is intentional, though perhaps a little disconcerting to those seeking details on how to implement the model.

Newmann and his colleagues recognize that their model is most useful as a tool for planning and reflection, a place to start in developing local adaptations of the ideas. They include a useful appendix (Newmann et al., 1995, pp. 80–102) that educators can use to analyze their work in relation to the model.

WHERE—An Instructional Design Tool

Criteria. In their book *Understanding by Design*, Grant Wiggins and Jay McTighe (1998, p. 115) offer guidelines for designing instruction under the acronym WHERE, which stands for

- *Where* are we headed?
- *Hook* the students
- *Explore* the subject and *equip* the students
- *Rethink* our work and ideas
- *Evaluate* results

As was the case with Newmann's framework and criteria for authentic achievement, Wiggins and McTighe present WHERE as criteria for instructional design, not a step-by-step chronology. In a "misconception alert," they explain (p. 116):

To use an analogy in story telling, a story needs a plot, characters, and setting. Those are story elements, just as WHERE summarizes the design elements. But how should those elements be fashioned into the most engaging and effective whole? There are many possible beginnings, middles, and ends.

To help students understand the purpose of tasks they will undertake, they must know where they, and their teacher, are headed. What standards, concepts, and questions drive this course of study? What is the rationale for the content and skills to be learned within this course of study? What will they have to do, at the end of the course and along the way, to demonstrate what they have learned? In general, students need to see the purpose of any particular assignment in the broader context of an overall plan.

The second element of the criteria, hooking the students, asks educators to use "engaging and provocative entry points" as motivators for learning. Motivating students to tackle big, organizing ideas requires more than just emphasizing tests, grades, and success in high school or college. Those extrinsic factors, though energizing to some, leave many students unmoved. Instead, "education should be an itch, not a scratch" (Lyman, 1992, pp. 169–181), eliciting a sense of excitement and urgency to figure things out, solve problems, and satisfy curiosity. Students are, by nature, "problem solvers and problem generators" (Bransford et al., 1999, p. xv).

Wiggins and McTighe suggest a few generic "hooking" strategies that set up important questions and ideas for a unit as a whole. The following list reflects Wiggins and McTighe's summary (1998, pp. 121–122) of what they have learned about engaging students:

- Subject students to "instant immersion" in questions, problems, paradoxes, and stories that require them to use their wits, not just formal school knowledge. This reflects a central tenet of "problem-based learning" and the notion of education as an itch, not a scratch.
- Introduce "anomalies, weird facts, counterintuitive events or ideas, and mysteries," which appeal to natural human curiosity.
- Challenge students to tackle problems, feelings, or obstacles to complete a task, sort of an "intellectual Outward Bound."
- Expose students to differing points of view on a single issue—for instance, the controversy over whether Shakespeare actually wrote the plays attributed to him.

The third criterion calls for providing students with opportunities to explore the key ideas and equipping students to demonstrate what they know and are able to do. Exploration should lead to in-depth, or enduring, understanding. As a practical matter, teachers ask students always to look deeper, from various perspectives, and to pursue answers to the essential questions driving the unit.

Equipping students requires carefully examining "what kinds of knowledge, skills, habits of mind, and attitudes are prerequisites for successful final performance, then deciding what instructional activities will give all students the chance to be successful, while also engaging their interest and allowing for exploration " (Wiggins & McTighe, 1998, p. 124). Wiggins and McTighe argue that active learning is more effective and more engaging in preparing students for success on assessments. Although they list a few strategies (debates, role play, discussions, and so on), they, like Newmann and his colleagues, are short on specifics. Whatever the strategy, they argue that the performance goals must always be kept at the forefront.

Giving students multiple opportunities to rethink and reflect on key ideas is the fourth of Wiggins and McTighe's criteria for instructional design. Students should be allowed to revise their work, rehearse for the assessment tasks, and refine their thinking as their understanding becomes more sophisticated (Wiggins & McTighe, 1998, p. 125).

In calling for rethinking and reflection, this criterion mirrors the notion of a "spiral curriculum": "The idea of the curriculum as a spiral is that big ideas, important tasks, and ever-deepening inquiry must *recur*, in ever-increasing complexity and through engaging problems and sophisticated applications if students are to understand them" (Wiggins & McTighe, 1998, p. 135). People learn by constantly returning to what they thought they understood to check that understanding against new experiences, different perspectives, and apparent paradoxes. Learners must decide if their initial understanding still works or if they should modify it somehow, given the new information. For example, students and teachers may begin with a statement or understanding that seems straightforward, black and white, and then gradually "see the shades of gray" as they revisit that idea again and again (Wiggins & McTighe, 1998, p. 136).

To encourage students to rethink their initial conceptions, theories, and explanations, teachers can raise puzzling questions, expose students to multiple opinions, and ask students to apply their understanding to related but dissimilar problems. Teachers should also require their students to revise their work, to practice using new skills and ideas, and to return to an analysis of their understanding and skills after they have tried to put them into practice (Wiggins & McTighe, 1998, p. 137).

The final element of this instructional design tool calls for students to exhibit what they have learned through authentic products and performances and to evaluate their own learning using some means of self-assessment. The products and performances should be set in a meaningful context, involve a clear purpose, and have an audience outside the school (Wiggins & McTighe, 1998, p. 126).

This element relates to Wiggins and McTighe's view that "what and how we assess signals what we value" (1998, p. 127). As students monitor and adjust their own learning, their knowledge of how they will be assessed and what evidence of their understanding should look like will help them make decisions about where and how to invest their effort. Wiggins and McTighe (1998, p. 124) contend that "The most overlooked aspect of instructional design is the need to help students self-assess and self-adjust their work as they progress." Just as teachers use formative and summative assessments to monitor and adjust their instructional practices, so students should engage in formative and summative assessments of their own learning, with guidance from rubrics, examples of student work, their peers, and the teacher to inform their self-adjustments. The goal is to move students away from being "constantly dependent on the judge to know how they did" (Wiggins, 1998, p. 49).

Wiggins (1998, p. 50) describes an example that—though drawn from a high school, not a middle grades, course—effectively demonstrates the notion of encouraging self-assessment and self-adjustment:

> In Ralph's welding course he works with thirty students at once and uses a system of effective feedback that requires no adult intervention. The first task is straightforward. Each student must produce a ninety-degree corner weld to industry specifications. The standards for this weld are written out on paper, but the feedback system involves something more. Ralph tells the students that when they believe their weld is up to standard, they should bring it over to a table, pick up a magic marker, and write their name on the weld. By so doing they signify, first, that they understand the standards, and second, that they believe their work is up to standard. There is a catch, however. On the table are welds from previous years, ranging from excellent to awful. Students routinely come up to the table thinking they have finished the task and then think twice after inspecting other welds. I watched one boy look around furtively to see if Ralph was watching before he snuck back to his station. This is a feedback system that works, based as all good feedback systems are on activating each person's ability to self-assess and self-adjust when he or she gets clear feedback and sees clear standards.

Brief Analysis. Like Newmann and his colleagues, Wiggins and McTighe focus on intellectual quality. Where Newmann talks about authentic achievement, Wiggins and McTighe (1998, pp. 38–62) describe six facets of understanding, the kind of in-depth understanding that they believe should characterize teaching and learning (see Box 4.1).

Wiggins and McTighe (1998, pp. 162–163) describe WHERE as an instructional design tool, then very briefly outline three basic methods of teaching: didactic (lecture or direct instruction), coaching (feedback and guidance as students work), and constructivist (based on concepts and inquiry). They see all three methods as valid, depending on the content to be taught and how students will be assessed.

Wiggins and McTighe argue that WHERE is a guide for instructional planning and reflection, not an instructional recipe, and their "questions for the teacher" can be used to gauge how well lessons are meeting WHERE's instructional design criteria (see Box 4.2). The bottom line for Wiggins and McTighe is that all students should be supported in reaching understanding and being able to demonstrate that understanding. The WHERE model is one way to design instruction that will engage, guide, and ultimately equip every student for success in attaining those two goals.

Differentiated Instruction

In explaining the need for differentiated instruction, Carol Ann Tomlinson outlines the problems with heterogeneous classrooms, as they are typically

Box 4.1 The Six Facets of Understanding

When we truly understand, we

- Can *explain:* provide thorough, supported, and justifiable accounts of phenomena, facts, and data.
- Can *interpret:* tell meaningful stories; offer apt translations; provide a revealing historical or personal dimension to ideas and events; make it personal or accessible through images, anecdotes, analogies, and models.
- Can *apply:* effectively use and adapt what we know in diverse contexts.
- Have *perspective:* see and hear points of view through critical eyes and ears; see the big picture.
- Can *empathize:* find value in what others might find odd, alien, or implausible; perceive sensitively on the basis of prior direct experience.
- Have *self-knowledge:* perceive the personal style, prejudices, projections, and habits of mind that both shape and impede our own understanding; we are aware of what we do not understand and why understanding is so hard.

Source: Wiggins & McTighe (1998), p. 44. Reprinted with permission.

structured. The education offered in typical heterogeneous classrooms is assumed to benefit everyone, in a one-size-fits-all model of instruction (Tomlinson, 1999, pp. 21–22). Struggling learners are left to "catch up" on their own, without support that meets them where they are. And advanced learners are often just given *more* work to do, on the assumption that since they are up to standard already, they will be fine without any "special provisions." Although the quantity of their work increases, the quality of the challenges they face does not, so they, too, are left to learn on their own. In fact, the model only fits some, while it pinches others in various ways that diminish their growth as learners.

Tomlinson offers an alternative for heterogeneous classes in the form of differentiated instruction, which provides students with many different avenues for learning, based on their diverse

- *Levels of readiness,* their entry points to learning particular skills and ideas
- *Interests,* the things and ideas for which they have a built-in passion or curiosity
- *Learning profiles,* how they learn best, which may be shaped by their cultural background, past experiences, preferences for group or individual

Box 4.2 **Questions for the Teacher—Unit Instructional Design Considerations, WHERE**

W: How will you help students know ***where*** they are headed and why (e.g., major assignments, performance tasks, and the criteria by which the work will be judged)?

H: How will you ***hook*** the student through engaging and thought-provoking experiences (issues, oddities, problems, and challenges) that point toward essential and unit questions, core ideas, and performance tasks?

E: What learning experiences will engage students in ***exploring*** the big ideas and essential and unit questions? What instruction is needed to ***equip*** students for the final performances?

R: How will you cause students to reflect and ***rethink*** to dig deeper into the core ideas? How will you guide students in revising and refining their work based on feedback and self-assessment?

E: How will students exhibit their understanding through final performances and products? How will you guide them in self-***evaluation*** to identify the strengths and weaknesses in their work and set future goals?

Source: Wiggins & McTighe (1998), p. 190. Reprinted with permission.

work, learning style, gender, and so on (Tomlinson, 1999, p. 11). (See Box 4.3 for more on learning styles.)

In a differentiated classroom, teachers are diagnosticians, "prescribing the best possible instruction for their students" (Tomlinson, 1999, p. 2). The instruction is intended to make certain that all students improve their knowledge and skills, moving substantially beyond where they began. Tomlinson contends that differentiated instruction is effective for both advanced and struggling learners, "maximizing their capacity" by appropriately challenging them to improve their performance (1995, pp. 13–15).

Teachers can differentiate on three dimensions, given their diagnosis of what will work best for their students (Tomlinson, 1999, p. 11):

Content—what they expect students to know and be able to do and the materials students will use to support their learning

Process—the activities that will help students make sense of what they are learning

Product—the evidence students will provide of what they have learned

Box 4.3 Learning Styles

How many times have you tried some home repair project, become frustrated, but then seen a picture of how to do it and understood it? Or think of a time you called the help desk when you were mired down in a computer problem. Though some of us will be successful following the instructions from the disembodied voice at the other end of the line, most of us would probably prefer another approach. How much easier would it be if we could just turn to a colleague and say, "Can you show me how to do this?"

That we each learn differently is the idea behind learning styles: "the notion that people are distinctly different in ways that they learn and make meaning for themselves." Whatever label is used to identify this approach (learning style, cognitive style, multiple intelligences) or the styles themselves (auditory, visual, concrete/sequential), what matters is that "individual student differences are respected and accommodated" (Guild & Garger, 1998, pp. 4–5).

By keeping in mind the different ways that students learn, teachers can vary their instructional strategies and reach more of their students. Some evidence suggests that when instructional methods and students' primary learning styles mesh, students have more positive attitudes toward school and learn more, improving their chances of success (Sims & Sims, 1995).

We recommend that educators review a variety of resources on learning styles, using an expanded understanding of the theories to make good decisions about instruction. We are not advocating for any particular model or approach, but instead for deliberate consideration of several approaches, with an eye toward what your own experience also says about what works best with your students. For more information on learning styles and their implications for instruction, here are a few sources to consider:

Barbe, W. B., & Swassing, R. H. (1994). *Teaching through modality strengths: Concepts and practices*. Columbus, OH: Zaner-Bloser, Inc.

Bargar, J. R., Bargar, R. R., & Cano, J. M. (1994). *Discovering learning preferences and learning differences in the classroom*. Columbus, OH: Ohio Agricultural Education Curriculum Materials Service. (The Ohio State University, 2120 Fyffe Road, Columbus, OH 43210).

Gardner, H. (1991). *The unschooled mind: How children learn and how schools should teach*. New York: Basic Books.

Gregorc, A. F. (1987). *Inside styles: Beyond the basics*. Maynard, MA: Gabriel Systems, Inc. (P.O. Box 357, Maynard, MA 01754).

Guild, P. B., & Garger, S. (1998). *Marching to different drummers* (2nd ed.). Alexandria, VA: Association for Supervision and Curriculum Development.

McCarthy, B. (1987). *The 4MAT system: Teaching to learning styles with right/left mode techniques*. Barrington, IL: Excel, Inc. (200 West Station St., Barrington, IL 60010).

Witkin, H., & Goodenough, D. R. (1981). *Cognitive styles: Essence and origins*. New York: International Universities Press, Inc. (Available from Consulting Psychologists Press, Inc., 577 College Ave., Palo Alto, CA 94306).

Teachers can adjust content, process, or product to match their students' levels of readiness, interests, or learning profiles. Although it sounds like a very complicated chemistry experiment, which could blow up if done incorrectly, the underlying idea of differentiation is quite simple: work *with* students' variability instead of ignoring it.

Teachers should differentiate instruction so that, over time, all students are given access to different avenues for learning and have opportunities to learn that best suit them in relation to critical knowledge and skills. Teachers need to be sensitive to students who have skill gaps, realizing that they may need to pay more attention to these students and be sensitive to how well such students grasp the underlying purpose of each lesson and activity. Do they need extended time, for example, or reinforcement of some underlying ideas and processes? Are they constructing meaning as they tackle a project or simply mucking about with scissors and paste? Differentiated instruction does not mean 25 different lesson plans, but instead accommodating differences with a set of learning activities that is robust enough that all children are learning, though perhaps at different rates and with more or less direction from the teacher and their peers: "While it is true that differentiated instruction offers several avenues to learning, it does not assume a separate level for each learner. It also focuses on meaningful and powerful ideas for all students" (Tomlinson, 1995, p. 4).

Characteristics of Differentiated Classrooms. Tomlinson outlines the characteristics of differentiated classrooms, though she acknowledges that no single formula works for all situations:

- The teacher focuses on the essentials. Like Newmann, Wiggins, and McTighe, Tomlinson advocates concentrating on in-depth understanding of critical concepts and principles, not discrete and disconnected facts. "Focusing on key concepts and generalizations can ensure that all learners gain powerful understandings that serve as building blocks for meaning and access to other knowledge" (Tomlinson, 1995, p. 20).
- Assessment and instruction are inseparable. Ongoing assessment (see Box 4.4) is used to diagnose students' levels of readiness, interests, and learning profiles, and those diagnoses are used to differentiate instruction, in a continuous feedback loop (Tomlinson, 1999, p. 10).
- The teacher modifies content, process, and products based on what the assessment data say about students' readiness, interests, and learning profiles. A teacher decides to modify content, process, or products only when he or she sees a student need and is convinced that the adaptation will help the learner grasp important knowledge or skills (Tomlinson, 1999, p. 11).
- All students participate in respectful work, work that respects their level of readiness, challenges them to grow in their mastery of essential concepts and skills, supports their growth by consistently escalating the degree of difficulty, and offers "equally interesting, equally important, and equally engaging" tasks (Tomlinson, 1999, p. 12).

Box 4.4 Examples of Ongoing Classroom Assessments

- Index card summaries and questions—students write on one side the big idea that they understand from the unit and on the other side describe something about the topic that they do not yet fully understand. This idea is similar to the "minute paper," in which students respond in writing to some variation on two questions: "What was the most important thing you learned during this class?" "What important question remains unanswered?"
- Hand signals—if students understand and can explain a specific concept, principle, or process, they give a thumbs up, if they do not yet understand, they give a thumbs down, and if they are not completely sure, they wave their hands.
- Question place—a box, bulletin board, etc. where students can post questions about concepts, principles, or processes they do not yet fully understand.
- Analogy prompt—this (concept, principle, or process) is like _____ because _____.
- Web or concept map that students create to show the elements of the topic or process.
- Misconception check—present students with common misconceptions about a concept, principle, or process and ask whether they agree or disagree and why.

Source: Adapted from Wiggins & McTighe (1998), pp. 166–167. Many different classroom assessment techniques also appear in Angelo & Cross (1993).

- The teacher and students collaborate in learning. Differentiated classrooms must be student-centered, with teachers serving as organizers of instruction, materials, time, and space. Together, teachers and students plan, set goals, and try to learn both from what went well and from what did not. As students get better at self-assessment and self-adjustment, as Wiggins and McTighe would argue, the teacher becomes more effective (Tomlinson, 1999, p. 13, Wiggins & McTighe, 1998, p. 124).
- The teacher balances group and individual norms. Success according to group norms, like standardized end-of-course tests, can make advanced learners who have not progressed look successful and make struggling learners who have made amazing gains look unsuccessful. For both the advanced and the struggling learners, teachers must balance individual goals, which require building skills and knowledge as rapidly as possible, with group goals that establish one finish line for everyone (Tomlinson, 1999, p. 13).

- The teacher and students work together flexibly, moving fluidly back and forth, for example, from whole group to small groups and individual work, single sources of information to multiple sources, one time frame to varying time frames, teacher-directed activities to student-directed activities. Teachers use "a wide range of instructional strategies to focus on individuals and small groups, not just the whole class" (Tomlinson, 1999, p. 13).

Tomlinson places the perfectly differentiated classroom on one end of a spectrum, with the perfectly traditional classroom on the other end, and admonishes educators to remember that virtually every classroom will fall somewhere in between the two extremes. She invites teachers to compare the characteristics of each type of classroom (see Box 4.5) and decide where their teaching is now and where they would like it to be.

Like the other two instructional organization models described in this chapter, differentiated instruction does not provide much detail on which instructional tools should be used when, though it does offer more suggestions of tools that will help match instruction to the students. Tomlinson (1995, pp. 29–33) also provides some key strategies for managing a differentiated classroom:

- Have a strong rationale for differentiating instruction based on student readiness and interest, and share that rationale with both students and parents so that they understand the "fluidity" of the differentiated classroom and can begin to discard their preconceived notions.
- Begin differentiating at a pace that is comfortable for the teacher's level of readiness. For example, teachers can start trying differentiated instruction in the class where they feel most at ease, or with the subject they enjoy best. They can differentiate using multiple resources, or have students work from a single text but at different paces.
- Time differentiated activities for student success. Some students work better in groups, while others work better independently. All students should learn to increase their attention span for either group or independent work. To help a student stretch his or her attention span for independent work, for example, the teacher should first give the student just a little less time for an independent activity than the student's attention span typically lasts. Starting with a shorter time frame allows the student's attention to outlast the task and gives him or her a sense of success in that task. Then, gradually, the time allotted for similar tasks should increase, pushing the student to lengthen his or her attention span for independent work and strengthen his or her intensity and concentration, as his or her confidence in his or her own ability to work diligently grows.
- Use an "anchor" activity to free up time to work with students. Anchor activities—reading silently, writing in journals or learning logs, practicing skills like spelling—allow students to work independently and quietly. These anchor tasks should be differentiated based on students' levels of readiness and interest. Gradually move from getting the whole class accustomed to working on anchor activities to having first half the class, and eventually only a third,

Box 4.5 Comparing Traditional and Differentiated Classrooms

Traditional Classroom	Differentiated Classroom
Student differences are masked or acted upon only when they present problems.	Student differences are studied as a basis for planning.
Assessment is most common at the end of learning to see "who got it."	Assessment is ongoing and diagnostic to understand how to make instruction more responsive to learner need.
A relatively narrow sense of intelligence prevails.	Focus on multiple forms of intelligences is evident.
A single definition of excellence exists.	Excellence is defined in large measure by individual growth from a starting point.
Student interest is infrequently tapped.	Students are frequently guided in making interest-based learning choices.
Relatively few learning profile options are taken into account.	Many learning profile options are provided for.
Whole-class instruction dominates.	Many instructional arrangements are used.
Coverage of texts and curriculum guides drives instruction.	Student readiness, interest, and learning profile shape instruction.
Mastery of facts and skills out of context are the focus of learning.	Use of essential skills to make sense of and understand key concepts and principles is the focus of learning.
Single-option assignments are the norm.	Multioption assignments are frequently used.
Time is relatively inflexible.	Time is used flexibly in accordance with student need.
A single text prevails.	Multiple materials are provided.
Single interpretation of ideas and events may be sought.	Multiple perspectives on ideas and events are routinely sought.
The teacher directs student behavior.	The teacher facilitates students' skills at becoming more self-reliant learners.
The teacher solves problems.	Students help other students and the teacher solve problems.
The teacher provides whole-class standards for grading.	Students work with the teacher to establish both whole-class and individual learning goals.
A single form of assessment is often used.	Students are assessed in multiple ways.

Source: Tomlinson (1999), p. 16. Reprinted with permission.

engaged in those "quiet" tasks. While part of the class is anchored, the teacher is free to work more closely with students who have newer and more unpredictable differentiated tasks. Over time, teachers can alternate students through the anchor tasks and the more active differentiated activities.

- Create and deliver instructions carefully. Since students will be engaged in different activities at the same time, it can be too confusing to give all the directions for their work orally. Instead, use task cards or activity sheets, give directions to group representatives who can then share with their respective groups, and set up learning centers containing varying instructions depending on the student task.

- Have a "home base" for students, basically a seating chart students use at the beginning and at different points during the class to allow the teacher to organize people and materials more quickly.

- Give students as much responsibility for their learning as possible as part of encouraging them to become more independent, and motivated, learners. Related to the notion of self-assessment and self-adjustment that Wiggins and McTighe described, responsibility can also include distributing and collecting materials, organizing the classroom itself for various activities, reviewing peers' work, establishing goals for their own learning, and developing some of their own tasks.

- Be sure students have a plan for getting help when the teacher is busy with another student or group. For example, students can ask for help from the other members of their group or from an "expert of the day," a position that should rotate among students, depending on the area of expertise required. In general, students should seek out help, not just wait or disrupt, and be able to judge when they really need to call the teacher.

- Engage students in talking about classroom procedures and group processes to help them understand the teacher's thinking in structuring activities and help the teacher understand the students' perspective on those same activities.

- Use flexible grouping, sometimes assigning students to groups based on their level of readiness, interests, or learning profiles, sometimes having students work on a brief task with whoever is nearby, and sometimes allowing students to set up their own groups. These changes in grouping strategies prevent the implicit labeling of long-running groups.

Brief Analysis. Differentiated instruction is probably the most intricate of the three instructional organization models included in this chapter. While all three models address connecting instruction to curriculum and assessments, neither authentic instruction nor the WHERE design tool provide much specific guidance on how to attend to student differences. Differentiated instruction intentionally pays attention to the third element that instruction must connect with—the students—and, in particular, to their variability on multiple dimensions.

Because it considers how instruction interacts with students of diverse needs and backgrounds, Tomlinson's model can truly and appropriately support all students in maximizing their learning. The characteristics of a differentiated classroom are grounded firmly in the latest research on how people learn

(Tomlinson, 1999, p. 18). The devil is in the details, however. Differentiated instruction must confront two realities about current schools: teachers may find it difficult to acquire the time, skills, tools, and resources to implement the model effectively; and schools, students, and their parents are suspicious of differentiation. Many people associate sameness with equality and equity, and thus are leery of any plan that requires difference in order to work.

With regard to Tomlinson's final strategy recommendation, on flexible grouping, let us be clear about the difference between tracking, discussed earlier, and short-term flexible grouping and other forms of differentiated instruction within a heterogeneous classroom. Tracking refers to long-term placement of students in academic tracks that are qualitatively different in the breadth and depth of the curriculum offered, in the instructional and assessment strategies used, and in the kind and amount of resources allocated for teaching (including teachers' level of experience and competence). Under no circumstances is tracking an acceptable educational practice. Flexible grouping and other examples of differentiated instruction refer to *short-term* differences in content or instructional strategies specific to particular units of instruction. Such strategies can significantly benefit student learning and motivation to learn. However, the goal of differentiated instruction, of all instruction, is the same: enabling all students to meet or exceed higher academic standards and develop their full intellectual potential.

OUR RECOMMENDATIONS FOR ORGANIZING INSTRUCTION

Each of the three instructional organization models—authentic instruction, WHERE, and differentiated instruction—addresses instruction's key connections: curriculum, assessments, and the students. Each model, however, focuses predominantly on one of three connections. Newmann's authentic instruction places more emphasis on curriculum, specifically the intellectual quality of what and how students learn. The WHERE model highlights instruction's connection to assessment, given Wiggins's and McTighe's idea that instruction should be organized around ensuring that students are able to demonstrate what they have learned. Finally, Tomlinson's differentiated instruction concentrates on attending to the students, specifically how their variability can be effectively addressed so that all students maximize their capacity. Interestingly, despite their different emphases, these three instructional models do not contradict each other on any major point.

Although they provide distinct frameworks, they all suggest organizing instruction in ways that reflect the latest research findings on how people learn best. We recommend organizing instruction around key commonalities across the three models. Educators should

- Meet students where they are, since people learn best by connecting new information to old.
- Center classrooms on the students, not the teachers, since people also learn best when they exercise some control over their learning.

- Provide rich learning environments, since intelligence is fluid, not fixed, and will increase, given access to a diversity of materials, opinions, and options.
- Organize content around concepts, since the brain searches for meaningful patterns, connecting parts to wholes.
- Engage students in challenging work, grounded in higher-order thinking, since people learn best when they have to stretch to succeed.
- Connect what happens in the classroom to the students, either directly or by helping them discover links to the world beyond the classroom, since people learn best when what they are learning has relevance to themselves or their society.

Besides the recommendations above, which reflect common ground among the three instructional organization models, we also recommend that educators

- Attend to student differences purposefully and consistently by differentiating content, process, and product based on learners' varying levels of readiness, interests, and learning profiles.
- Stress learning that is experiential, since students "learn most powerfully from doing, not just hearing about, any subject" (Zemelman, Daniels, & Hyde, 1998, p. 9).
- Provide opportunities for students to work collaboratively, thus both enhancing their learning and allowing them to develop an invaluable skill (Zemelman et al., 1998, p. 12).
- Encourage students to reflect on what they have learned, to seek out those shades of gray in experiences and ideas that initially seemed black and white.
- Assess students' understanding and skill using authentic means and products, and be sensitive to where to begin an instructional unit, given the characteristics of the students. Teachers may be tempted to jump into complex, authentic tasks that turn out to require a level of reading or math skill that is at the frustration level for several of their students, thereby risking alienating such students from the start (Margaret McLaughlin, personal communication, January 15, 2000).
- Look at student work, in addition to other means of ongoing assessment, to get a clear sense of what students are understanding, and misunderstanding, with the goal of modifying instruction as needed.
- Collaborate with teaching colleagues and specialists in the school in designing instructional activities. For example, special education teachers can be wonderful resources for their peers in developing inclusive lessons for students with disabilities. Fellow team members can offer useful insight into planning instruction for particular students, in addition to their more overarching role as fellow curriculum designers.

None of the models prescribe specific instructional strategies, and neither will we. Instructional strategies proliferate in the world of schooling—

cooperative learning, complex instruction, reciprocal teaching, Socratic seminars, discovery learning, problem-based learning, hands-on learning, even old-fashioned lecture and workbooks, to name but a few. As Ruth Mitchell and her colleagues (Mitchell et al., 1995, p. 89) put it, "No single teaching strategy is good or bad as such—it is either useful or not useful." As to the choice of which strategy to use when, it depends on the three key connections for instruction: the curriculum to be learned, the assessments to be used to show what the students have learned, and the students themselves. In short, the answers to the questions of what, to what end, and for whom will shape decisions about specific instructional strategies. (See Box 4.6 for a list of recommended resources for specific instructional strategies.)

TECHNOLOGY AS A RESOURCE FOR INSTRUCTION

Although an in-depth examination of technology and its multiple uses in schools is beyond the scope of this book, we do want to point out the results of an important study that looks at whether using computers as an instructional resource is making a difference in mathematics. The results of that study may have implications for computer use across the disciplines. Harold Wenglinsky (1998) of the Educational Testing Service's Policy Information Center conducted the study using data from the 1996 National Assessment of Educational Progress. Although the research revealed many interesting results, we will focus on a few findings related specifically to the eighth grade.

First, and perhaps most important: for eighth graders, "the use of computers to teach lower-order thinking skills was negatively related to academic achievement and the social environment of the school" (p. 3). Lower-order activities in-

---

Box 4.6 Resources for Specific Instructional Strategies

For more information on specific instructional strategies, we recommend the following resources:

Erickson, H. L. (1998). *Concept-based curriculum and instruction: Teaching beyond the facts*. Thousand Oaks, CA: Corwin Press, Inc.

Joyce, B., & Weil, M. (in press). *Models of teaching* (6th ed.). Needham Heights, MA: Allyn & Bacon.

Marzano, R. J., & Pickering, D. J. (1997). *Dimensions of learning: Teacher's manual* (2nd ed.). Alexandria, VA & Aurora, CO: Association for Supervision and Curriculum Development and Mid-continent Regional Educational Laboratory.

Saphier, J., & Gower, R. (1997). *The skillful teacher: Building your teaching skills* (5th ed.). Acton, MA: Research for Better Teaching.

cluded drill and practice primarily, though some learning games could be either higher or lower order and the use of computers to demonstrate new math topics could also be either higher or lower order, depending upon the topic. Higher-order activities included simulations and applications, along with some learning games and some topic demonstrations. We believe that this negative relationship between lower-order computer activities and academic achievement has implications for how computers are used in all subject areas. Apparently, "drill and kill" is still deadly even when it comes with bells, whistles, and a flashing cursor.

Second, the study found that "professional development [for eighth-grade teachers] in technology and the use of computers to teach higher-order thinking skills were both positively related to academic achievement in mathematics and the social environment of the school" (p. 3). As we will discuss in Chapter 5, substantive, ongoing professional development is vital to a successful school. This study provides evidence that professional development tied to technology and higher-order thinking yields improved student outcomes.

Finally, in a finding with implications for equity, the researcher found that black eighth grade students "were less likely to be exposed to higher order uses of computers and more likely to be exposed to lower-order uses than white students. Similarly, poor, urban, and rural students were less likely to be exposed to higher-order uses than non-poor and suburban students" (p. 3). Given our focus on ensuring success for every student, it seems evident that, when computers are available, every student should have opportunities to use technology to support higher-order thinking skills.

INSTRUCTIONAL REFORM AND BROAD-BASED INTERVENTION FOR LANGUAGE MINORITY STUDENTS

Since language minority students are at high risk for dropping out of high school, the middle grades are the critical period for instructional and emotional intervention with these students. It is during these years that adolescents solidify their perceptions of themselves as students and when negative feelings toward school tend to become cemented. The emotions experienced and opinions formed during the middle school years set the stage for what is to come in high school. Academic, emotional, and social problems should be addressed when they first show up; educators should not wait until high school to intervene.

Parental involvement is also critical to the success of language minority students. Students need to see that their family members support the instruction they receive at school, and English language learners in particular need reassurance that the school's priorities are complementary, not competing, with their family's values, even though they may seem dramatically different.

In addition to parental support, schools that strive to support children in all aspects of their lives by having counseling, health-care, and social service staff on site are particularly beneficial for English language learners. Especially in the case of nonnative English speakers and students from low socioeconomic backgrounds, the most successful schools recognize that even the most engaging curriculum with the most effective instruction will fail if delivered to a child who is experiencing severe emotional or health problems outside school (Kenji Hakuta, personal communication, January 2000).

SPECIAL FOCUS: TEACHING READING IN MIDDLE GRADES SCHOOLS

We advocate ensuring that all students achieve the Turning Points vision, in detracked classrooms, through the use of powerful curriculum relevant to student concerns, varied and purposeful assessments, and effective instruction. A critical obstacle to our goal, however, deserves further examination: 30 percent of young adolescents leave the primary grades without basic reading skills (Showers, Joyce, Scanlon, & Schnaubelt, 1998, p. 27).

Reading is a crucial tool in the effort to build equity and excellence in society as a whole. As G. Reid Lyon (1998, p. 14) of the National Institute of Child Health and Human Development argues, "Learning to read is critical to a child's overall well being. If a youngster does not learn to read in our literacy-driven society, hope for a fulfilling, productive life diminishes. In short, difficulties learning to read are not only an educational problem; they constitute a serious public health concern."

Indeed, both equity and excellence would seem to suggest that adolescents should have an inalienable right to read. However, reading is not often a focus of instruction in the middle grades, despite the statistics on the number of students who are poor readers (Irvin, 1998, p. 230). Why don't middle grades schools make a better, and more focused, effort to improve the reading skills of their students? Perhaps it boils down to *when* students are expected to learn to read and then to develop the ability to read to learn.

Specifically, educators, parents, and even students typically expect that children will learn to read in elementary school. They also expect that students will enter the middle grades ready to use their reading skills to learn new content through reading expository text, like that found in social studies and science. When teachers ask students to read a text or any other resource to learn new information, they are doing so on the assumption that their students can read.

Since educators have too often assumed that students have "mastered" reading in elementary school, the middle grades learning community has never set itself up to improve adolescents' literacy. In fact, as Judith Irvin points out, "Most reading instruction stops entirely after fifth grade. But, we never really stop learning to read—adding more complex text, different genres, etc. Also, we become more and more proficient at understanding expository text. . . . It should be every middle grades teacher's joy to extend the literacy learning of his/her students" (personal communication, February 14, 2000).

Middle grades teachers, however, typically are not prepared to teach reading (Cooney, 1999, p. 6). Parents, though deeply concerned about their children's literacy, are often no better equipped than educators to support teenagers in improving their reading skills. Within this climate of nonsupport, students who do not read well have often given up on learning how, given up on their academic careers and, in effect, given up on their success as adults.

Who Should Teach Reading?

The reading debate in the middle grades is even more basic than the controversy over phonics versus whole language that swirls through the early grades. Why should middle grades teachers be responsible for teaching reading at all when they feel that students should have learned that skill in elementary school? More concretely, given an obvious need for reading instruction, who should teach reading in the middle grades?

The most obvious answer is that reading specialists should teach reading. Both Joan Lipsitz (personal communication, November 1999) and Judith Irvin (personal communication, February 14, 2000) argue that schools should consider directing more resources toward supporting reading specialists. Putting more reading specialists in middle grades schools helps build expertise in how to teach reading to young adolescents among school faculty members whose pre-service experiences and training have not prepared them to support improved literacy.

However, reading specialists are only part of the answer. Middle grades schools should teach reading across the curriculum as part of a system of supports to improve students' reading skills and enhance their enjoyment of reading. Research shows that when students have many chances to read and write in the content areas—like history, math, and science—they become better readers, writers, and critical thinkers (Dickinson & DiGisi, 1998, p. 24; Many, Fyfe, Lewis, & Mitchell, 1996; Tierney, Soter, O'Flahavan, & McGinley, 1989).

A middle grades reading program should include targeted training and ongoing support for all teachers. Reading specialists, for example, should devote part or all of their day to supporting other teachers in implementing reading strategies through their content (Judith Irvin, personal communication, February 14, 2000). The reading program should also include intensive supports for students whose skills are weak and reading recreation activities that weave the enjoyment of reading into the fabric of the school day for every student. So, who should teach reading? Essentially every teacher, since reading skill is essential in every subject, though students who are significantly far behind will need additional interventions that require specialized knowledge and skills.

We recommend that our readers review "Adolescent Literacy: A Position Statement" (March 18, 1999) for more specifics on how to improve reading instruction for young adolescents. Produced by the International Reading Association's Commission on Adolescent Literacy, the statement is available for a nominal fee from IRA's website (www.ira.org) and goes into more depth than we can here about how to support adolescents' literacy growth. For exciting ideas about improving reading comprehension, we recommend *Mosaic of Thought: Teaching Comprehension in a Reader's Workshop*, by Ellin Oliver Keene and Susan Zimmermann (1997).

Teaching Reading Across the Curriculum

Content-area teachers should teach reading strategies along with the content. As Judith Irvin (1998, p. 241) points out, "Sole emphasis on content leaves students with isolated information and without strategies for learning new content; sole emphasis on reading process leaves students with little about which to think or write." Teaching reading across the curriculum does not mean abandoning content for reading skills instruction, but rather weaving reading strategies into content as a way of helping students learn the content better. Irvin contends that if teachers support reading strategies in their content areas, "students' reading levels actually rise . . . because they have a purpose for reading, they have built some prior knowledge on the topic, and see some relevance in the assignment" (personal communication, February 14, 2000).

Research has also revealed what schools should *not* do in the name of teaching reading in the content areas. A study of 12 middle grades schools purportedly teaching reading across the curriculum (Allington, 1990, pp. 34–35) found instructional methods that led to further fragmentation of the curriculum, not cohesion:

> Most of the academic work required students to work alone, reading a text and responding to tasks that required them to simply locate or remember literate information from the text base. With the text in front of them these students performed a variety of tasks ranging from "copying out" text information to supplying missing words, selecting the appropriate multiple-choice response, spelling from memory . . . or answering teacher questions about the text.

Instead of fragmented exercises that may undermine comprehension rather than improving it, reading instruction should stress transfer of skills across texts and disciplines. A tight focus on skills alone can yield short-term success but long-term failure, as Davidson and Koppenhaver (1993, p. 43) described in their review of successful adolescent literacy programs:

> Researchers found that some widely acclaimed programs, boasting high test scores, may address the skills needed to perform specific literacy tasks in one context but may ignore the variety of contexts in which students will need to exercise those skills. For instance, students who are carefully drilled in the decoding skills used on a certain test may perform well on that test but may not be able to transfer that decoding knowledge to literacy tasks outside the test format.

One challenge for content-area teachers can be finding materials for their discipline(s) that are suitable for different reading levels. Tomlinson (1995, p. 49) advocates offering varied text and resource materials, ranging from simple to complex in readability but addressing the same underlying concepts and principles within the unit of study. She recommends "building a classroom library from discarded texts of various levels (or requesting that textbook money be used to buy three classroom sets of different books rather than one copy of a single text for everyone), and by collecting magazines, newsletters, brochures, and other print materials."

Reading specialists can support content-area teachers by providing information about students' reading skills, demonstrating strategies for teaching reading, providing follow-up support as teachers try out new strategies, evaluating texts for their readability, and so on (Irvin, 1998, p. 241). A curriculum coordinator or facilitator can also serve a supportive role for the faculty, becoming a school "expert" on improving reading (see Chapter 5 for more on the role of a coordinator or facilitator).

Even with support from specialists, intensive staff development, and varied resources, content-area teachers cannot do everything necessary to improve the reading skills of every student significantly. Robert Slavin (1999, p. 14) divides middle grades students into three groups according to their reading skills: "one group is reading at or above reading (grade) level, a second is reading significantly below grade level, and a third group is barely reading at all."

All three groups will benefit when their content-area teachers teach reading strategies in the context of meaningful content and offer a wide range of resource materials to support the curriculum. However, students who enter the middle grades significantly behind their peers in reading ability require more, and more intensive, assistance if they are to achieve success.

How to Teach Reading

Research and our experiences over the past ten years have revealed very little about how to improve, substantially and rapidly, the reading skills of students who enter the middle grades significantly behind their peers. As a result, our suggestions for helping such students draw on a relatively new program for middle grades students (the Success for All Middle School's Reading Edge) and strategies that have been proven effective with elementary students and seem to us to hold promise for young adolescents.

The Reading Edge Program. The Success for All Middle School's Reading Edge is grounded in the Success for All elementary school program, which has proven effective in schools across the country (Herman, 1999, p. 2). In a description of the Success for All Middle School pilot project, Daniels, Madden, and Slavin (2000, pp. 12–13) outline how the Reading Edge program will improve students' reading skills.

The Reading Edge requires that all middle grades students devote 40–60 minutes a day to reading. All members of the faculty conduct Reading Edge classes, after receiving targeted training in the teaching of reading. Students are grouped by reading level for the Reading Edge classes and are reassessed frequently, every eight weeks at the most. The results of these frequent assessments are used to reconfigure instruction, the student groups, and the use of materials (Success for All Foundation, 1998, p. 3). The recurring assessments enable teachers to move students into different reading groups as they progress, avoiding the kind of semipermanent residence in a particular group that could smack of tracking. We reiterate what we said above: flexible grouping to differentiate instruction is acceptable; tracking by any name is not.

Daniels et al. (2000, p. 12–13) explain that the Reading Edge

> is designed to help students who are reading below grade level build a
> strong phonetic skill base and then move quickly to develop comprehen-
> sion, metacognitive strategies, study skills, vocabulary, and a love of
> reading. . . . Nonreaders learn basic decoding and literal comprehension
> strategies using a sequence of stories with phonetically regular text that
> become gradually more difficult. [Students who can read but still are below
> grade level] use stories, novels, magazine articles, and other sources as
> the basis for instruction.

Students who are reading at or above grade level still need to extend their
literacy learning, as Irvin points out (personal communication, February 14,
2000). During the daily Reading Edge classes, for example, those middle grades
students who are reading at or above grade level could devote their attention to
more advanced comprehension strategies and to reading more complicated
texts—they might, for example, develop strategies for reading college-level texts
in history. More advanced learners also might spend some of the reading acceleration time learning a foreign language, tutoring younger students, or engaging in other activities connected to the curriculum (Daniels et al., 2000, p. 13;
Slavin, 1999, p. 15).

We recommend a concentrated, daily class focused on reading for middle
grades students, like the classes provided in the Reading Edge. Such classes have
proven quite effective in improving the skills of elementary school children and
put a crucial spotlight on improving the reading skills of all middle grades students. We further recommend that reading acceleration classes make connections to the curriculum of students' regular classes as much as possible, so that
content and process are tied closely together. Teachers from all disciplines can
be trained to lead reading classes, a strategy that keeps those classes small and
strengthens the skills of teachers from all disciplines in reading instruction.

One-to-One Tutoring. Because one-to-one tutoring is the most effective
educational intervention known (Success for All Foundation, 1998, p. 4), we
recommend that it be used for students who have significant reading deficits to
supplement the reading instruction they receive in regular classes and a reading acceleration class. Reading Recovery, the tutoring program used to improve
the reading of first graders, has a very strong record of positive results (Slavin &
Fashola, 1998, pp. 59–62). When students in Reading Recovery are reading at
grade level and can continue to do so without further tutoring, they are moved
out of the program (Slavin & Fashola, 1998, p. 59), again mirroring the philosophy that initial ability need not destine a student to permanent placement.

The Success for All elementary program uses daily 20-minute tutoring
sessions for the weakest readers, a part of the package of Success for All improvements that has demonstrated impressive results (Herman, 1999, p. 2). It makes
sense to us that such a program of assistance, as a supplement to reading instruction in all the content areas and to reading acceleration classes, would have

success with middle grades students who are reading significantly below grade level. Again, we would add that tutoring should make strong connections to the curriculum of students' regular classes, so students strengthen their reading skills within a meaningful context.

Content, Process, and Choice. Besides teaching reading across the curriculum and offering reading acceleration classes and one-to-one tutoring, schools can extend learning time for reading through before- and after-school programs, homework centers, and intensive summer school programs. In all these reading instruction opportunities, teachers should balance their attention to content and to reading process and should give their students some choice in what they read. For example, tutors might work with students using materials that are also being used in their content-area classes and allow students to select other things to read that may or may not be related to the curriculum. Content-area teachers should use reading instruction in the context of tackling resources within or across their content areas. They should also allow students to choose what materials to use in support of their studies, drawing from the kind of rich classroom libraries Tomlinson (1995, p. 49) advocates in support of differentiated instruction. Teachers can also make connections to the multiple texts with which young adolescents are already engaged, from cereal boxes and the covers of music CDs to websites on the Internet.

Reading Instruction and Language Minority Students

The inability of English language learners to read in English seemingly poses a challenge to our assertion that every student can achieve excellence. To further complicate matters, while English language learners do require special attention and instruction in order to become literate in English, not all language minority students have the same needs. Some students may be unable to speak, read, or write English but may have strong literacy skills in their native language. Other students who cannot speak, read, or write English may also be illiterate in their native language, and still others may speak and understand English well but may be experiencing problems with English literacy.

New immigrant students who already have strong literacy skills in their native language will be at an advantage when it comes to developing these same skills in English. After learning English phonemes, graphemes, and basic vocabulary, these students will be able to transfer the reading skills they possess in their native language to English. Educators can help these students by providing native language support for their reading in the curriculum so that their literacy development will not be static while they are learning English. This is particularly important in the middle grades, because students will miss out on critical content if they are required to "take time out" to learn English. Any additional literacy and content skills gained during this time can be transferred to English later.

For new immigrant students who are not English-proficient and who are not literate in their own language, experts speculate about whether it is better to teach them literacy in their native language and then transfer those skills to English or to teach them immediately to read in English. Given that our focus here is the middle grades, educators should consider the following possible explanations for the student's delay in reading before deciding how to proceed: the student may be from a culture that has no written language, the student may not have been exposed to a literate environment, or the student may have been exposed to a literate environment but has some type of learning disability that has inhibited his or her ability to learn to read. Depending on the situation, teachers would be able to determine an appropriate curriculum. At the middle grades level, the focus should be on getting the students to read in English as quickly as possible and ensuring that they have access to appropriate-level content in the meantime.

For language minority students who have a high level of English proficiency but seem to be struggling with reading in English, the problem could actually be unrelated to their language-minority status; it could have more to do with decoding, comprehension, etc. Assessments should be administered to determine the specific area of the problem, and the results should guide a personalized intervention.

Supporting and Staffing Reading Instruction

To staff these various reading support efforts effectively, schools will need to offer substantive and ongoing professional development to teachers from all disciplines, with follow-up support from a reading specialist or curriculum coordinator. Schools may also train volunteers in reading instruction, especially as part of an effort to build the school's capacity to offer one-to-one tutoring. Volunteers may be drawn from among older students, parents, community members, and paraprofessionals (teacher aides). However, whoever they are, all volunteers require intensive training in reading instruction. Otherwise, as Davidson and Koppenhaver (1993, p. 164) point out, volunteer tutors can actually limit reading progress. "Tutors who have minimal skill levels themselves may reinforce incorrect information, or unwittingly mislead beginning readers because of their own lack of information on the subject."

Though focusing on academic content is vital, a school's efforts to promote improved reading skills should also include reading appreciation activities. As Irvin (1998, p. 238) points out, "[It] is clear that students will not become lifelong readers unless they enjoy reading." Increased proficiency will likely lead to further enjoyment, but schools can also supplement their more academically focused reading programs with what Irvin (p. 242) calls "recreational reading programs." Such programs can include "book fairs, reading break time, book exchanges, and any special school-wide reading activities." However, these recreational reading efforts, though important, are no substitute for reading instruction across the content areas and substantial support for students whose reading skills are below grade level.

Excellent teachers anchor all efforts to improve teaching and learning. The next chapter describes a continuum for preparing teachers to support young adolescents in fulfilling all aspects of the Turning Points vision.

5 Expert Teachers for Middle Grades Schools: Pre-service Preparation and Professional Development

TEN YEARS AGO, *Turning Points* argued that specific professional preparation for middle grades teachers is necessary to improve student learning and to promote the healthy development of young adolescents. It is no less true today. Increasing middle grades teachers' knowledge and skills before and during their tenure in the classroom is critical to the success of middle grades education.

The whole of a teacher's career should be a seamless continuum of learning and development focused always on improving student learning. Critical steps along the continuum include high-quality pre-service teacher preparation, carefully designed mentoring and induction programs, initial certification and licensure, and ongoing professional development, perhaps leading to advanced certification by the National Board for Professional Teaching Standards (see Box 5.1 for definitions of key teacher preparation and development terms). In turn, as teachers progress through the stages of the continuum, they can assume

Box 5.1 Defining Key Terms in Teacher Preparation and Development

Educators and policymakers use an array of terms to talk about the various stages of teacher preparation and development.

- *Pre-service teacher preparation* refers to all university-based education and training that precedes a teacher's first paid position as a classroom teacher.
- *New-teacher mentoring* refers to any activities or relationships created to support a first- or second-year teacher as he or she begins teaching in a particular school, or a high school or elementary school teacher who is entering middle grades teaching for the first time.
- *Induction* refers to any formal or informal activities offered to acquaint any teacher new to the school to the rules, procedures, norms, and expectations of the school and the district.
- *Professional development* (often called in-service training or continuing education) refers to the entire range of activities and learning that teachers engage in, both inside and outside the school, on school time and their own time, in order to improve their teaching knowledge and skill. The term encompasses both activities designed to teach a particular pedagogical skill—often referred to as training activities—and those intended to advance teachers' conceptual knowledge of curriculum, instruction, assessment, and other key elements of middle grades education.
- *Advanced certification* is the outcome achieved by experienced teachers who meet or exceed standards of excellence in teaching established by the National Board for Professional Teaching Standards. Board standards reflect rigorous analysis by teachers and other educators of excellent practice in each subject area and grade level. Board certification is voluntary, and teachers seeking it must engage in a rigorous year-long process of self-analysis, including the preparation of portfolios of their students' work, videotapes of themselves teaching, and written analyses of their teaching and its connection to student learning. Teachers also undergo formal assessments of their professional knowledge. Currently, pass rates are under 50 percent per year. However, the majority of teachers undergoing the process report that it is a powerful professional development experience (National Commission on Teaching & America's Future, 1996, p. 74; Rotberg, Futrell, & Lieberman, 1998, p. 463).

positions of professional leadership—such as mentor to new teachers, instructional coach, curriculum specialist, or principal—that enable them to share the knowledge, skills, and attitudes that make them successful teachers. This chapter describes proven and promising approaches for enhancing each stage of a middle grades teacher's education.

PRE-SERVICE PREPARATION OF MIDDLE GRADES TEACHERS

We make the argument here, as in the original *Turning Points*, that programs geared toward the specialized preparation of middle grades educators will produce expert teachers who are best qualified to teach young adolescents.

Middle grades teachers should come to their first teaching experience with

- A strong conceptual grasp of their academic disciplines and skills in developing and using assessments to guide instructional decisions (Chapter 3)
- Instructional knowledge and skills grounded in how people learn best (Chapter 4)
- An understanding of how effective interdisciplinary teams work and how they can best contribute to effective teams (Chapter 6)
- Substantial comprehension of young adolescents' developmental characteristics and needs (Chapters 1 and 6)
- Willingness and the preparation to participate actively in the school's governance system (Chapter 7)
- Knowledge and skills to support a safe and healthy school environment (Chapter 8)
- Capacity to engage parents and community members in support of students and the school (Chapter 9)

In short, we believe that new middle grades teachers should be prepared to become part of the Turning Points design system we are describing in this book. Teachers affect and are affected by the implementation of every recommendation we make for improving middle grades schools.

From a practical standpoint, however, aren't teachers who have been educated in high-quality high school or elementary school pre-service programs adequately prepared for teaching in the middle grades? Not according to middle grades teachers, principals, and other stakeholders. A number of studies have shown that middle grades teachers and principals support the specialized professional preparation of middle grades school teachers (Jenkins & Jenkins, 1991; McEwin, Dickinson, & Hamilton, 2000; Scales & McEwin, 1996), and 100 percent of the first group of teachers certified by the National Board for Professional Teaching Standards as Early Adolescent/Generalists believed that middle grades teachers should receive specialized middle grades professional preparation (McEwin et al., 2000). Professional organizations (the National Middle

School Association and the National Association for Secondary School Principals, for example) have also backed specialized preparation, as have boards and policymaking groups, such as the Southern Regional Education Board. Some states—among them North Carolina, Georgia, and Ohio—have established strong initiatives focusing on specialized middle grades teacher licensure and teacher preparation processes. State and national assessments that focus directly and exclusively on middle grades teaching are now available and are being used by some states as they move toward separate preparation and licensure of middle grades teachers.

Two other documents illustrate the growing consensus that middle grades teachers should receive professional preparation that focuses on the knowledge, skills, and attitudes needed to be highly successful teachers of young adolescents. The National Association of State Directors of Teacher Education and Certification (NASDTEC) includes separate outcome-based middle grades teacher education standards in its widely utilized publication *NASDTEC Outcome-Based Standards and Portfolio Assessment* (1994). The National Middle School Association and the National Council for the Accreditation of Teacher Education (National Middle School Association, 1997) have released the *Approved Curriculum Guidelines Handbook*, which focuses on the middle grades and has proven tremendously popular.

Do teachers who have experienced specialized middle grades preparation value it once they're in the classroom? According to a national study involving 2,139 middle school teachers in six states (Scales & McEwin, 1994), the answer is yes. This study found that the greater the number of courses devoted to the middle grades, the more favorably middle grades mathematics, language arts, social studies, and science teachers rated their preparation programs.

Despite the need for specialized teacher preparation, most middle grades teachers in the nation do not receive this preparation at the pre-service level. Several studies have revealed that fewer than one in four middle grades teachers have received specialized preparation before they begin their careers (McEwin, Dickinson, & Jenkins, 1996; Scales, 1992; Scales & McEwin, 1994). This percentage is likely to be much smaller in states where specialized middle grades teacher preparation and licensure are unavailable. Many experienced middle grades teachers bemoan the lack of specialized training:

> I definitely believe middle level teacher preparation should be different from elementary or secondary. I spent time in elementary preparation courses and learned only through experience about teaching middle school students. After 10 years of experience, I hunger for methods courses that are specifically for middle school teachers. I have had to try to learn on my own and from other teachers.... (Scales & McEwin, 1994, p. 47)

> I was not prepared for the middle school. I was prepared as an elementary teacher.... I am afraid I have had to learn the hard way to become a good middle school teacher (which I believe I really am).... It would have been wonderful to have been prepared back in 1982 when I started out, but I just was not. (Scales & McEwin, 1994, p. 7)

In states committed to middle grades preparation and licensure (for example, Georgia, Missouri, North Carolina), the majority of middle grades teachers in the basic subject areas have either received initial middle grades preparation and licensure or have taken advantage of graduate programs that lead to advanced middle grades licensure. A study by Scales and McEwin (1994) found that 55 percent of middle grades mathematics, science, social studies, and language arts teachers in six states with specialized middle grades teacher programs and supporting licensure had received specialized middle grades professional preparation (22 percent initial and 33 percent graduate).

One major reason that relatively few middle grades teachers have graduated from middle grades preparation programs, even in these six states, is that such programs are or were unavailable in their region or state. However, more and more teacher preparation institutions are now establishing middle grades programs. The percentage of institutions with special middle grades courses, add-on programs, or full programs has increased from approximately 23 percent in 1972–1973 (Gatewood & Mills, 1973) to 51 percent in 1995–1996 (McEwin, Dickinson & Swaim, 1997). Despite the increasing availability of middle grades teacher preparation programs, however, many thousands of prospective and practicing middle grades teachers find these programs inaccessible or even nonexistent.

The current teacher shortage appears to be complicating the effort to place expert, or at least adequately prepared, teachers in schools. As Lynn Olson (2000, p. 12) noted in a recent article for *Education Week,*

> As the ultimate arbiters of who is permitted to teach, states . . . raise standards for who can enter the profession on the front end, while keeping the door cracked open on the back end to ensure that every classroom will be staffed come September. . . . States have a critical choice: they can take steps now to ensure a qualified teaching force for years to come, or they can scramble to fill classrooms with mere warm bodies and be stuck with the results of those lax policies for decades.

THE CONTENT AND STRUCTURE OF PRE-SERVICE PROGRAMS

A wide variety of individuals, professional associations, foundations, special councils and boards, policymaking groups, and other stakeholders have reached a strong consensus on the essential components of middle grades preparation programs (McEwin & Dickinson, 1995; McEwin, Dickinson, Erb, & Scales, 1995; National Association of State Directors of Teacher Education and Certification, 1994; National Middle School Association, 1995). We begin our look at middle grades pre-service programs with these agreed-upon components, but we go beyond the present consensus to propose a radically different teacher preparation program, a comprehensive course of study that reflects the holistic nature of the Turning Points design.

According to the current consensus, the essential components of highly effective middle grades teacher preparation programs are

- Comprehensive study of early adolescence and the philosophy and organization of middle grades education
- Early and continuing field experiences in a variety of middle grades settings (usually grades 5–8)
- Preparation in two or more broad teaching fields (e.g., mathematics and science)

A Comprehensive Course of Study

The "consensus" course of study focuses on what teachers in middle grades schools will uniquely need to know: the nature of early adolescents and the philosophy and organization of middle grades schools. We agree that these are essential components of pre-service instruction, and we examine them in some detail below. However, we have observed over the past decade that advocates for middle grades pre-service training, in their efforts to carve out a niche for the middle grades, typically have not given as much attention as they should have to issues and topics that cross over levels of schooling, such as engaging parents or participating in decision making.

We propose a comprehensive course of study for middle grades pre-service that includes adolescent development and the philosophy of middle grades schools, but that goes further in encompassing all the *Turning Points 2000* principles we outline in this book. Like a teaching program at the University of California–Los Angeles, we do "not approach teaching as a technical profession with a set of skills, but rather as a commitment to higher academic achievement for all children, or, in the words of Associate Dean Jeannie Oakes . . . 'teaching to change the world'" (Education Development Center, 1999, p. 17).

A *Turning Points 2000* middle grades pre-service program would include:

- Developing curriculum grounded in standards for what students should know and be able to do
- Developing and using multiple means of assessment to provide ongoing, useful feedback, to both students and teachers, on what students have learned and to guide instructional decisions to improve student learning
- Differentiating instruction in classes with students of diverse needs, interests, backgrounds, and learning styles
- Integrating technology effectively into curriculum, assessment, and instruction
- Becoming involved in and support ongoing professional development, grounded in ensuring success for every student
- Participating effectively in an interdisciplinary team
- Becoming a good citizen of the school as a learning community by taking part in the governance system, using data to drive decisions, and assisting in developing and carrying out school improvement plans
- Creating and supporting a safe and healthy school environment
- Engaging parents and community members in support of the school itself and of student learning

The significance and substance of all these topics are dealt with in other chapters. We focus here on two facets of the course of study we are recommending: adolescent development and the philosophy and organization of middle grades schools.

Middle grades teachers must be well grounded in the development and needs of young adolescents if they are to be successful. Prospective middle grades teachers attain this expertise through a formal study of young adolescent development and through opportunities to work directly with young adolescent students to apply their knowledge. Teachers should know about how developmental realities play out against a backdrop of race, ethnicity, religion, gender, socioeconomic status, family, and community. The intended outcome is the creation of developmentally responsive programs and practices for young adolescents (McEwin & Dickinson, 1996). Authentic opportunities to translate issues of development into appropriate instructional plans that emphasize the diversity of learners and their needs should be included in all middle grades teacher preparation programs (see Chapter 4 for more on instruction).

Just as middle grades teachers need to know how, specifically, young adolescents are different from young children and older adolescents, they also need to understand that middle grades schools are different from elementary and high schools. This difference is much more than the sign in front of the school; it lies in the philosophical foundations of middle grades education and the organizational structure that grows from and supports this philosophy. A thorough study of middle grades philosophy and organization, not merely a superficial exploration, should be a main element of middle grades teacher preparation programs.

Prospective middle grades teachers should also be given many opportunities to learn about middle school philosophy. Formal study of middle grades philosophy should include an analysis of statements of middle school philosophy, like the National Middle School Association's 1995 publication, *This We Believe: Developmentally Responsive Middle Level Schools,* or the National Association of Secondary School Principals' 1985 *Agenda for Excellence at the Middle Level.* Students should also investigate the origins and development of the junior high school movement as the foundation of current middle grades practice.

Field Experiences in Effective Middle Grades Settings

High-quality field experiences provide a learning laboratory where prospective teachers can apply knowledge gained through university course work in settings where education faculties (from schools and universities) can teach, supervise, and advise. Fieldwork by prospective middle grades teachers should follow a pattern of increasing complexity and involvement, culminating in an extended internship or practicum during which prospective teachers are responsible for groups of young adolescents.

Prospective middle grades teachers should have opportunities to interact with young adolescents in a variety of situations, beginning when the prospective teachers are in their sophomore year of college. These learning experiences could include, for example, shadow studies, in which a prospective teacher observes one student for an entire school day; interviews with young adolescents and practitioners (classroom teachers, principals, guidance counselors, school nurses); and observations of classroom, team, and administrative practice. Interns could also assist in after-school programs and other extracurricular activities, like sponsoring clubs, coaching teams, or teaching short "interest" courses on, for instance, photography or travel (McEwin & Dickinson, 1996).

McEwin and Dickinson (1996, p. 24) describe a promising practice advanced by Savario Mungo of Illinois State University:

> Dr. Mungo treats the study of young adolescents as a study of a different culture. He advances the position that prospective middle level teachers must immerse themselves within that new culture to understand it, and therefore prospective middle level teachers observe and study young adolescent language, watch their movies, read their books, play their games.

An extended internship or practicum of 12–16 weeks should give prospective teachers real-world practice in all the areas we described under the comprehensive course of study. For example, such field experiences should include involvement in an interdisciplinary team, including creating integrated units of study, developing assessments, planning and delivering instruction, and analyzing student work; participation on school governance committees; involvement in student-led parent-teacher conferences, and so on. All student teaching experiences should include considerable feedback from mentors and peers, and interns should be required to reflect on their own practice.

The Southern Regional Education Board (SREB), in its 1998 report (Cooney, 1998, p. 11) on improving middle grades teaching, recommends that states "require prospective teachers in the middle grades to have a student teaching experience with middle grades students." We advocate taking that a step further: all field experiences for prospective middle grades teachers, from the most simple school visits to the extended practicum, should involve immersion in a middle grades learning community of students, educators, parents, and community leaders. We agree with McEwin and Dickinson (1996, p. 31) that these field experience placements should include "structurally different schools and schools with diverse populations of young adolescents." The SREB report noted that administrators believe that many middle grades teachers in the region leave the profession because "they do not want to teach the middle grades [or they] have had no [prior] exposure to middle grades students" (Cooney, 1998, p. 10). Our recommended field experiences would provide the "shakedown cruise" that would bring beginning teachers into middle grades classrooms much better prepared to chart their own successful course of study for their students.

Preparation in Two or More Teaching Fields

Prospective middle grades teachers will almost certainly teach in schools that emphasize the basic subject areas of mathematics, science, language arts, and

social studies. It is important to remember, however, that middle grades instruction should focus both on in-depth disciplinary knowledge *and* on concepts and
principles that cut across different subject areas. To accommodate both these
important goals, the content preparation of middle grades teachers should
extend beyond one field (discipline) to two or more teaching fields, or at least
to a major in one field with a minor in a related subject.

   As noted in *Turning Points*, prospective teachers should gain in-depth
knowledge of the subjects they will eventually teach during their undergraduate studies, en route to a bachelor's degree that will prepare them for graduate-
level training in teaching or for further study in a range of other fields. We highly
recommend that teachers continue their development in one- or two-year graduate programs, with a strong focus on methods of teaching specific to the two
(or more) academic disciplines they will teach, along with cross-disciplinary
connections. Again, in field settings, postgraduate interns should apply what they
have learned by working in interdisciplinary teams, teaching in their own disciplines, and drawing connections across disciplines, thus integrating two or more
subject areas.

Tying Middle Grades Pre-service Programs to the Future

We have outlined what we believe to be a strong middle grades pre-service program, one that represents a clear trajectory toward success in a school based on
our *Turning Points 2000* design. However, we recognize that much of what we
have described regarding teacher preparation will require changes inside the
ivory towers of higher education, changes that will undoubtedly be inexorable
but slow. So, how do we avoid creating teacher preparation programs that are
stuck in 2000, continuing to offer courses and experiences that will soon no
longer represent what is known about how people learn and teach best? We argue
that it will always be useful to look at what student outcomes need to be, whether
the outcomes are behavioral or academic, and then use those targets to work
backward toward an appropriate course of study and field experiences in teacher
preparation. This strategy is much like the "backward design" planning process
described in Chapters 3 and 4 in regard to classroom practice.

MIDDLE GRADES TEACHER LICENSURE/CERTIFICATION: IS IT NECESSARY?

With a few notable exceptions, high-quality middle grades teacher preparation
programs simply do not exist in states without mandatory licensure for teaching
in the middle grades that is separate and distinct from licenses for elementary
education and secondary education (e.g., grades 5–8). In 1997, for example,
88 percent of all institutions with specialized middle grades preparation programs
or middle grades courses were in states with specific middle grades licensure or
endorsement requirements (National Middle School Association, in press).

   Without a middle grades license to acknowledge their special professional
preparation, a great many prospective teachers will not select middle grades

teaching as a career. Altruism alone is seldom sufficient motivation for prospective or practicing teachers to seek out specialized professional education when they receive no recognition for their efforts to enhance their knowledge and skills. Whether it should be so or not, licensure requirements drive teacher preparation programs, exerting a powerful force on program development.

The Status of Middle Grades Licensure

At least 42 states have either middle grades teacher licensure or a middle grades endorsement (Useem, Barends, & Lindermayer, 1999). However, in many states, this credential is "voluntary" or is available to teachers with little or no specialized professional preparation. In some states, for example, the only requirement for obtaining a middle grades license is to have an elementary or secondary credential and teach one year at the middle grades level. These kinds of policies make a mockery of one of the primary purposes of teacher licensure, that of ensuring that all students are taught by teachers who have the specialized knowledge and skills to do so effectively.

An additional significant problem with many current middle grades teacher licensure plans is that the patterns of grades included in the various teaching licenses contain large overlaps that negate the significance of the separate middle grades license. An overlapping plan (e.g., K–8, 6–9, and 7–12) sends the clear message to all that the middle grades option is relatively unimportant, since both elementary and high school teachers are also licensed to teach in the middle grades. As a result, most current teacher preparation programs focus either on the elementary or high school levels, with the assumption that graduates of either group are, in some magical way, also well prepared to teach young adolescents (McEwin & Dickinson, 1996, p. 11).

Prospective teachers should have the opportunity to decide upon a career that focuses on a single developmental age group and should receive rigorous preparation in the subjects they will teach. This specialized professional preparation for the middle grades should be rewarded by a distinctive license that accurately informs all concerned that the teacher holding it has demonstrated his or her abilities to teach young adolescents effectively.

The "distinctive versus overlapping" grade-level issue also has implications for those who employ middle grades teachers. In some states, efforts to design and implement mandatory, nonoverlapping middle grades licensure have been blocked by representatives of districts that have difficulty employing enough licensed teachers. The argument against middle grades licensure that is usually put forth holds that some school districts are already having trouble finding teachers and that if the span of grade levels included in the license is "restricted," they will have even more difficulty. Efforts to move to separate and distinct middle grades licensure patterns are also sometimes opposed by teacher organizations or unions because of their members' concerns that the range of grade levels to which they can be assigned to teach is narrowed.

These are legitimate concerns. However, to allow them to dictate policy with regard to the qualifications and training of middle grades teachers violates the one rule that is absolutely essential if a middle grades school, or any school, is to be successful: Do what is right for the children. Expecting teachers educated to teach five-year-olds to teach young adolescents makes no more sense than expecting history teachers to teach algebra. In emergencies, schools and school districts may well be forced to allow teachers to teach outside their area of competence, but no one would advocate establishing policies that encourage emergency actions to become permanent, acceptable practice. As Kati Haycock of the Education Trust said, "Just like I don't want an emergency-credentialed surgeon to operate on my child, I also don't want an emergency-credentialed teacher to teach my child" (Education Development Center, 1999).

Just as it does in economics, we believe it likely that demand will drive supply. If those people who hire teachers for young adolescents do not demand the kind of preparation and licensure we describe, then the supply of such expert teachers will remain inadequate. The concerns of districts, unions, and even some principals about the availability and employability of middle grades teachers are important, but they need to be addressed through greater efforts and incentives to recruit new, highly qualified teachers rather than by denying young adolescents' need for specially trained teachers.

Overlapping licensure patterns, where both elementary and secondary education overlap middle grades licensure, also mean that teacher preparation institutions can choose to offer only elementary/middle (K–8) and middle/secondary (7–12) programs without establishing separate middle grades teacher preparation programs. In states like North Carolina, where the grade overlap has been eliminated, however, virtually all public and private institutions have developed separate middle grades teacher preparation programs. Clearly, licensure regulations can encourage, and even require, teacher preparation institutions to develop specialized middle grades teacher preparation programs, which will benefit both young adolescents and their teachers.

What About Middle Grades Teacher Endorsements?

Turning Points recommended that, in the absence of middle grades licensure or certification, states should at least provide teachers with the opportunity to earn a middle grades endorsement voluntarily. The experience of the past ten years suggests that this is one of the *least* effective methods of ensuring special preparation for middle grades teachers. In a typical endorsement plan, a prospective teacher must first earn a degree and license in elementary education, a secondary subject area, or some other teaching field. Then, by extending their study, prospective teachers can also receive an endorsement to teach in the middle grades. These endorsements are rarely required for teaching in the middle grades, since many states allow elementary and secondary prepared teachers to teach young adolescents without a middle grades license or endorsement. A major problem associated with middle grades endorsement plans is that they often amount to little more than two or three courses that may or may not focus directly on middle grades teaching (for example, one psychology class and one reading or methods class). Some states have more extensive middle grades endorsement plans that include specialized middle grades courses and field experiences, but these extensive plans typically require an extra semester or more of preparation. In light of all this, it should not be surprising that few prospective teachers select the middle grades endorsement route.

If the endorsement route has been so unsuccessful, why does it continue to reappear year after year, decade after decade? The answer is that it is a politically expedient solution (or "nonsolution") to the kinds of highly charged issues of teacher employment and assignment noted earlier. In our view, the Task Force on Education of Young Adolescents that produced *Turning Points* simply did not adequately recognize these political dynamics. All too often, policymakers and other influential individuals and groups agree to leave existing licenses as they are (i.e., K–8, 7–12) while adding a voluntary endorsement that includes the middle grades (e.g., 5–8, 6–9). Unfortunately, since the endorsement is not required, few teacher preparation institutions create such programs and few teachers bother to apply for the endorsement. After a few years, most or all of the few teacher preparation institutions that developed middle grades endorsement programs drop them because of low enrollments. State licensing agencies eventually drop the license endorsement because "it is not being used." The result is that young adolescents continue to be taught by teachers with a wide range of professional preparation, some of which is far removed from their middle grades teaching assignments.

Specialized education for middle grades teachers is the first key step in the continuum to develop highly effective teachers of young adolescent students. The following section addresses the next critical step—when a teacher begins his or her professional career.

MENTORING AND INDUCTION PROGRAMS FOR MIDDLE GRADES TEACHERS

A good pre-service education is only as good as the follow-up and support the teacher receives as he or she tries to make the transition to full-time teaching responsibilities. The daunting challenges of the first teaching assignment, particularly classroom management and curriculum planning, too frequently lead unsupported beginning teachers to adopt practices contrary both to their educational philosophy and to the instructional strategies they learned in pre-service education. New teachers often struggle just to get through the day.

All new teachers need mentoring from expert veteran teachers to translate the lessons of university classrooms into the practical artistry of excellent teaching. Comparing teaching with other professions, one university director of teacher-credentialing programs (Evans, 1999, p. 35) wrote,

> In no profession other than teaching are inexperienced and untried beginners left to their own devices and allowed to have autonomous responsibility to make substantive professional decisions. In law, the approach

to a complex legal issue is either devised or carefully reviewed by a senior partner; in medicine, the treatment of a puzzling medical condition directly involves the consultation and judgment of the chief of staff; . . . and in police work, the rookie cop is paired with an experienced, streetwise officer. In each of these organizational settings, less experienced individuals are under the direct daily guidance, tutelage, and supervision of more experienced and successful mentors. Differentiated levels of decision-making authority based on experience and success are taken for granted. This is the case even when the new practitioner has completed a formal pre-service training program.

Strong evidence reveals that comprehensive mentoring and induction programs can make a tremendous difference in the skills, attitudes, and self-concepts of new teachers, determining both their decision to stay in the profession and their long-term effectiveness. In summarizing a range of studies, the National Commission on Teaching and America's Future (1996) concluded that, "research shows that beginning teachers who have had the continuous support of a skilled mentor are much more likely to stay in the profession and much more likely to get beyond classroom management concerns to focus on student learning" (pp. 80–81). "They become more effective as teachers because they are learning from guided practice rather than trial-and-error" (p. 40).

Many local districts implementing California's Beginning Teacher Support and Assessment Program (BTSA) report that only 10–15 percent of teachers who have gone through the program leave the profession within the first five years (Archer, 1999, p. 20), well below the more typical rate of 30 percent or higher. This is particularly significant, since the majority of the teachers in some of California's local BTSA programs enter teaching under emergency credentials, having received no formal teacher training at all. Although mentoring is never an adequate substitute for high-quality teacher preparation, mentoring programs are vital to ensure even a minimum level of quality in some of the highest-need districts.

Unfortunately, formal mentoring programs are relatively rare. New teachers are left to sink or swim, often given the heaviest teaching loads and the worst-prepared students. In urban and rural school districts serving the poorest students, 5-year teacher attrition rates of 50 to 60 percent are not uncommon (Archer, 1999, p. 20; Fideler & Haselkorn, 1999, p. 4; Huling-Austin, 1989, pp. 7–8; Ruenzel, 1998, p. 34). To make matters worse, evidence shows that the most academically talented teachers may leave in the greatest numbers (Huling-Austin, 1989, p. 8).

High teacher turnover jeopardizes student learning because essential attachments between teachers and adolescents are interrupted. Behavioral problems are exacerbated if students assume that a teacher will not be around long. Many young adolescents undoubtedly read such situations as yet another example of uncaring adults not taking them seriously, and the disillusionment shows in their behavior and in their lack of motivation to learn. Effective teaching and learning under these conditions is extremely difficult.

Content of Mentoring Programs

Effective mentoring and induction programs can take many forms. However, they are defined by several common characteristics (Fideler & Haselkorn, 1999; National Commission on Teaching & America's Future, 1996). Novice teachers are paired with experienced, highly skilled mentor teachers, preferably from the same grade level or subject area and preferably for two years, but at least for the first full year of service. The relationship is intended both to develop the skills of the new teacher and to provide essential emotional support during the trying early stages of teaching.

Neither the new teacher nor the mentor should be assigned a full teaching load. A new teacher's job of translating largely theoretical knowledge about teaching into skillful curriculum planning, assessment, instruction, and classroom management requires enormous time and practice, as does the mentor's role of providing in-depth feedback and advice. Mentors should have their teaching load reduced incrementally for each new teacher under their supervision. New teachers should teach no more than 80 percent of what a veteran teacher would be expected to teach, leaving them sufficient time to work with their mentors and engage in curriculum planning and other professional development activities. Although seminars, orientations, and other group meetings may be part of the mentoring program, most of the mentor's time should be spent meeting individually with the one or more new teachers under his or her tutelage.

Ideally, mentors and new teachers are paired before the school year starts so that the new teachers have help as they prepare for the very important first days and weeks of school. Then, by meeting with their mentors on a weekly or even daily basis if needed, new teachers can continue to gain specific, regular advice and feedback on all aspects of their teaching. For example, to develop curriculum planning and instructional skills, the new teacher and the mentor might jointly identify a specific instructional technique to focus on improving. Then the new teacher plans a class incorporating that skill, shares the plan in advance with the mentor for feedback and modification, teaches the class with the mentor observing and perhaps even videotaping, and finally discusses the results with the mentor.

The mentoring relationship is one step in the continuum of professional preparation and growth. The materials, methods, and processes used in the mentoring relationship build upon what was learned in the pre-service phase and begin to inculcate in the new teacher the skills and inclinations to engage the sort of career-long inquiry, reflection, and growth envisioned by, for example, the National Board for Professional Teaching Standards.

A number of middle schools have tried to develop mentoring programs themselves by pairing experienced teachers with beginning teachers. These efforts are commendable, but in the absence of district support in the form of release time for mentors and opportunities for training for the role, the potential effect of such efforts is diminished. Thus, while school-based efforts are definitely worth doing, it is vital to advocate for a systematic, districtwide approach to mentoring beginning teachers (see Box 5.2).

Box 5.2 One District's Effort to Support Beginning Teachers

The Cincinnati Public Schools mentoring program illustrates many of the elements of a successful mentoring and induction program. The mentoring component is part of an overhaul, aimed at improving student achievement, of the district's entire system for teacher preparation and recruitment, professional development, and instructional leadership. Central to the reforms is the creation of a career ladder for teachers that includes opportunities to provide instructional support to colleagues. One professional leadership role excellent experienced teachers may assume is that of mentor to new teachers. (Another role for mentors is to provide support for tenured teachers who are experiencing serious instructional deficiencies and who thus may face dismissal.)

To become mentors, teachers must first apply to become "lead teachers" through a rigorous process involving classroom observations, interviews by other teachers and principals, and detailed documentation of their educational philosophy, their instructional and leadership skills, and their efforts to grow professionally. Certification by the National Board for Professional Teaching Standards also makes teachers eligible for lead teacher status.

Becoming a lead teacher is a challenging process. Fewer than 40 percent of those who apply to be lead teachers make it through all the steps. Every lead teacher position is reopened every two years. Current lead teachers may reapply for their positions, but because no lead teacher may be out of the classroom full time for more than two years, reappointment can be on a part-time basis only. Besides mentoring, lead teachers may act as curriculum development specialists, middle school interdisciplinary team leaders, high school department leaders, or instructors in specific professional development programs.

All new teachers in the district are assigned mentors from within their subject area or grade level. The mentors are responsible for helping the new teachers refine their teaching skills; orienting them to district goals, curriculum, and structure; and making them aware of sources of professional and personal support, including opportunities available through the district's newly created professional development academy. In terms of instructional assistance, mentors

- Help new teachers locate classroom materials
- Help new teachers plan curriculum and set appropriate instructional goals
- Observe new teachers and make recommendations on teaching and classroom management techniques
- Do demonstration lessons
- Arrange for the beginning teachers to observe veteran teachers

In recognition of their additional responsibilities and expertise, all lead teachers receive additional compensation of $4,500–$5,500 a year. While most lead teachers remain in the classroom, full-time mentor teachers do not. They are assigned a maximum caseload of 14 new teachers each. Part-time mentor teachers remain in the classroom but receive release time equivalent to 12 substitute days for each new teacher in their care. Mentor teachers must engage in professional development in such areas as adult learning and course work related to their mentoring responsibilities. In addition, a program facilitator coordinates the entire program, including the training for mentor teachers.

The mentoring program is designed as both a support and an accountability system. Mentors also evaluate the performance of new teachers and recommend their continued employment or dismissal to a peer review panel of teachers and administrators. This panel, in turn, votes on these reports and makes recommendations to the superintendent of Cincinnati public schools, who sends his recommendations to the Cincinnati board of education, which makes a final determination.

Inducting New Teachers into the School Culture

Although the terms "mentoring" and "induction" are often used interchangeably, some schools and districts have developed formal programs to induct or to welcome beginning teachers or teachers new to a school's professional community. Schools are cultures, with their own norms and "folkways," and they function best when they have organized ways of accepting new members, and of transmitting their values, mission, and practices to novice teachers and experienced educators new to the school.

Some local districts provide several days of orientation for all teachers new to the district. Such large-scale sessions are useful as long as all the schools in the district share a common mission, standards, curriculum, and assessment scheme. When schools vary on these dimensions, each school should provide its own introductory program. Formal induction programs can provide an overview of such issues as

- The school and district philosophy, mission, and structure
- Performance standards and assessment practices used in the school
- Organizational issues such as the school calendar and scheduling practices
- School policies on issues such as discipline, parent communication, and referrals for health or mental health services

In addition to formal programs, many good middle schools develop a more personalized way of inducting new team members. Not surprisingly, different teams within a school will develop different subcultures. Moreover, teams can come unraveled by turnover in membership if they have no mechanism for transmitting expectations for students and norms and routines for collaborative work to new members. As with any culture, teams (and schools) induct new members through ongoing informal communication, but organized approaches to welcome new members are also valuable.

PROFESSIONAL DEVELOPMENT

Mentoring and induction programs are part of a broader array of learning opportunities that must be available to teachers throughout their careers. Thus it comes as somewhat of a surprise, in hindsight, that *Turning Points* paid little attention to middle grades educators' need for effective professional development opportunities. Although high-quality pre-service preparation is critical, ongoing staff development is equally essential to ensure that teachers build on the knowledge and skills necessary to assist all their students to learn at high levels.

It is safe to say that professional development is a problem in virtually every middle grades school in the country, and in many schools it is a major one. But the problem is not that teachers are not engaged in professional development in some way or another. A 1993–1994 survey by the National Center for Education Statistics (1998b) found that 96 percent of public school teachers had participated in some professional development during the school year. The problem is that much of what passes for professional development is of poor quality, of such limited duration as to be ineffective, and often only marginally connected to the most pressing classroom challenges that face teachers. Recalling the much-maligned practice of taking students out of their regular classrooms for remedial instruction, Sparks (1998) describes the typical staff development experiences as "adult pull-out programs."

Key Elements of Effective Professional Development

Effective professional development in middle grades schools is results-driven, standards-based, and embedded in teachers' daily work (Sparks, 1997). It grows out of understanding the principles of adult learning and organizational development, and it also involves follow-up assistance in implementing new instructional strategies (Bransford et al., 1999, pp. 178–193).

Middle grades staff development that is results-driven begins with three central questions:

> What do we expect all middle grades students to know and to be able to do?
> What must teachers know and be able to do to support their students' achievement of these expectations?
> How must staff development be designed to support high levels of learning for all staff and students?

Judith Renyi (1996), executive director of the National Education Association's National Foundation for the Improvement of Education, writes that the goal of professional development in schools must be to improve results in terms of student learning, not simply to enhance practice. Unfortunately, professional development is all too often evaluated solely on the basis of the number of teachers involved and the amount of time they spend participating.

An expectation that professional development activities can be effectively focused to improve outcomes for students makes professional development a serious endeavor for all involved. Rather than a frivolous activity, or one designed only for individual enhancement, results-oriented professional development implies a collective approach by teachers targeted toward solving a significant learning challenge. Studies of successful school improvement efforts have repeatedly shown that good results depend on the building of a collaborative community of adult learners who accept joint responsibility for student achievement (Joyce & Showers, 1995; Little, 1997; Newmann & Wehlage, 1995). For example, once a school has identified an area of instruction in need of improvement (through an inquiry process like that described in Chapter 7), teachers should be required to participate actively in professional development designed to increase their competency in the instructional area. Principals and district officials have a reciprocal obligation, of course, to provide the time and support necessary to develop this capacity (Elmore & Burney, 1997; Guskey, 1994, p. 46).

Because it is so important for all teachers to engage in results-oriented professional development, school improvement plans that identify the school's most pressing learning challenges should specify the kinds of professional development activities that teachers will be expected to participate in. In turn, teachers should be expected to develop annual (at least) professional development plans linked to school- or districtwide instructional and student performance goals. Progress in implementing the plan should be an important part of a teacher's annual performance review. To ensure that teachers have the support they need to meet their learning goals, the school principal should be held accountable by district officials for providing the time and other resources that teachers need (Elmore & Burney, 1997). (See Box 5.3 for an example of professional development in practice.)

Implicit in the key questions driving results-based professional development is the requirement that in-service training be based on standards, standards for what both teachers and students should know and be able to do, and standards for the quality of the professional development activities themselves. A majority of states have defined or are defining the knowledge and skills that middle grades students must have in order to pass certain courses or state tests. As described in Chapter 3, these state standards provide direction for locally developed standards of student achievement. Standards for teaching—such as those developed by the National Board for Professional Teaching Standards— describe the knowledge and skills expected of accomplished teachers. Staff development standards define the nature of high-quality professional development experiences.

The National Staff Development Council (1994), in collaboration with ten leading education associations, produced middle grades staff development

Box 5.3 Schoolwide Professional Development Fosters Improved Learning

In 1994 Colonel Richardson Middle School was warned for the third year in a row that it would be reconstituted by the state if it did not improve. A small school in rural Caroline County on Maryland's Eastern Shore, Col. Richardson has 461 students, 45 percent of whom qualify for free or reduced lunch, and 30 percent of whom are members of minorities, mostly African American. Today the school is listed as one of the most improved schools in Maryland and posts test scores, in some subjects, above state averages.

In Maryland, each school is required to have a school improvement committee, which draws up a school improvement plan that sets out the school's objectives and ways to meet those objectives. In 1994, Debbie Chance, Colonel Richardson's newly appointed principal, chose to focus school improvement efforts on writing. Chance, who had been an English teacher in a neighboring county for 18 years, felt comfortable with the topic and wanted something that would have an immediate effect on instruction and student achievement. Chance knew that she was initially viewed with suspicion by most of the teachers, who had seen many principals come and go during a very short time, leaving the school rudderless—without continuity or direction. In fact, when Chance arrived in 1994, Col. Richardson had just posted alarmingly low scores on the Maryland School Performance Assessment Program tests (MSPAPs), with only 22 percent of its students registering as satisfactory in writing. Perhaps even more alarming was the teaching staff's indifference to the threat of state reconstitution, a possibility they felt was very remote and unrealistic.

Chance drew up a two-year plan, during the first year of which teachers learned about the topic; the second year was the implementation year, when teachers were expected to use what they had learned. One of the key supports for at-risk schools' improvement plans is an "MSPAP coordinator" who is assigned by the district to each elementary and middle school. The coordinator's job is to support the instructional program of the school. She acts as a teacher of teachers and a coach and provides support, which includes helping with scoring of papers and teaching of classes when needed. Chance calls the MSPAP coordinator her "assistant principal for instruction."

The coordinator has also been the key organizer of the formal professional development activities, which take place in three venues. The first are statewide and national training conferences which teachers attended with grant funds from Carnegie Corporation's Middle Grade School State Policy Initiative. The second are the school's in-service days, between one and one-and-a-half days per grading period. The third are team meetings. Chance organized the school into three grade-level teams that meet one period every day. Because the teams are small, the six or eight teachers are able to look at each other's lesson plans and discuss which new strategies and teaching techniques worked with which classes and why in more depth than is possible in a larger group.

During the first year of the cycle, professional development consisted of classes and workshops, including presentations by experts, discussions of assigned readings, and presentations by Chance and the MSPAP coordinator. During the second year, teachers were expected to begin using what they had learned and to bring to the team meetings examples of ways they had implemented new ideas and strategies that had been discussed in the previous year. Teachers were required by Chance to put together portfolios of the writing assignments they gave and examples of student work.

A breath-stopping moment came when the 1996 state assessment scores were released: 46.3 percent of the students had performed at a satisfactory level in writing. That was still well below the state goal of 70 percent, but it was a little above the average state performance, which was considered a triumph. Even more dramatic, in the category of language usage the number of students performing at a satisfactory level grew from 42.9 percent in 1995 to 64.7 percent in 1996—within spitting distance of the state goal of 70 percent. And, reflecting the fact that the state assessments require students to write about mathematics and the students were now used to doing so, the mathematics scores shot up as well, from 23.6 percent performing at a satisfactory level to 42.3 percent.

Because of a state emphasis on reading, Chance, in consultation with the school improvement committee, has most recently focused improvement efforts in this area. The staff has spent a year learning about new ways to improve the analytic approach students bring to reading a variety of materials. During the 1999–2000 school year, teachers have begun using some of those techniques. Each department is choosing two or three techniques to concentrate on, depending on how well they conform to the subjects, and teachers will be expected to have common performance criteria for all their students.

Even after a two-year professional development cycle is completed on a given area of need, the teachers are expected to maintain the portfolios demonstrating their continuing use of techniques that were learned in previous years. Also, the MSPAP coordinator provides occasional updates on the previous topics by distributing new information or articles of interest; the coordinator also uses after-school workshops to bring new teachers up to speed. In this way, the professional development program retains its freshness and relevance to the teachers and classroom.

Teachers have especially appreciated the focused, sustained nature of the professional development and its emphasis on bringing improvements to the classroom. Many of the teachers have been teaching for ten or more years and have sat through many one-shot professional development classes and workshops that they felt didn't necessarily translate to their classrooms. The other thing teachers said they appreciated is how much of the professional development has been available during the school day, rather than after school and on weekends, which is particularly a burden for teachers with children. Although it is still not perfect, Col. Richardson has tackled its problems in a focused, sustained way, concentrating on the professional development of its teachers. And it has seen real results.

standards that provide direction for the planning, delivery, and evaluation of staff development activities. The standards address three areas: content, process, and context.

Staff development content standards describe what is important for all educators to know and be able to do to facilitate high levels of student learning. They address issues such as curriculum, instruction, adolescent development, classroom management, assessment, service learning, interdisciplinary teaming, and parent involvement.

Process standards describe the learning processes that best enable adults to gain the knowledge and skills required to ensure high levels of student learning. These standards address issues of individual and organizational change, models of staff development, evaluation, data analysis, and group development.

Context standards provide guidance on the organizational structures and culture that support professional learning. Furthermore, they address issues of continuous improvement, leadership, advocacy, and the use of resources and time.

Focused on results and based on standards, effective professional development should also be a daily part of teachers' work. Unfortunately, this is more often the exception than the rule. Judith Warren Little (1997) notes that, although research over the past decade confirms the link between professional development and student learning when teachers work in professional communities, staff development is still typically seen as something external to the ongoing work of teaching, something that one "does" or that is "provided" in the form of discrete activities or events. Yet when professional development is built into the daily, weekly, and yearlong job of teaching, it results in changed practice and student success (Renyi, 1996).

As will be discussed in Chapter 6, middle grades teaching teams and other small-group structures are excellent ways of embedding professional development in the daily routine of teachers. With teams in place, common planning time becomes a vitally important period when teachers can discuss ways to improve teaching and student learning. Additional time can be set aside each week, or at least every two weeks, for teachers to come together in disciplinary or grade-level groups, or perhaps in groups focused on a common problem concerning student learning.

The need to embed professional development in the daily lives of teachers raises an issue that educators consistently identify as one of the most critical factors determining the quality of professional development activities: time. Numerous studies of school change conclude that the availability of time to learn about and implement new instructional methods is a key issue in successful school improvement (Corcoran, 1998, p. 6; Fullan & Miles, 1992, p. 750; North Central Regional Educational Laboratory, 1997). McDiarmid (1995, p. 2) argues, "The changes teachers must make to meet the goals of reform entail much more than learning new techniques. They go to the core of what it means to teach. . . . To learn what they need to know and to change their roles and practices, teachers need time and mental space . . . to concentrate their thinking on teaching away from the physical and mental demands of the classroom."

As with any resource, time might be used more efficiently in middle grades schools to "free up" a few minutes here and an hour there that can be dedicated to teacher learning opportunities. Such efforts may be helpful in the short run, but the long run, toward all students meeting or exceeding high standards, demands that significant time for both individual and collective learning and reflection be incorporated in teachers' regular workday. Undeniably, this will ultimately cost more money or require the redirection of funds from current uses that do not provide teachers with ongoing professional development opportunities. High-quality education does not happen "on the cheap," and the sooner we acknowledge this fact, the more likely we will be to reach our goals for educating young adolescents in the 21st century.

Finally, it has been said that professional development without follow-up assistance in the classroom where new knowledge is to be applied is akin to malpractice. Teachers need "at-the-elbow" assistance in implementing many new instructional strategies. Joyce and Showers (1995, p. 110) estimate that successful implementation of a complex model of teaching requires as many as 25 trials in the classroom over eight to ten weeks, coupled with opportunities to reflect and to receive feedback, before the new strategies become part of a teacher's regular repertoire of practice.

Impact on Teaching and Student Learning

The goal of professional development is to improve student learning, and the means to that end is continuous development of teachers' knowledge and skills. A critical aspect of this development is the strengthening of teachers' content knowledge. Middle grades teachers are being asked today to teach students to reach high content standards for which their own preparation may be inadequate or outdated, or they may find themselves teaching in subject areas in which they received little formal academic education. Recent findings from a 17-year synthesis of the impact of federal investment in professional development show that deeper understanding of academic content and its application in real-world settings is necessary if all teachers are to be successful in helping students master challenging academic standards (Koppich & Knapp, 1998). The data show two crucial components of improving student achievement: teachers' knowledge of subject matter and their ability to translate that knowledge into classroom learning activities appropriate to learners at different developmental levels and of different backgrounds.

In addition to helping teachers attain a deeper understanding of the key concepts, principles, and methods of inquiry within their subject area, professional development should increase their knowledge of instructional strategies specific to the discipline. (See Chapter 4 for more information on improving instruction.) Such discipline-specific instructional strategies have been termed "pedagogical content knowledge" (Bransford et al., 1999, pp. 143–177). Closely linked to the development of instructional strategies, professional development should provide teachers with the classroom assessment skills that allow them to monitor gains in student learning regularly. Student achievement increases substantially in schools that continuously use student performance data to guide changes in instructional practice (Newmann & Wehlage, 1995).

High-quality professional development builds a culture among educators within a middle school, and between "like-minded" schools, that supports innovation, experimentation, and collegial sharing. Collaborative planning and inquiry activities such as team- or subject-based curriculum planning, collaborative analysis of student work, peer observation and coaching, study groups, and action research all contribute to breaking down norms of privacy and isolation that prevail in many schools. For a school to engage seriously in collaborative inquiry—to get teachers permanently out of "private practice"—requires opportunities for open and critical discussions of instruction (Little, 1997). Such collaborative work redefines teaching as an ongoing process of problem identification and problem solving (Haslam, n.d., p. 9). (See Box 5.4 for an example of professional development embedded in collaborative inquiry.)

Powerful opportunities to reduce teacher isolation and enhance collaborative learning can also be created outside the school. Teacher networks (both face-to-face and electronic) can serve as important sources of information, materials, and support. Networks enable teachers to learn from colleagues, to connect to research and best practices beyond their schools, and to enhance their feelings of professionalism among other educators who share their passion for improving student achievement.

When the principles of effective professional development are put into practice, teacher knowledge and skill demonstrably improve, resulting in improved student learning. A study of more than a thousand school districts concluded that every additional dollar spent on more highly qualified teachers netted greater improvements in student achievement than did any other use of school resources (Ferguson, 1991). An analysis of data from 60 different studies found that investments in high-quality teacher education and training improve student achievement more than a range of other reforms, including increasing teacher salaries or decreasing teacher–student ratios (Greenwald, Hedges, & Laine, 1996; National Commission on Teaching & America's Future, 1997). A recent study by the National Staff Development Council showed that the content, process, and quality of professional development programs are related to improvement in teaching practice and student achievement (Killion, 1999). In addition, recent studies of the implementation of "whole school" reform designs document the centrality of high-quality professional development to school improvement (Bodilly, 1998; Nunnery, 1998).

The best-documented evidence of the impact of professional development on the quality of teaching and student outcomes comes from New York City's Community School District 2. A decade of significant investment in comprehensive professional development in this predominantly low-income district has dramatically improved the instructional skills of teachers in core curriculum areas, leading to steady gains in achievement scores (Elmore & Burney, 1997).

The Professional Development Facilitator

One of the most significant lessons of the past decade regarding school reform is that, to effect lasting change, nearly every school needs sustained assistance

Box 5.4 Looking at Student Work

"Four years ago we might have thought we knew it all," acknowledges Mary Massich, an eighth-grade history teacher who chairs the history department at Hoover Middle School in Long Beach, California. "We'd received many grants. We were a model history department in the state of California. We had incredible staff development and we felt so cutting edge. And then we started looking at our student work. And we became these humble teachers becoming humbler by the minute! When we really thought about how this all trickles down to kids, we realized we have so much more to learn."

Over the past several years, a diverse array of schools, practitioners, and intermediary organizations have developed strategies for using the assessment of student work as a vehicle for improving classroom instruction. Approaches vary in emphasis, philosophy, and process. Supported by the DeWitt-Wallace Readers' Digest Fund, three organizations deeply involved in school reform—the Coalition of Essential Schools, Harvard University's Project Zero, and the Academy for Educational Development—have been working with a select number of schools and districts around the country to train school faculties in assessment methods and to develop promising staffing and scheduling models that free up in-school time for teacher talk about curriculum and instruction.

Another intermediary organization, the Washington, D.C.–based Education Trust, has aligned the process of looking at student work with the movement for standards-based reform. Working with cities and districts across the country that have produced educational standards, the Trust's "Standards in Practice" (SIP) process engages teachers, parents, and school leadership staff in several hour-long sessions that are scheduled weekly or biweekly, on-site, and during the school day. In these structured forums, small cross-disciplinary groups analyze teachers' assignments to see whether and how they align with standards expectations; do the assignments themselves to understand the skills and knowledge required of students; design a "scoring guide" to evaluate student work based on the assignment's particular priorities and the standards it purports to address; score the student work reviewed; and develop intervention strategies based on what they've found.

Though the organizations' approaches to reviewing student work differ in important respects, they share the fundamental assumption that engaging teachers in conversation about student work can be a powerful tool for improving teaching and learning in the classroom. What's critical about looking at student work is not the scoring process itself but the conversation it engenders. For many teachers, these conversations—though humbling and at times downright difficult—can spark "aha" moments that become transformative teaching events. As Hoover's Mary Massich puts it: "Having a group of teachers work with me, and having seven to ten different pairs of eyes look at my work and my kids' work, has helped me define what it is I want my students to do. It's helped me see the big picture."

BOX 5.4 CONTINUED

Hoover Middle School houses 1,100 primarily low-income students who qualify for Title I status. It is part of the Long Beach Unified School District (LBUSD) in California, one of four districts in the country that received substantial funding from the Edna McConnell Clark Foundation to implement standards-based reform in middle school settings.

Hoover's approach to looking at student work contains strands of various groups' methods. Reflecting the work of the Education Trust, Hoover's history teachers are highly cognizant of LBUSD's middle school social studies standards as they assess their own teaching tasks and the work students produce. Their scoring of student work is premised on students' meeting standards criteria, rather than on teachers' prior knowledge of an individual student's strengths and weaknesses. The particular scoring rubrics used by Hoover's history teachers have been adapted from a theoretical assessment framework developed by University of Wisconsin professor Fred M. Newmann and his colleagues (Newmann, Lopez, & Bryk, 1998; Newmann, Marks, & Gamoran,1995; Newmann, Secada, & Wehlage, 1995). Hoover's teachers also occasionally review scholarship by practitioners and theorists in the field. And their discussions inevitably lead to decisions about actions they will take to retool assignments or reteach material so that all students—and particularly low-end per- formers—will be more likely to meet standards expectations.

What actually happens when teachers sit down over sodas and snacks to talk about student work? Typically, Massich explains, two or three teachers present samples of work to be considered. Sometimes teachers ask for guidance in examining the tasks they have assigned; sometimes they ask for help in reviewing a sample of student work. Two different scoring rubrics, both adapted from Newmann, provide three overarching assessment criteria (and associated four-point scores) for teacher task and student work assessment. Criteria address disciplinary knowledge (the degree to which tasks ask students to demonstrate knowledge of subject matter content); construction of knowledge (the degree to which tasks ask students to engage in higher-order thinking tasks); and value beyond the school (the degree to which the task has relevance in real-world settings beyond the life of the school).

Teachers typically ask each other to review proposed assignments *before* they have been delivered to students; this gives teachers time to refashion their assign- ments before they are introduced in the classroom. As Ruth Mitchell of the Education Trust often says, "Students can do no better than the work they're assigned." In the past, when teachers identified problems in student work, Massich explains, they found that it "always related back to a flaw in the task" that had been assigned. Now teachers look at the task first, articulate its relevance to the standard, and score it on how well it asks students to demonstrate content knowledge, high-order thinking, and relevance. "We've cut down a lot on the frustration!"

Guidelines for looking at examples of student work follow a modified version of the Newmann rubric. Teachers identify the standard the work was intended to address and articulate what "proficiency" might look like in meeting that standard. They then examine a sample of student work, score that work according to the criteria, discuss differences in teachers' assessments, and eventually home in on intervention strategies.

Of course, it takes a lot to open oneself up to criticism willingly. As Ruth Mitchell puts it, the process is both a "personal and professional self-examination. If I'm a 25–year veteran teacher and suddenly see that what I'm doing has flaws, that's tough. And if I'm a new teacher, I may be incredibly frustrated because nobody taught me a different way of doing things." To work through these challenges and be truly effective, proponents argue, teachers need *support* (financial support to honor teachers' investment of time, as well as emotional support from parents and school leadership to help them be willing to open themselves up for public scrutiny); *time*, ideally during the school day, to engage in substantive conversation; *leadership* from school or district-level staff to prioritize this professional development activity among the many other demands placed on teachers; *access to high-quality teaching materials* to turn to when critical reflection leaves them dissatisfied with the way they have been doing things; and a *professional climate* that values collaboration, honesty, and critical exchange. Though these conditions may be difficult to put into place, the potential rewards are worth it: heightened teacher camaraderie, energy, and commitment; increased rigor and demand in teacher assignments; and, ultimately, higher student involvement and performance.

from at least one individual whose role is to facilitate staff members' professional development. A comprehensive evaluation of the first phase of implementation of the New American Schools whole-school reform designs found that one of the key ingredients in the most successfully implemented school designs was the presence of one or more site-based facilitators, or "coaches," who provided intensive classroom-level assistance to teachers on a consistent basis (Bodilly, 1998). Similar results were found in Nunnery's analysis of six of the most comprehensive studies of school change (1998) and in Haslam's analysis of lessons learned from New American Schools projects about the centrality of professional development to successful implementation (Haslam, n.d.).

Middle grades faculty members interviewed for this book who had received assistance from an outside professional development facilitator or who had benefited from a highly skilled teacher in this role had improved their teaching and raised their students' achievement. Especially in schools with high concentrations of low-achieving adolescents, assistance from one or more instructional coaches is invaluable.

In all but the smallest schools, the facilitator's role should be a full-time position. The facilitator should not be involved in official district or school-based teacher evaluation. The school principal has a key role to play in supporting instructional change, but virtually no middle grades principal has the time to work with individual teachers on a sustained basis while also attending to administrative responsibilities. Also, it is the principal's role to evaluate teachers, which will, unfortunately, in many instances inhibit candid discussion by teachers of their difficulties and questions regarding practice.

The professional development facilitator has several important responsibilities:

- Keeping abreast of and gaining access to outside sources of information, research, and support for school staff members
- Coordinating site-based professional development activities
- Helping teams or subject area teachers plan agendas and organize materials, presentations, and activities for extended planning and professional development opportunities
- Modeling excellent practice in the classroom through demonstration lessons
- Observing individual teachers and providing feedback
- Arranging for teachers to observe each other's practice
- Mentoring new teachers where a formal mentoring program does not exist within the district
- Leading action research or study groups and helping to connect groups of teachers with experts in universities or reform networks

A professional development facilitator should have expertise in the content and instructional strategies of at least one of the areas in which the school is trying to improve. Good communication skills are also vital. The facilitator's knowledge and ability to communicate what he or she knows helpfully and clearly will determine his or her credibility with staff members, although prior status as a valued member of the school faculty will also certainly help (Haslam, n.d.; Nunnery, 1998; Showers, Joyce, & Bennett, 1987).

THE BOTTOM LINE

In Chapter 1, we noted that our "bottom line" on what it takes to transform a dysfunctional middle grades school into a high-performance middle grades school is continuous, high quality pre- and in-service professional education that is integrated into teachers' daily work. In this chapter, we have tried to describe the content of a seamless flow of professional development and its ultimate effect on student learning. Embedding professional development in teachers' daily work means not only that it takes place regularly, but that the school is organized in ways that promote the kind of collaborative professional problem solving that is the hallmark of effective professional growth. The next chapter focuses on the organization of the middle grades school as a learning environment, for both students and adults.

6   Organizing Relationships for Learning

A N INTERESTING PARADOX exists in American education. When educators and the public consider how to improve students' performance in schools, the focus is usually on changing the curriculum, teaching methods, or assessment strategies. Clearly, improvement in these key aspects of education is essential, and it is the central focus of several earlier chapters of this book. Yet when successful adults are asked what aspect of their education most influenced their later accomplishments, they often cite a special relationship with a teacher.

Middle school educators have long recognized an essential truth about children's learning: relationships matter. For young adolescents, relationships with adults form the critical pathways for their learning; education "happens" through relationships. Many middle grades teachers intuitively recognize the importance for students of being known well by at least one adult within the school, and ideally by many. Why, though, from the young person's perspective, are relationships critical to learning?

The influence of the quality of adult relationships on children's learning begins long before the middle school years. Studies show that the strength of attachment to parents and other caregivers is crucial to children's later development (Watson, Battistich, & Solomon, 1997). Close attachments to parents provide a secure emotional base from which infants can actively explore the world around them. Through early exploration, children add information to the basic intellectual constructs present at birth to create more complex knowledge over time. Throughout childhood, a child's relationships with parents and caregivers provide both an anchor and an audience for the child's intellectual voyages.

Although more elaborate in its manifestations, the connection between young adolescents' ability to learn and the security that comes from close, trusting relationships with adults and peers in the middle grades school is similar to the need of infants and children for attachment as a basis for early learning. A key difference, though, reflects the vastly expanded range of relationships available to young adolescents. For young adolescents, the need for attachment expands to a need for affiliation and belonging to a valued group. Building on early parent–child relationships, students' sense of belonging at school—of being known, liked, and respected by peers and adults—strengthens and expands their capacity for learning. Just as a nurturing parental relationship leads to confident children who identify with parents and are most likely to become contributing citizens, a nurturing school community leads children to identify with the community and commit to its values and goals (Watson et al., 1997, pp. 571–572).

Belonging within a supportive web of relationships motivates young adolescents to make the effort and to take the intellectual risks that produce high-level learning. Young adolescents derive much of their academic motivation from their sense of the supportiveness of others within the school environment (Goodenow, 1993, p. 37). Put simply, students try harder and achieve at a higher level if they feel that their teacher is interested and supportive and that they belong to a group of peers and adults that encourages them to succeed and provides help when it is needed (Goodenow, 1993, p. 25, p. 37).

Expectations for success are transmitted through the relationships a student has with adults and peers. When students care about what others think about them and expect from them, they feel a personal stake in meeting those expectations (Arhar, 1992, p. 147). Conversely, students who feel that no one knows or cares what they are capable of doing, who believe that they are viewed by others as incapable of high-level achievement, will lower their expectations of themselves to "fit" what they sense is the prevailing view of their own incompetence (Kramer, 1992, p. 29).

The relationships established within the middle school affect both the quality of student learning and the quality of teaching. When teachers have the opportunity to know students well, they are more likely to make the kind of intense investment in their students, the tailoring and targeting of teaching strategies to students' interests and learning needs, that fosters greater student achievement (George & Alexander, 1993, p. 335). In turn, as teachers become more effective in helping a broader range of students learn, student motivation increases, creating a "win–win" upward spiral toward improved student performance (Eccles & Wigfield, 1997, p. 22; Erb & Stevenson, 1999b, p. 65).

Not all of adolescents' motivation to learn can be attributed to their sense of belonging to a middle grades community. Yet research has shown that the degree to which students are engaged and motivated at school depends to a great extent on the quality of the relationships they experience there (Eccles & Midgley, 1989, p. 140; Lee & Smith, 1993, pp. 164, 180). Supportive relationships are necessary, although not sufficient without high-quality curriculum and teaching, to foster high performance among young adolescents.

Unfortunately, upon entering the middle grades, young adolescents often encounter a glaring lack of opportunities to create close relationships with adults and peers, which seems clearly related to a corresponding downturn in interest and valuation of schoolwork (Goodenow, 1993, p. 25). A decade ago, *Turning Points* warned (p. 32), "A volatile mismatch exists between the organization and curriculum of middle grades schools, and the intellectual, emotional and interpersonal needs of young adolescents." The report recommended that middle grades schools should be restructured on a more human scale. Students and teachers should, upon entering the middle grades school, join a small, ethical community in which adolescents and adults get to know each other well and so create a climate of intellectual development and a community of shared educational purpose.

In the ten years since the release of *Turning Points*, an enormous amount has been learned from schools across the nation about how these kinds of middle grades learning communities can be created. It is to these changes in the organization of middle grades schools that we now turn.

SMALLER IS BETTER

No one would actively seek out a large, traditional junior high school as a place to learn. Student populations in middle grades schools exceed 1,000 in many jurisdictions and reach as high as 2,000 in some urban areas. Along with size, the fragmentation of instructional time into periods of 50 minutes or less and the requirement for teachers to teach 150 or more students over the course of a day make the traditional junior high school structure—still found in many "middle schools"—a dysfunctional learning environment for many teachers and students.

It is essential that very large middle grades schools be redesigned as smaller institutions. At the middle grades level, we believe from our observations over the past decade that no school should exceed 600 students; ideally, a school should serve an even smaller number of young adolescents. The key principle is to create groupings of students and educators small enough to stimulate the development of close, supportive relationships. While not sufficient in themselves to create a learning community, such relationships are a necessary precondition.

A growing body of research documents the advantages of small schools for all students, including young adolescents (Darling-Hammond, 1997b, p. 136). Small schools tend to be safer, to have higher attendance rates, and to have better participation rates in a wide range of school activities; at the high school level, they have significantly lower dropout rates (Farber, 1998, p. 7). They are repeatedly found to benefit students' achievement, attitude toward school, social behavior, interpersonal relationships, self-esteem, and feelings of "belongingness." In addition, teachers' attitudes and collaboration are more positive in small schools than in large ones (Cotton, 1996, p. 3). Students from low-income families have been found to benefit the most from being educated in small schools (Farber, 1998, p. 7).

Large middle schools can be restructured into smaller learning environments in a number of ways, including subdividing them into "houses," a term often used synonymously with "schools-within-schools" (CCAD, 1989, p. 38; CCAD, 1995, p. 76; Fenwick, 1996, p. 14). Both terms describe any of a variety of organizational plans used to divide schools into smaller groups or units in order to obtain the benefits associated with small schools outlined above. The primary difference between the two arrangements is that houses are not separate schools in their own right; together they form one school, although, in many cases, houses have their own instructional and disciplinary plans. In contrast, schools-within-schools are more like minischools unto themselves, usually co-existing in one building under one central administrator, but with separate governance systems. In either case, distinct communities are created within the larger school, allowing small groups of teachers and students to coalesce and "experience on a daily basis the spirit of traditional neighborhoods in which group loyalties, individual integrity, and concern for the well-being of self and others are highly valued outcomes of human interaction" (Fenwick, 1996, p. 14).

Since houses should accommodate 125 to 250 students, and no more, they tend to be smaller than schools-within-schools. Otherwise, the same indicators of quality apply to both houses and to schools-within-schools:

- The composition honors and reflects the demographic and developmental makeup of the larger school community.
- Students remain together in the same unit as long as they are enrolled in the school.
- Any necessary reorganization of the school's physical plant is logical, well-planned and functional, with a clearly named and marked area within the larger building designated for each unit.
- All instruction in core subjects takes place within each student's assigned unit.

While houses are a viable option for many middle schools, more and more schools, especially very large ones, are opting for restructuring into two, three, or four separate, autonomous schools-within-a-school. In fact, the "small schools movement" is perhaps the most exciting development of the past decade in the organization of middle schools. In New York City, for example, a $25 million challenge grant from the Annenberg Foundation has leveraged systemic reform throughout the city's school system, largely by creating and strengthening individual small schools. This reform effort, known as the New York Networks for School Renewal (NYNSR) project, had, through the combined efforts of four organizations—the New York Association of Community Organizations for Reform Now, the Center for Collaborative Education, the Center for Educational Innovation of the Manhattan Institute, and New Visions for Public Schools—resulted in the creation of 130 new small public schools by the 1997–1998 academic year. Some of these separate schools operate within a single building (see Box 6.1), while others operate in separate buildings within the same community.

A TEAM APPROACH

Creating smaller schools is an important strategy for fostering supportive relationships between teachers and students. In large schools or small, however, creating teams of teachers and students is a vital part of developing a middle grades learning community.

A team consists of two or more teachers and the group of students they commonly instruct. Together, teachers on a team teach all the core academic subjects; in some instances, teams also cover special subjects and special education (Arnold & Stevenson, 1998, p. 2). In practice, the characteristics of teams vary widely. There is no single right way to establish middle grades teams. Excellent teams do, however, have common characteristics and functions, elaborated below, that facilitate both student and teacher learning.

Like small neighborhoods within a bustling city, teams within a middle grades school enable young adolescents and educators to interact daily on a formal and informal basis. Teams offer students the most direct path for forging stable relationships with teachers and peers. In many schools, a team provides the valued group that young adolescents need to support their intellectual and interpersonal development. Teams provide a psychological home within the school that helps reduce the stress of isolation and anonymity.

The team can provide the peer group affiliation noted earlier as important to young adolescents' emotional development and school success. When students feel they are genuinely cared for by a group that they themselves value, they develop more positive attitudes about school, and disruptive behavior drops dramatically (Erb & Stevenson, 1999b, p. 66). Schools with teams report significantly fewer office referrals or suspensions than school without teams (Pounder, 1998, p. 73).

Within the team, it is possible for each student to receive both the attention of a group of concerned adults and the individual attention of one teacher whose aim is to become the school "expert" on that particular student. This happens when teachers on the team agree that each of them will take special care to know and act as advocates for a subset of students on the team. The

Box 6.1 Small Schools in Big Cities: Getting There from Here

A significant body of research demonstrates that school size matters and that the creation of smaller, more connected, and more integrated school communities can indeed facilitate the relationship building, personalization, and mentoring deemed critical to healthy development in the adolescent years. Yet large traditional middle grades schools still dominate much of the educational landscape, particularly in urban settings, raising the question of how the transition to smaller schools can be achieved.

In the past several years, with support from the Annenberg Foundation and other institutions, a number of small school experiments have been launched in New York City and elsewhere. These experiments have sought to put many of the recommendations of *Turning Points* into practice and thereby create the relational frameworks that indirectly help strengthen academic performance and broader life skills. Some efforts have focused on creating new small schools from scratch; others have sought to transform existing structures, breaking big schools down into smaller ones by establishing multiple "houses" or "academies." These latter efforts are particularly instructive of how reform-minded principles can be adopted in seemingly daunting educational contexts.

The transformation of the Ditmas School (IS 62) in Brooklyn, New York, into four distinct "schools of choice" within the "Ditmas Educational Complex" offers a good illustration of this second model. Before its restructuring in 1991, Ditmas was in all respects a "failing school." Its dingy, dimly lit, cheerless school building housed 1,500 sixth-, seventh-, and eighth-grade students, nearly all of whom were poor, members of minorities, and struggling with their school work. Ditmas's largely veteran teaching staff was unprepared to handle the rich mix of linguistic and ethnic cultures that mingled in the school's crowded hallways. Student performance was far below standard, attendance was low, disciplinary incidents were high, and staff morale was dismal. According to Nancy Brogan, who joined IS 62 as principal in 1991, "Many teachers in the building simply didn't have the skills necessary to teach these kids. They felt terribly ill-equipped, and because their own needs weren't being met, there was lots of invective in the building."

In 1991, Brogan pulled together a team to compete for a $26,000 Annenberg planning grant. At the same time, the district superintendent brought in the Manhattan Institute's Center for Educational Innovation, a sophisticated intermediary organization involved in numerous primary and middle school restructuring efforts throughout the city, to help Ditmas plan for and institute change.

By identifying students' needs and building on teacher expertise and other resources, four discrete "schools of choice" were ultimately created. Three of these schools—the Institute for Law and Community Service; the Institute for Math, Technology, and Environmental Science; and the Institute for Academics, Performing, and Visual Arts—stress particular academic concentrations and offer integrated community partnerships while covering comprehensive curricular requirements. The fourth—Ditmas's International Middle High School—provides Ditmas's newly arriving immigrant population with instruction in their first languages as well as bilingual support; a recently awarded $1.2 million U.S. Department of Education Title VII grant provides weekly ESL and citizenship classes to the parents of these same students. Each of the four schools of choice has its own governance structure: each is run by a three-person leadership team composed of a director, a teacher, and a parent. These teams report to Brogan, who describes herself as a "superintendent of a middle school village." A cross-school governance body, made up of each school's leadership team, Brogan, and a representative from the United Federation of Teachers, ensures cross-school accountability and coordination.

Such wholesale change did not come about easily. It required a great deal of painstaking and time-consuming discussion, consensus building, and planning that involved diverse members of the school community. "We had to change both our mental model and our physical model," Brogan explains. And not everyone in Ditmas favored its radical transformation. Brogan estimates that although roughly 60 percent of her teachers were actively on board, 10 percent were actively in opposition. Eventually, the small but vociferous opposition left the school altogether, either transferring out or retiring.

The teachers who did stay—and they were the overwhelming majority—stayed later and later, worked harder and harder, and became more and more invested in the school as they increasingly "owned" the changes they helped to bring about. "I got a call from the police department at 10 one night saying that one of my teachers was locked in the building," Brogan remembers. "She had forgotten to go home! She was doing her work." As teachers were given the freedom as well as the training to move forward with their vision, Brogan argues, they developed as leaders, collaborators, grant writers, peer coaches, and practitioners. As parents saw the school become more responsive to their children's needs, they participated more in school activities and began to avail themselves of the school's resources. Most important, school- and citywide test records indicate that as Ditmas's students became more connected, engaged, and challenged, their attendance went up, their disciplinary suspensions went down, and their performance on standardized measurements in various disciplines improved. These findings are consistent with the research literature on small schools, which has found that students in small-school settings—particularly students from low socioeconomic backgrounds—are typically less alienated and more engaged and perform higher on standardized tests.

Reflecting on how Ditmas's story may help inform other schools as they consider implementing strategies for change, Brogan suggests that certain strategies—like having teachers lead reform efforts—are constants, while others must reflect each school's unique population, characteristics, and circumstances. "It's like a Betty Crocker box," she explains. "There are the same ingredients and the same recipe that you always use. But if you're at a different altitude, or using a different oven, you'll have to change things a bit to make it come out right."

teacher might, for example, serve as the primary faculty contact for the student in relation to other school staff members or facilitate contact between the team and the student's parents.

For teachers, teams provide the kind of collaborative work group that is increasingly viewed as vital to organizational productivity across a wide range of professions. Peter Senge, one of the nation's leading experts on organizational behavior, calls workplace teams essential to enable professionals to learn together and to take advantage of collective thought that goes beyond any one individual's understanding (Senge, 1990, pp. 10, 233–269). Increased professional contact and dialogue fosters joint learning and problem solving and enables teachers on teams to develop "high teaching efficacy"—the belief that they can have a positive effect on student performance regardless of the students' abilities, family background, or academic history (Erb & Stevenson, 1999b, pp. 65–66). As teachers receive emotional, moral, and intellectual support from a network of colleagues they are better able to focus their attention and coordinated action on student learning and behavior.

Without the opportunity for collaborative planning, academic standards represent just another set of unreachable expectations for teachers and students. Teams provide the essential mechanism for translating academic standards into engaging, interdisciplinary learning activities and assessment strategies (Guiton et al., 1995, pp. 91–92) that help young adolescents realize their full learning potential. As noted in Chapter 3, teaching a standards-based intergrated curriculum relies on the collaboration of teachers of different subject areas who have the prerequisite knowledge, skills, and experience (Erb, 1997, p. 42). Teaming also enables teachers to create a composite picture of each student's approach to learning and to identify the instructional strategies that are required to reach each and every student on the team (see Chapter 4 for more information on differentiating instruction).

The ongoing dialogue of teachers on a team, especially when it is regularly focused on looking at student work to assess student learning and guide instructional strategies, is potentially the most powerful source of professional development for middle grades teachers. (Effective strategies for looking at student work are described in Chapter 5.) The shared insights, critique, conjecture, search for evidence, discussion of lessons learned, prodding, probing, and small celebrations of success that permeate the conversation of effective teams are the primary means by which teachers *create* their professional knowledge about teaching. This is the promise of middle grades teams.

It is important to recognize, however, that collaboration on teams in middle grades schools, as in most organizations, is not the norm. Relatively few schools nurture schoolwide teaming as a standard way of doing business, and many individuals will not immediately embrace a team approach. Whether teams reach their full potential as small learning organizations depends on a number of key structural characteristics and the quality of interaction among teachers on the team. For example, the quality of team interactions—group cohesion and harmony, team decision making, and other characteristics—is rated higher by teachers on teams with high levels of common planning time than by those with little or no common planning time (Mertens et al., 1998).

The Anatomy of Effective Teams

Although educators have not discovered a single right way to organize effective teams, schools have found several research-based principles useful (Erb & Stevenson, 1999a, p. 50):

- Keep teams small, in terms both of the number of teachers and students involved.
- Provide sufficient team and individual planning time to teachers.
- Allow team teachers to design the bulk of their students' daily schedule.
- Designate team areas in the building.
- Allow for team continuity over a number of years.

The presence and, more importantly, the interaction of these structural characteristics, provide the basis for effective teaming.

Team Size, Student–Teacher Ratio, and Composition. As with school size, it is extremely difficult to determine precisely "how small is small enough" with regard to the number of teachers and students on a middle school team. *Turning Points* suggested that no team should be larger than 125 students and 5 teachers, although no specific research could be cited at the time to support this conclusion. Now, early data from the Project on High Performance Learning Communities being conducted at the University of Rhode Island's National Center on Public Education and Social Policy provides support for *Turning Points'* assertion. This research indicates that teams of 120 or fewer students, with a ratio of no more than 25 students to one teacher, engage in the kind of instructional practices that are linked to positive student outcomes more often than larger teams or teams with higher student–teacher ratios (Erb & Stevenson, 1999a, pp. 48–49). Data from the W. K. Kellogg Foundation's Middle Start initiative in Michigan indicate that on teams of 90 or fewer students, the use of desirable instructional practices and the quality of team members' interactions is substantially higher than on larger teams (Flowers, Mertens, & Mulhall, 2000).

Over the past decade, middle grades educators have increasingly recognized the value of even smaller "partner teams" consisting of two or three teachers with 40 to 75 students (Arnold & Stevenson, 1998, p. 10). Teams of this size magnify the advantages of teaming by substantially reducing the number of students a teacher is expected to know. Moreover, with fewer teachers and students, communication is enhanced, instructional goals are more easily identified, changes in scheduling are more easily made, and, most important, the smaller structure facilitates curriculum integration across subject areas (Arnold, 1997, p. 444; Arnold & Stevenson, 1998, pp. 10–11).

In fact, two- and three-person teams generally require teachers to teach more than one subject, so the possibility of curricular integration is obviously enhanced. For example, in a two-person team, one teacher may teach both language arts and social studies, and the other mathematics and science. Such small teams are very appealing, but they require teachers to have in-depth content knowledge in two areas, which, while desirable, is still rare (in Chapter 5 we recommend that teachers should be trained in at least two content areas). The rule of thumb, then, is to keep the size of teams as small as possible given the strengths of the teachers involved.

Smaller teams are worth striving for, but uniformity in the size and composition of teams within the school is not. "One size fits all" makes no sense as an approach to schoolwide teaming; the objective is to find the best match of teachers and students (Arnold, 1997, p. 445). Moreover, effective teams reflect more than content expertise and small size: they also have good interpersonal chemistry. Good chemistry does not mean that teachers on teams always agree. A heated debate over how to improve student work may well reflect the strength of a team rather than its weakness. Moreover, when students witness emotionally charged but reasoned discourse concerning *their* intellectual development, it sends a powerful message about the importance of learning while providing a model for peaceful conflict resolution. More important than congeniality are mutual respect, trust, and an appreciation of divergent perspectives and experiences (Klemp & Special Guests, 1997).

Determining which teachers will work best together must be done with great care and deliberation. A cookie-cutter model will not produce good teams, nor should they be put together in an arbitrary fashion or based solely on academic expertise, disciplinary background, or existing friendships. Many school principals, with significant teacher input, systematically analyze teachers' personalities, adult learning styles, beliefs and knowledge about teaching and learning, teaching and teaming experience, and cultural awareness and understanding, especially in relation to the school's ethnic and socioeconomic population (Thomas, 1997, p. 112). Principals have called this "matchmaking," a process of creating well-balanced teams with complementary personalities, working styles, and areas of expertise in order to advance reform evenly across the school (Guiton et al., 1995, pp. 102–103). By the same token, teachers on teams should be expected to learn to work well together, even when personalities clash, because effective teacher collaboration is essential to student learning.

The composition of students on the team is no less important than the mix of teachers. Each team should be a microcosm of the overall school population, which means grouping heterogeneously with regard to ethnic and socioeconomic background, gender, special education status (if possible), and past academic achievement. To do otherwise is to invite academic tracking, which has no place in middle grades schools, given its disastrous consequences for those young adolescents relegated to the lower tracks (Mac Iver & Epstein, 1993; Wheelock, 1992, pp. 9–12). (Effective approaches to teaching heterogeneously grouped students are addressed in Chapter 4.)

Time for Planning and Teaching. Time is perhaps the most important but least available resource in American education. Teachers need time to plan curriculum and develop assessments, refine instructional strategies, and engage in collaborative inquiry to improve student work. Teachers in the United States teach more hours per year and are given less planning time than teachers in any of 15 European countries (Dickinson & Erb, 1997, p. 525). The National Commission on Teaching & America's Future reports that in Germany, Japan, and China, teachers spend 15 to 20 hours a week working with colleagues, observing other teachers, and participating in study groups. These teachers say that they could not succeed if forced to work under the conditions that prevail in most American schools (Holland, 1997, p. 12).

In American middle grades schools, a key issue is a lack of common planning time for teachers on a team. Few middle schools provide teachers with nearly enough time for the focused, ongoing conversations required to craft instructional strategies that will enable every student to reach substantially higher performance standards. The National Center for Public Education and Social Policy reports that to affect student outcomes positively, teachers need three to four hours of common planning time per week, divided, for example, into four or five daily periods of at least 45 minutes, preferably an hour. The center's ongoing research suggests that when teams have adequate planning time, they are better able to integrate curriculum across subject areas; coordinate student assignments, assessments, and other aspects of instruction; involve parents in their children's education; and contact health and other services to address behavioral issues or other concerns that affect learning (Erb & Stevenson, 1999a, pp. 47–48).

Research from the Michigan Middle Start Initiative also shows that as the amount of common planning time increases, the quality of team interactions and the frequency of desired instructional practices increases. Moreover, the highest increases in average seventh-grade reading and mathematics scores over a two-year period were recorded by schools that provided high levels of common planning time, defined as a minimum of four meetings of at least 30 minutes each week (Mertens et al., 1998).

A particularly vexing problem in middle grades schools is that of ensuring adequate communication and collaboration between teams of teachers of what are considered "core" subjects—English, mathematics, science and social studies—and teachers of "exploratory" subjects, like art, music, foreign language, and physical education. Although often considered outside the core of the curriculum, there is important new evidence of the importance of the arts in improving student learning. In one recent study, for example, analysis of data from the National Educational Longitudinal Survey showed that all eighth-grade students, especially those from low-income families, who were highly involved in the arts had higher grades and achievement scores on standardized tests than similar students who were not highly involved in the arts (Catterall, Chapleau, & Iwanaga, 1999). Box 6.2 offers some suggestions for effective integration of core and exploratory subjects.

Teachers' shared time should not, however, come at the expense of their individual preparatory periods. When common planning supplants individual

Box 6.2 Interdisciplinary Teaming Beyond Core Subjects

One of the thorniest issues in middle level education is how to ensure meaningful communication and collaboration between teams of core subject teachers and teachers of "exploratory" subjects such as art, music, drama, foreign languages, and physical education. These subjects are at times mistakenly seen as less important than the core curriculum subjects. The National Assessment of Educational Progress 1997 Arts Report Card indicates that most American children are infrequently or never given serious instruction in music, the arts, or theater (Manzo, 1998, p. 1). Yet these disciplines often provide the very spark that excites many youngsters about school when math, language, arts, social studies, or science simply do not (Jones, 1997, p. 223). Not only do exploratory classes frequently engage students in different modes of thinking and hands-on activities that appeal to diverse learning styles (Arnold, 1997, p. 446), but exploratory teachers often bring fresh perspectives to instruction and have more experience teaching heterogeneous groups of students (Guiton et al., 1995, pp. 100–101).

The most common barrier to integrating core and exploratory subjects within the middle grades curriculum is scheduling time for core team teachers and exploratory faculty to meet. In many schools, common planning time for core team members occurs when students are in exploratory classes, which means that exploratory teachers cannot participate. Unconnected to the work of teams, exploratory teachers tend to feel isolated, undervalued, and even unnecessary (Serna & Guiton, 1996, p. 42).

Middle grades schools have identified a number of effective strategies for overcoming the lack of communication between exploratory and core teachers. For example, in some schools, exploratory teachers form a team of their own and designate a team leader who meets with other core team leaders each week (Bergman, 1992, p. 189). Alternatively, exploratory teachers may affiliate with one or more core teams, with both the core and exploratory teachers making special efforts to communicate regularly even if they all do not share common planning time. A third approach is for exploratory teachers to "rotate in" to an established core team of teachers as the students move through an exploratory "wheel." For example, students on a team may have art and computer instruction during one semester or trimester and music and dance in the next, and the teachers of those subjects integrate instruction with core teachers during that time (Anglin, 1997, p. 394; Arnold & Stevenson, 1998, p. 114).

Effective integration of core and exploratory subjects requires the school principal and the core subject teachers to keep exploratory teachers informed of pertinent team issues by circulating team plans, minutes, and newsletters and involving them in team activities whenever possible. Teams can also designate one teacher as the team's liaison to exploratory teachers or the exploratory team. To create regular opportunities for core and exploratory teachers to meet, administrators can cover exploratory teachers' classes or arrange for substitute teachers or "guest artists" from the community to step in. It may be necessary for meetings to take place before or after school, during lunch hours, and on professional development days, but the extra effort will be rewarded by a more balanced and engaging curriculum for students.

time, collaborative work suffers because teachers predictably are concerned about their own workloads. Offering teachers a "choice" between common or individual time is no choice at all. In effect, it requires educators to decide how the school will fail its students.

Scheduling. Teachers on teams also require sufficient time for instruction, which is too often thwarted by a standardized schedule of 45- or 50-minute class periods. A more effective approach is for students to spend most of their school day with other students on the team, allowing the team's teachers to decide how to use most or all of the time available for instruction. Through flexible scheduling of blocks of time, teachers are able to vary the frequency and order of classes, and to lengthen or shorten class periods to reflect instructional goals and students' changing needs.

Team Areas. Flexible scheduling is much easier if teamed teachers' classrooms are near each other. Little time is lost to changing classes, and students have fewer opportunities to encounter problems in the halls. The minutes gained can be used for learning activities. In addition, a greater sense of unity is achieved when a team is given control over an area in the school that the students and teachers can call their own (Erb & Stevenson, 1999a, p. 50; 1999b, p. 64; George & Alexander, 1993, p. 287). Another benefit of such proximity is the increased opportunity for informal teacher-to-teacher contact.

Continuity Through Looping. In addition to how much time a team spends together during the school day and how that time is spent, the amount of time teachers and students are able to spend together on a team over the years can affect the quality of their experience together and the outcomes for students. It is not uncommon for teachers to need three or more years to develop strong teams, and changes in membership of teachers on a team can slow progress considerably (Arnold & Stevenson, 1998, p. 18). Michigan Middle Start schools engaged in teaming for five or more years (which does not guarantee but suggests more firmly established teams) had higher frequencies of desirable instructional practices and team interactions than schools engaged in teaming for less than five years (Flowers, Mertens, & Mulhall, 2000; Mertens et al., 1998).

Continuity in the student composition of teams is also an important element in the creation of a powerful teaching and learning community. As noted in *Turning Points* (p. 40), teams of students and teachers should remain together for at least two years, and preferably for students' entire middle grades experience. In many other countries teachers typically stay with their students for more than one year—in Japan and Germany, for example, teachers and students are together for two to four years (Darling-Hammond, 1997b, p. 135).

This practice, often called "looping," enables students and teachers to deepen their knowledge of and trust in each other. Teachers tend to invest more of themselves in their students when they know them longer and better, and they tend to persist in finding solutions to academic and other problems because they have more time to do so. Also, teachers are more likely not to "write off" students who are difficult to teach because they know they will be working with those students again (Arhar, 1992, p. 155; George & Alexander, 1993, p. 335). In addition, teachers do not lose valuable time in the beginning of each year learning a new set of names, establishing basic rules, and figuring out exactly what was learned the previous year (Darling-Hammond, 1997b, p. 135). From the perspective of students and their parents, looping provides the time needed to get to know teachers well and to develop the healthy emotional attachments that are critical to effective learning.

Teams as Interactive Systems

Finally, if this were an examination of human anatomy rather than the anatomy of effective middle grades teams, it would be laughable to suggest that the mere presence of bones, muscles, organs, and other critical "parts" indicated the adequacy of a person's functioning. The way anatomical structures interact over time is obviously critical to one's health. Similarly, the elements of effective teaming described above are interactive; the "health" of a school's teams cannot be assessed by simply noting their size, composition, time for planning, or any other characteristic. Teams are small systems, and their functioning mirrors the complex interplay of structures and processes of the school itself, as described in Chapter 2.

Because it is an interactive system, a deficit in any one critical element will inevitably affect the quality of the team's overall functioning. Indeed, when schools attempt to implement teaming but do it "on the cheap" (e.g., only one or two common planning times a week, or large teams), they often see no effects or even negative effects, especially on teacher attitudes and student performance (Felner et al., 1997, p. 548). For example, a team may be small enough to enable students and teachers to develop strong feelings of mutual support and connectedness but be severely hampered by teachers' lack of planning time or control over the scheduling of classes. Another team may have adequate planning time but lack a sense of cohesion because of a school policy of changing student and teacher membership on teams every year. In both cases, student achievement is likely to fall or, at best, to remain unaffected.

The point here is simply that a school does itself and its students a grave disservice if it claims to have implemented teams when it has done so in name only. The development of strong teams requires sustained attention to both the quality of key structural elements and the quality of interaction among team members. The next section addresses critical steps in the development and implementation of teams.

CREATING AND SUSTAINING EFFECTIVE TEAMS

The creation of effective teams is an evolutionary process. It takes time to develop the skills, relationships, beliefs, and practices that engage young adolescents routinely in powerful, interesting learning experiences. It is not feasible to "install" or decree teams by imposing teaming on a school, training staff, informing students and parents of the change, and expecting it to work (Mohrman, Cohen, & Mohrman, 1995, p. 27). Members of a school community have to believe in the potential of teaming and "buy in" to its use. If the seeds of ownership for teaming are to take root, teachers must have a solid understanding of what is to be undertaken, why it is needed, and how teams will be implemented.

As part of a school's ongoing discussion of how to improve student learning, the entire faculty should be given the opportunity to consider a move to teaming. It will usually fall to the principal to articulate clearly and with conviction the benefits of teaming for the staff, students, parents, and other community members. Patience and a willingness to take the necessary time to explain—and explain again—in simple and concrete language are absolute requirements (George & Alexander, 1993, p. 336). Anxiety is inevitable, especially among those teachers who are the most accustomed to working alone behind closed classroom doors. These teachers face a tough task: to begin to view themselves as interdependent professionals rather than as individual practitioners (Maeroff, 1993, p. 9).

One of the best ways to convince the faculty of the potential benefits of teams is for schools to host conversations with teachers from other schools who are actively engaged in effective teaming and then send teachers to observe teaming at those schools for themselves. Also, collecting and distributing written materials about teaming, including the excellent sources cited in this chapter, will help the school build a professional knowledge base. Broader discussions about the merits of teaming that include the entire school community of students and families can occur in "town hall" meetings and other public forums.

The principal and school staff members should be prepared to make the case for teaming to district officials, the local school board, and leaders of teachers' unions. They must emphasize that effective teams do not develop in a vacuum. As noted earlier, strong teams require changes in the use of time and other resources in the school. Moreover, teaming will have limited impact on student learning if teachers do not control curriculum, assessment, and instruction. It is important, therefore, to present teaming as a critical element of a dynamic, comprehensive school reform model that will require fundamental change in the operation of the school, not tinkering around the margins, in order to succeed. This level of change requires support from decision makers outside the school just as it does from those within the school community.

Many of the key criticisms of teaming are predictable, and information from this book and other sources can be used to respond effectively. One of the most common battles principals fight with district personnel, school boards, and teachers' unions is over gaining the necessary planning time for teams during the school day (Guiton et al., 1995, p. 95). Another familiar hurdle is the misconceived notion that interdisciplinary teaming eliminates the need for disciplinary knowledge, or somehow even prohibits teachers from developing such knowledge. As teams are implemented, a school may or may not eliminate formal subject-area departments, yet the need for teachers of the same discipline to collaborate on matters specific to their subject area will continue unabated and will need to be accommodated in the overall school structure.

As Tom Erb, editor of the *Middle School Journal*, noted in a recent editorial, the term "interdisciplinary" has two distinct meanings; one that refers to the organizational structure of teams that include teachers from different disciplines and another that refers to curriculum design that makes connections across disciplines. An interdisciplinary team is certainly well suited to teaching an interdisciplinary (or "integrated") curriculum, but such a team could also deliver a subject-centered curriculum. In short, people may refer to interdisciplinary teaming without implying interdisciplinary curriculum. However, teachers would find it very difficult to create an interdisciplinary curriculum in the departmental organizational structure, since that structure does not give them opportunities to coordinate "student support, curriculum, instruction, their own workloads, or [much] else in their professional lives" (Erb, 1999).

Once an informed decision has been made in support of teaming, implementation should be deliberate, at a pace that reflects staff members' "developmental readiness." Moreover, decisions on the pace of implementing teams and their composition should reflect substantial input from teachers, since they are the ones who will work within this structure.

Many schools spend a full year or more preparing and training teachers for the transition to interdisciplinary teacher teams (Arnold & Stevenson, 1998, p. 25). If a school has staff members who are already experienced with teaming, the transition should move faster. However, some teachers may have had negative experiences on ineffective or poorly supported teams. In these instances, these teachers' concerns should be recognized publicly and addressed in the newly designed teaming system.

Some schools will prefer to plan over the summer months and implement teams all at once to stimulate a strong sense of momentum. Other schools, with little or no experience with teams, may elect to move more gradually. A school may, for example, begin with a pilot team in the first year that then serves as a resource for broader implementation during the following year. Another school may begin teaming in one grade and add a grade each year.

Schools commonly take two or three years of experimentation and professional development to develop a schoolwide system of strong teams (Pounder, 1998, p. 78). However, while most schools are reasonably thorough in their initial professional development activities, many falter when it comes to "ongoing training and consultation to help teams through the natural developmental stages to becoming a fully functioning team" (Pounder, 1998, p. 84). Especially in schools just moving from departmentalized and tracked organization to teaming, teachers may have a particularly strong need for substantial training in how to integrate curriculum and work with heterogeneous groups of students (Arnold & Stevenson, 1998, p. 122).

Also, as teams evolve, their professional development needs are likely to vary over time—typically, teams begin with a focus on relationship building and management issues and then progress to a focus on collaborative teaching and curriculum integration (Pounder, 1998, pp. 77–78). As will be described next, the principal, with the aid of other professional support staff, must provide a steady flow of relevant information, resources, and support to help teams continuously improve the quality of their decision making and planning.

TEAM ROLES AND RESPONSIBILITIES

Principals and Teams

The school principal is not a member of an interdisciplinary team, yet team success often depends on the administrator's leadership skills. A principal must be prepared to be the key source of information within the school on effective teams, always available to serve as a guide, troubleshooter, and relentless supporter.

Teams must have substantial autonomy in decisions about student instruction. Nevertheless, the school principal generally needs to be closely involved in the work of teams (Arnold & Stevenson, 1998, pp. 37, 39). For example, the principal might meet on a weekly basis with teams or a group of team leaders to look at student work in relation to an instructional focus, such as literacy (Center for Collaborative Education, 1998). Principals frequently require teams to turn in minutes documenting their team discussions and decisions. They then write comments on the minutes, providing constructive criticism or recognition of work well done, or directing teams to address a particular issue related to curriculum and instruction (Guiton et al., 1995, pp. 102–103). This practice also enables principals to identify critical questions about teaching and learning that are affecting teams schoolwide (Kruse & Louis, 1997, p. 285).

Principals often act as facilitators by helping teams deal with conflicts and confront issues that may be seen as threatening to the "family" feeling many teams strive to create. The principal can help team members tackle tough issues, ranging from personality clashes to disagreements over educational matters (Kruse & Louis, 1995, p. 283). The principal should hail the successes of teams and talk frankly about what is not working well and needs to be changed.

The principal is responsible for seeing that each team reflects and puts into practice the school's overall vision and goals (Arnold & Stevenson, 1998, p. 40). The principal must, therefore, attend to cross-team issues and help teams use each other as resources while working to avoid creating a competitive environment or "cross-team rivalry" (Guiton et al., 1995, pp. 99–100). Communication among teams is an important part of the overall communication flow in the school that produces a unified, coordinated school improvement effort. A strong sense of team community need not and should not weaken or replace a "whole school family feeling" (Guiton et al., 1995, pp. 100–101) or create "a balkanized school culture" (Ryan, Guiton, & Gong, 1996, p. 39). Principals must help teachers balance the demands of being team members with the demands of membership in the larger school community (Kruse & Louis, 1997, pp. 271, 284).

The principal is also the key figure in creating a schoolwide focus on student learning (Kruse & Louis, 1997, p. 285). He or she is central to keeping all eyes on the prize: enabling every student to learn how to use his or her mind well and to meet or exceed high academic standards. If a principal neglects this role, teaming can degenerate into multiple, uncoordinated points at which autonomous and conflicting decisions are being made (Kruse & Louis, 1995, pp. 283–284).

Leadership Roles for Teachers

Teams operate most productively when team members have designated roles, including a team leader (Pounder, 1998, p. 78). While the principal provides some leadership, as just discussed, a successful team depends on leadership from within. The principal, no matter how supportive and involved, is not a team member and will not be there each day as a team gets down to business. Teams must lead and manage themselves, not only out of necessity, but also to deepen their sense of ownership and commitment to the work of the team.

The team leader's role differs from that of the more familiar department chairperson and assumes added importance as middle grades schools increasingly move from departments to teams and from departmental chairs to team leaders. Unlike a department chair, the team leader faces something of a paradox—how to assert leadership without compromising the equal-status nature of teachers as colleagues. In theory, the answer is simple: team leaders are facilitators, and their primary responsibilities are to guide day-to-day team functioning and to keep the team focused on team- and school-level tasks related to improving teaching and learning. In practice, it is considerably more complex because many teachers, if not most, have little training or experience as facilitative leaders.

Most team leaders learn on the job. As they do, they have the opportunity "to help establish a new paradigm of teacher collaboration" (Kain, 1997, p. 420). Picture a small group of teachers "with shared responsibilities and clear accountabilities strategizing together, reaching decisions by consensus, and coordinating implementation" (Senge, Kleiner, Roberts, Ross, & Smith, 1994, p. 436). What distinguishes the leader in this scenario? At first glance, the leader may be the person ticking off items on an agenda or asking if everyone has had a chance to speak up on a certain issue. However, he or she may be harder to spot because the team leader is not motivated by the desire to control or be noticed. Rather, satisfaction for a team leader lies in fostering learning for everyone and being part of a group that produces results that they truly care about and own (Senge, 1990, p. 341). "The baseline [for team leaders] . . . is that leadership always be directed to effective teaming . . . to the relentless pursuit of continuous improvement" (Kain, 1997, p. 419).

Another major difference between the role of department chair and team leader is that team leaders operate more as co-leaders of the school, requiring the principal to cede some responsibilities and authority to them and to trust their judgment (Kain, 1997, p. 405) As will be discussed in Chapter 7, one of the team leader's key roles is to serve as the team's representative to schoolwide decision-making bodies. As described in Chapter 7, middle grades schools should have a central leadership team made up of the principal, team leaders, and other school and community representatives. At regularly scheduled meetings, each team leader can report on his or her team's major activities, learn what other teams are doing, discuss schoolwide issues, and work with other team leaders to improve teaming throughout the school (Arnold & Stevenson, 1998, p. 65).

In turn, the team leader can communicate decisions made by the leadership group to the team for discussion and implementation. When team leaders facilitate an ongoing dialogue across teams, knowledge and insight grounded in the work of teachers and students guides the direction of the school. For this to happen, team leaders must operate in an environment—at the team and school level—of trust and real authority.

As noted earlier, it is critical that the creation of teams not fracture the school into disconnected camps. An isolated team fares no better than the oft-bemoaned isolated teacher. A team leader builds success for his or her team by establishing and maintaining relations with other teams and the school as a whole (Kain, 1997, p. 414).

Team leaders can be designated by the principal, or they can be chosen by their teammates, which is preferable except in situations where faculty members do not know one another well (Arnold & Stevenson, 1998, p. 191). The ideal selection method is for the team to reach a consensus on who will fill the leadership role. "Through this process the team will dialogue the pros and cons of the role, and come to a mutual agreement" (Shapiro & Klemp, 1996, p. 16). Usually, the position is rotated among team members each year, "ensuring that each teacher has the benefit of the distinct perspective of that leadership role" (Arnold & Stevenson, 1998, p. 65). Changing the position more frequently is recommended only if the leader is rotated in because of special talents or expertise needed for a particular phase of the team's work (Kain, 1997, p. 417).

Team leaders may take the lead on certain tasks such as gathering agenda items and facilitating meetings, but they do not set themselves apart by using their status in order to do more or less work. Effective team leaders count on all team members, including students, to participate, and to assume various leadership roles over time (Arnold & Stevenson, 1998, p. 66). Often, however, being a team leader does result in some extra time obligations (for example, meeting with other team leaders), so many schools arrange for team leaders to receive extra compensation.

Two additional roles are especially recommended for all teams: parent liaison and curriculum coach (Shapiro & Klemp, 1996, pp. 17–18). As will be emphasized in Chapter 9, parent involvement is critical to student learning. The team provides a focal point for communication between parents and the school. Parents get to know the small group of teachers who work with their child and always know to turn to them for information. A team can enhance this situation by designating one teacher—a parent liaison—who explicitly focuses on maintaining the quality and quantity of communication with parents. The parent liaison can also encourage parent involvement by working with colleagues to make parent conferences more effective, providing concrete ways to support learning at home, establishing regular phone contact, and possibly even sending out a weekly team newsletter published by students with announcements and samples of student work.

Teams should also select a curriculum coach. This teacher's responsibility is to maintain and invigorate a team's focus on curriculum, assessment, and instruction. The curriculum coach should be the catalyst for finding connections across subject areas (Erb, 1997, p. 48). For example, the curriculum coach facilitates curriculum coordination and discussions of teaching strategies, spearheads efforts to improve students' reading skills (see Chapter 4), and locates and shares professional development information.

WHAT EFFECTIVE TEAMS DO

Team Plans

In sports, great teams have great game plans. The same is true for great middle grades teams. A team plan for improving student learning provides a blueprint for success. An excellent team plan will identify goals for student learning, strategies and realistic timelines for implementing them, team members' roles and responsibilities, and the materials, professional development, and other resources that the team will require to reach its learning goals for students. Goals should be both short-term, relating to things the team would like to accomplish during the semester, and long-term, relating to what the team envisions itself accomplishing by the end of the year and beyond.

The process of creating a team plan is often as useful as the plan itself because it enables teachers to think through important issues together and to come up with an organized, comprehensive approach to teaching and learning (Arnold & Stevenson, 1998, p. 24). A good rule of thumb is that teachers should be able to hold in their heads both the goals and the primary strategies covered by the plan so that the plan truly guides everyday decisions. The plan does not need to be a polished-to-perfection manifesto. Moreover, an effective team plan should not be a compilation of individual plans for each student. Each student surely needs individual attention, but such a plan would be unwieldy and of little value as a guide for the overall work of the team.

A team plan is inevitably a "work in progress" that, without compromising its goals, will need to be revised from time to time as conditions and opportunities change. Teachers on a team should be given both the freedom and the responsibility to make ongoing adjustments and improvements in their instructional approach to reflect the individual needs of learners in the classroom. Sharing a team plan with the principal, other faculty, or family members should therefore carry with it an understanding that it is a "living" document, evolving as the team works to continuously improve its practice.

Teamwork to Improve Student Learning

The hallmark of an effective team is its ability to focus sustained attention on coordinating the curriculum and improving teaching strategies. What an effective team does *not* do is spend an inordinate amount of time on the behavior problems of a few students or on other issues that distract the team from the main business of the team: improving student learning. Teaming will not improve student achievement unless teams consistently focus on teaching and learning.

Why should teachers work collaboratively to improve instruction? Even the most experienced teachers believe teaching is inherently difficult and that teachers never stop learning to teach. Teaching is hard work. Success can be ensured for every student only when teachers pool their strengths and support each other by engaging in a common quest for continuous improvement (Fullan & Hargreaves, 1996, pp. 44–48).

Intellectual assistance is at the core of effective team practices (Kruse & Louis, 1997, p. 264). Joint planning and integration of curriculum and instruction by teachers with different perspectives, backgrounds, and learning and teaching styles leads to more effective learning experiences for students. Team members "fill in gaps in one another's base of knowledge and experience." They help each other "plan what they will do in their classrooms, serve as sounding boards for ideas, and add disciplinary and pedagogical expertise" (Darling-Hammond, 1997b, p. 167).

To work together effectively, teachers on teams need to be skilled in the group norms and operating procedures that enable efficient group functioning. Teams need expertise in interpersonal communication, group decision making, goal setting and evaluation, time management, team building, problem solving, and use of an inquiry process. Teachers and students must agree on key aspects of the instructional program, such as expectations for student assignments, grading criteria, procedures for flexibly grouping students, and policies for addressing disciplinary problems. When teachers on a team are consistent in their practices across classrooms, guidelines and expectations are reinforced, and both teachers and students experience the team as more coherent and unified (Burkhardt, 1997, p. 169). Teams that do not learn how to work together often fall prey to conflicts, confusion, and inertia.

As teams learn how to work together, collaborative inquiry and professional development often merge. Common planning time becomes a daily professional development "huddle" as teachers reflect critically on their purpose and approach to teaching, addressing issues that extend well beyond the simple sharing of resources, ideas, and other immediate practicalities. As mentioned earlier, at its best, the heart of the collaborative team process is the examination of student work to assess student learning and produce strategic changes in instruction (see Box 5.4 in the previous chapter for more on looking at student work).

Continuous Assessment of Progress

An educator must be a "reflective practitioner" who considers carefully how actions are implemented and what the resulting effects are (Fullan & Hargreaves, 1996, p. 67). Assessment and evaluation of progress and outcomes are the way that teams hold themselves accountable for adhering to their vision and meeting their goals and for making the inevitable improvements and revisions needed along the way.

Teams should engage in two kinds of assessments. First, effective teams critique how they work together to ensure that they are functioning in a way that enables them to achieve their goals (Klemp & Special Guests, 1998). Regular reevaluation of the teaming process benefits team effectiveness (Erb & Doda, 1989, p. 61). The team's evaluation of itself need not be overly formal and can be kept to very simple questions, such as whether the team stays on task during common planning time, whether everyone participates equally in team decisions, and what professional development is needed to improve team functioning. Often, members of more experienced teams can provide a useful outside perspective for newer teams or teams that are experiencing difficulties.

A second form of team assessment uses the team plan as a framework for evaluating student outcomes. Here, substantial emphasis is placed on analyzing the quality of student work as evidence of the team's impact. Thus, the utility of teaching strategies incorporated in the team's plan is assessed in relation to the team's bottom line: did student performance improve? Only by collecting data and evidence related to the goals established in the plan will the team be able to make informed decisions about instructional practices and prove to itself and others that improvement has occurred (Dickinson & Erb, 1997, p. 534).

A team should use the information from both forms of evaluation to plan changes that will remedy shortcomings and to set more ambitious goals in areas where it is already strong. Teams will naturally vary in the pace and manner in which they evolve. What is important is that the effort to improve never cease.

ADVISORY

Effective teams offer students and teachers a dynamic structure for forging close relationships. Yet even reasonably sized teams may not be able to meet all students' needs for individualized attention. As noted in *Turning Points* (p. 40),

> Every student should be well known by at least one adult. Students should be able to rely on that adult to help learn from their experiences, com-

prehend physical changes and changing relations with family and peers, act on their behalf to marshal every school and community resource needed for the student to succeed, and help to fashion a promising vision of the future.

When students make a lasting connection with at least one caring adult, academic and personal outcomes improve. A significant adult who provides support and direction during difficult times is an important factor in helping students avoid academic failure and a variety of other problems (Galassi, Gulledge, & Cox, 1997, p. 303). Among youth at risk from health or behavioral problems, family dysfunction, poverty, or other stresses, the most important school factor fostering resilience—defined as "successful adaptation despite risk and adversity" (Masten, 1994)—may be the availability of at least one caring responsible adult who can function as a mentor or role model (Bernard, 1993, cited in Miller, 1998, p. 12).

An advisory period during the school day is potentially an important time for educators and students in middle grades schools to develop strong interpersonal bonds. We say "potentially" because, although often recommended for middle grades schools, advisory programs are often among the most difficult structures to implement, both because of practitioners' lack of knowledge about what they are supposed to do, and, at times, because of parental and community concerns that educators are inappropriately intruding in their students' personal lives. When it is well implemented, our sense is that the advisory can be effective in developing relationships that support learning. Where the advisory is implemented in a perfunctory manner, which is unfortunately often the case, students' and educators' time is undoubtedly better spent in well-crafted instructional activities.

When they are done well, small-group advisories drawn from within the team provide a further opportunity for the personalized guidance and active monitoring young adolescents need. In the advisory, a teacher, administrator, or other qualified staff member meets with students, the advisees, and leads group activities that address a broad range of students' concerns. Ideally, these groups meet for 25 to 30 minutes each day, or, at the least, three times a week. The advisory often takes place at the beginning or end of the school day; it should not be squeezed into a lunch period, scheduled irregularly as time allows, or conducted when another activity is canceled. The effectiveness of the advisory depends on trust, forged through continuity in relationships over time.

The range of potential advisory topics is vast, from interpersonal issues to health-related questions or concerns about schoolwork. Student interest in the advisory group's work is greatest when they have a voice in selecting advisory activities. Advisory is a particularly important time to focus on personal development and social relationships. Middle grades students need continuing assistance in comprehending, analyzing, accepting, and coping with the various emotional and social components of their lives. They need help in getting to know themselves and sustained support in crafting relationships with peers and adults both in and out of school (Galassi et al., 1997, p. 307). Strong advi-

sory programs help students gain emotional strength, self-knowledge, and social skills through peer interaction and the acceptance and personal affirmation of trusted adults (Fenwick, 1996, p. 31).

Advisory is *not* a time for intensive personal counseling. The benefits of advisory complement the expert support provided by professional guidance counselors. Middle grades educators, other than professional guidance counselors, are
not qualified to engage in counseling on sensitive personal issues. Furthermore,
discussions within the advisory cannot and should not take the place of the candid dialogue between parents and young adolescents that is so vital to young
people. Advisory enables educators to provide responsible adult guidance and
extra support as middle grades students undergo normal, yet often turbulent,
developmental changes that directly and indirectly affect learning.

In schools where the advisory program is most effective, adult advisors
and guidance counselors work together. Counselors can often provide the professional development educators need to become competent advisors. The counselor, as an "advisor" to other educators, can serve as a guide to the dilemmas of
early adolescence. Also, if an educator believes that a student may need professional help to negotiate a serious problem, the counselor can provide such services when appropriate or can help the student get the needed support from
sources within the community.

CONCLUSION

Small schools, teams, and advisories are the structures commonly associated with
a successful middle grades school. Unfortunately, many middle grades schools
go no further than creating these structures, never connecting them to improving teaching and learning so that every student is able to meet or exceed high
academic standards. The structures become a foundation for a house that is never
built. In Chapters 3 and 4, we described the kind of curriculum, assessment, and
instructional strategies that can enable schools to complement structural changes
to engage every student in stimulating, high-level learning. We continue the journey in Chapter 7 by examining the democratic processes of decision making that
enable a school to strive constantly to become a true learning community.

7

Democratic Governance to Improve Student Learning

A MERICANS CONSIDER PARTICIPATION in the democratic process a fundamental right, founded in our belief in the equality of all men and women and the necessity of self-determination. We believe democracy is as vital to sustaining our way of life as the beating of the heart is to sustaining life itself. Most of us would also argue that the democratic process is an effective and equitable way of making decisions. That is, through an inclusive process of airing different perspectives, considering alternative options and reaching consensus, better decisions are made than if one person or only a few people were involved in the decision-making process. As Winston Churchill once said, "Democracy is the worst form of Government except for all those other forms that have been tried."

A democratic form of governance is as vital to the functioning of an effective middle school as it is to the governance of our nation. Democratic governance in middle grades schools may not be an "unalienable right," but it is clearly the right way to engage an entire school community in the pursuit of high academic achievement and bright futures for all young adolescents.

Turning Points recommended, and we agree, that a middle grades school should be organized and should function through a democratic governance system with structures and processes that are systematically inclusive, collaborative, and focused on the improvement of student learning. The system should give all "stakeholders" in the school—teachers, administrators, support staff, parents, students, and community members—a primary voice in planning and implementing school improvement efforts.

Democratic governance structures allow all faculty members and other constituency groups to be heard and to influence decisions, through both representation and direct participation (Glickman, 1993, pp. 37–39). Democratic participation enables schools to make lasting changes in practice with the full endorsement and engagement of all stakeholders (Darling-Hammond, 1997b, p. 163). When educators, parents, and students make important decisions regarding school matters, they share responsibility for implementing those decisions and for the outcome of those decisions (Hopfenberg et al., 1993, p. 24).

Democratic governance in middle grades schools is not synonymous with "school-based management," as managing a school, no matter how efficiently, does not automatically lead to improvement of the organization. Our analysis of decision-making processes in middle grades schools over the past ten years suggests that governance is better thought of as a schoolwide system for communication, planning, evaluation, and accountability. The governance system should continually draw on the experience of school staff members and others to enable the organization to behave more intelligently. Building on the collaborative work of teachers on teams who are constantly constructing and using knowledge about their students, schoolwide democratic structures and processes allow the entire school to become a learning community, improving its actions on behalf of students through the development of greater knowledge and understanding.

Research has demonstrated that schools that have restructured to function democratically "produce high achievement with more students of all abilities and graduate more of them with better levels of skills and understanding than traditional schools do" (Darling-Hammond, 1997b, p. 331). Studies also show that "student achievement increases substantially in schools with collaborative [democratic] work cultures that foster a professional learning community among teachers and others, focus continuously on improving instructional practices in light of student performance data, and link to standards and staff development support" (Fullan, 1998, p. 8). In other words, it appears that "when given support, time, and resources, democracy of, by, and with 'workers' works" (Glickman, 1998, p. 80).

While these findings are encouraging, we noted earlier (in Chapter 2) that organizational changes and democratization of school policies and procedures alone are not enough to raise student achievement. Democratic governance, involving direct or representative participation by all school community members, is but one of the *Turning Points 2000* recommendations, not a transformational silver bullet. Effective democratic governance is an essential part of the *Turning Points 2000* design system described in Chapter 2, but its contribution to ensuring every student's success hinges on its interaction with the other six recommendations.

Not only is democratic governance *not* sufficient to improve a school, but "there are often daunting barriers that render democratic governance ineffective or even—in some cases—counterproductive" (Douglas Mac Iver, personal communication, 1999). One of the greatest dangers facing schools is that the introduction of new structures and governance methods often diverts attention from the quality of teaching and learning (Newmann & Wehlage, 1995, p. 2). Furthermore, it is not uncommon, as a study by the University of Pennsylvania's Graduate School of Education highlighted, for reforming schools to overlook student learning as an explicit restructuring goal in favor of staff empowerment, changed decision-making processes, and improved stakeholder relationships (Summers & Johnson, 1995, p. 25). We believe that schools will realize more substantial gains in student achievement if they develop strong leaders while at the same time improving instruction. Over the past decade, we have repeatedly seen that the most significant improvement in student achievement occurs when all members of the school community focus simultaneously on transforming instruction and on developing the skills and practices of strong democratic leadership.

THE LEADERSHIP TEAM, INQUIRY GROUPS, AND STUDENT INVOLVEMENT

What is the best way for a school's governance system to work? There is no one "best" way, but our review of research and the experiences of reforming middle grades schools over the past decade leads us to the following conclusions.

Leadership Team

First, a middle grades school's leadership team is the heart of its governance system, the focal point for schoolwide communication and decision making. As noted in *Turning Points* (Carnegie Council on Adolescent Development, 1989, p. 56), the leadership team "coordinates and integrates all activities that occur within the school building and between school and community organizations." "Standing" members—that is, those automatically included—are the school principal and a representative from each team, most often the team leader. Many leadership teams also involve all other major constituency groups in the school community, including the building representative of the local teacher's union, health and social service professionals, parents, community members, and students. These members may be elected, or they may volunteer. To the extent possible, the leadership team should reflect the ethnic and cultural diversity of the school community. Meetings are open to all who wish to attend, although only regular members have a direct say (or vote) in decisions.

By maintaining open and direct lines of communication throughout the school community, the leadership team can identify the critical learning challenges students are facing schoolwide and find effective ways to address them. Input from team representatives, reflecting teachers' day-to-day interaction with students, is especially critical. Subject-area or grade-level faculty groups and committees may also identify important issues.

Like a team of teachers, a leadership team will function more productively when its members receive assistance in developing communication and other skills necessary for successful collaboration. Fostering the skills and practices of shared leadership and decision making enables the school community "to manage and facilitate change, and to stay focused on teaching and learning" (Center for Collaborative Education, 1998, p. 2).

Moreover, in an environment with clear, agreed-upon ground rules for discussion and decision making, where everyone is invited and expected to participate, leadership team members feel empowered to assume new roles and responsibilities, to try new ideas and take risks, and to openly assess the results. In a true learning community, no one is ridiculed for making a mistake (Senge et al., 1994, p. 51).

In addition to its role as a decision-making body, much of the leadership team's effectiveness hinges on its ability to communicate effectively with the school community. The leadership team keeps the school mission alive by regularly communicating what the school's goals are to those both inside and outside the school, how it is striving to reach those goals, and how well it is attaining them. It also serves as a clearinghouse of information, disseminating important news and acting as the hub through which individuals and groups can communicate and coordinate their actions.

Inquiry Groups

The leadership team continually identifies and prioritizes critical learning issues, and once priorities have been set, an effective leadership team establishes inquiry groups. An inquiry group is a committee created to investigate the causes of and potential solutions to one of the school's most pressing problems. By analyzing a variety of data on student outcomes, instructional practices, and so on, as well as research and other information describing the best available instructional options, an inquiry group develops an action plan to address a particular goal area and presents it to the leadership team. The leadership team can then make informed choices about how best to meet students' needs. As changes are implemented, inquiry groups assess progress toward the goal and make further recommendations: for example, professional development may be needed to strengthen instructional practices. In addition to formal inquiry groups, the leadership team may also convene short-term investigative committees to address rapidly emerging issues that warrant immediate action. Inquiry groups are important vehicles for maximizing direct participation from throughout the school community in school governance.

Every faculty member should serve on at least one inquiry group during the school year. Inquiry groups should also make use of expertise within the school community, by including, for example, a school psychologist and other health professionals to address student mental and physical health issues.

The interaction between the leadership team, inquiry groups, teams, and other committees allows ideas and information to be communicated effectively to everyone within the school, encouraging participation and ownership of a decision-making process that is focused on the school's overall improvement. Coherence and unity of purpose in the work of the school is maintained, and school community members have ongoing opportunities to develop shared perspectives and to learn from one another (Darling-Hammond, 1997b, pp. 163–164).

Student Involvement

The leadership team, inquiry groups, and other governance bodies offer important opportunities for students to become involved in meaningful democratic participation. Students need to "experience the change process, learn the skills of solving problems, of communication in groups, of leadership and membership" (Dalin, 1998, p. 1065). Moreover, middle grades students are mature enough to engage in thoughtful, sustained analysis and problem solving, especially on matters that clearly affect them. Their insights into existing conditions in the school and the improvements needed are a valuable source of information.

In many schools, the student council provides a student-led forum similar in form and function to the leadership team. Student councils enable students to participate actively in the democratic process on a wide range of issues. For example, a student council might review a draft school improvement plan and recommend changes, consider how to engage parents better in the life of the school, evaluate the quality of cafeteria food, and participate in drawing up school rules. As we will see in Chapter 8, students who help develop school rules are more likely to become "willing participants and enforcers rather than violators" (Darling-Hammond, 1997b, p. 139).

FUNCTIONS OF THE LEADERSHIP TEAM

Developing and Using a School Improvement Plan

What are the main functions of the leadership team, and how are they carried out? The leadership team's single most important task is to develop and communicate an annual comprehensive school improvement plan. This document states publicly how the school will ensure that every student fulfills the Turning Points vision. It describes the school's strengths and weaknesses, specifies learning goals, articulates strategies for reaching the goals, and establishes benchmarks for assessing progress. The school improvement plan aligns and integrates all school improvement efforts within one coherent strategy that can be adapted for use with various audiences, such as the federal government (to document the need for Title I funds under the Elementary and Secondary Education Act, for example), the state education agency, and the local school district.

A school improvement plan requires data-based inquiry and decision making. To be of any real value, a school improvement plan must reflect careful analysis of a broad range of information about students' work, teachers' instructional practices, the school's organizational structures, and its interpersonal climate. It is fundamentally not a statement of teachers' and administrators' opinions about students' needs, although educators' professional judgment is required to determine the best course of action to solve learning problems identified through analysis of data.

For many, the phrase "data-based inquiry and decision making" sounds both sterile and somewhat daunting. However, data-based inquiry and decision making should not be misunderstood as an intimidating, elitist, or cumbersome undertaking. It is merely a more deliberative process through which a school defines problems or issues thoroughly, examines and analyzes a range of related information and facts—data from multiple sources—and develops action plans to address them. Increasingly, schools are finding that this more systematic and analytical approach "is allowing them to build lasting change and improvement" (Rugen, 1998, pp. 1–2). As Lipsitz et al. (1997, p. 536) put it, "Schools need to move beyond brainstorming in a vacuum: it will never be as productive as assessing the impact of current practice and setting next steps based upon verified outcomes."

Plans based on the analysis of data enable schools to be proactive in their improvement efforts rather than reactive, crisis-driven, or drawn toward actions that reflect the views of an especially vocal minority. "Use of a systematic data analysis process also permits participants to review their decision making . . . to see where they might have gone wrong, omitted a step, or otherwise misused the process, and, therefore, made a poor decision or failed to solve a problem" (George & Alexander, 1993, p. 508).

Data-based inquiry and decision making also enables the school to investigate differences in outcomes for various groups of students systematically. It is, therefore, absolutely essential to disaggregate data by race, ethnicity, gender, and special education and income status to determine whether different things are happening for different groups of students. The school must then use this information to determine how to move the school toward greater equity in outcomes for students (Rugen, 1998, p. 2). If student assessment data are not disaggregated, improvements in a school's average test scores may mask slower rates of improvement, or even a failure to improve, among some groups of students. A school cannot rightly claim that it is committed to enabling all students to meet or exceed high academic expectations—the essence of the Turning Points model—if it does not look carefully at rates of improvement along racial, ethnic, gender, special education, and socioeconomic lines. (See Box 7.1 at the end of the chapter for an example of the way Texas uses disaggregated data to hold schools accountable for the success of all their students.)

An effective school improvement plan is a road map to help the school improve results for students. Written in accessible language, it sets attainable goals with realistic action steps, time lines, roles and responsibilities, and resources for accomplishing them, as well as benchmarks to assess progress and to plan for the future. It aligns the school's resources—human, time, and monetary—in the service of the school's overall improvement effort (Center for Collaborative Education, 1998).

To ensure broad "ownership" of the document, the entire faculty should be directly involved in its development through participation on the leadership team or inquiry groups that contribute critical elements. Often it is the process of planning, more than the plan itself, that is the catalytic force in a school change process (Ainscow, Hopkins, Southworth, & West, 1994, p. 30).

Development of a data-driven school improvement plan involves five key steps: creating a schoolwide vision, assessing current circumstances, setting priorities, developing strategies for action, and evaluating the effects of changes in order to monitor progress. The last step is critical to determine the extent to which improvement efforts are "on course" and to ensure that improvements continue to gain momentum.

Each step builds upon the information gathered or decisions made in the previous one. In practice, however, the process of developing and revising a school improvement plan is never so "linear." Some steps may occur simultaneously or in a different order. School improvement planning should be a continuing conversation focused on attaining better results for students (Center for Collaborative Education, 1998). The goal is a school in which everyone shares beliefs about the purpose of education, about rules of decision making for planning and implementing changes, and about the necessity of ongoing evaluation to assess the effect of changes on student performance (Glickman, 1998, p. 144). Clear in theory but "messy" in practice, the development and use of data-based plans are an effective way for labor-intensive organizations like schools to improve their productivity.

Creating a Shared Vision. A shared vision communicates the school's fundamental beliefs and expectations, which should be "firmly based on the characteristics and needs of developing adolescents" (George & Alexander, 1993, p. 469), on "what students should know and be able to do upon exiting the school" (Center for Collaborative Education, 1998, p. 8), and on supporting social equity.

How does a school create its vision? Unlike each of the other steps in creating a school improvement plan, this element does not reflect analysis of data. Instead, it emerges from a coherent and inclusive process of reflection and conversation on the best middle grades school that can be imagined by and for everyone in the school community (Hopfenberg et al., 1993, p. 74). Some schools have found it useful to begin this conversation by considering the simple but profound question, "How would I design a middle school for my own child?" Alternatively, a school may wish to start by considering existing mission or vision statements, such as that of the National Forum to Accelerate Middle-Grades Reform (see Box 1.1), as a basis for crafting its own vision.

Either through discussion or individual reflection, the entire school staff should be involved in developing draft "vision statements" (Hopfenberg et al.,

1993, p. 75). The goal is to craft a clear, concise, and bold declaration that defines the school's mission—its purpose for existing. Students and parents should also be encouraged to participate in the process. Many middle grades school students and parents have a well-developed sense of their dream school, and they are usually eager to contribute their ideas.

The leadership team synthesizes these focused reflections into a single draft vision statement that is shared with everyone in the school community to elicit feedback and suggested revisions. Several iterations of this stage of the process may ensue, but it is important for the leadership team to set reasonable but firm limits on the duration of discussions about the vision and come to a consensus as an executive body on what the vision statement will be. Once established, the vision statement will provide a kind of litmus test to determine if actions suggested to improve the school reflect the school's core beliefs. However, as school improvement efforts move forward, the vision statement itself will need to be reexamined to see if it is still an accurate rendering of the school's fundamental mission.

Creating a shared vision is not a "touchy-feely" exercise for dreamers. It is a critical part of a school improvement effort because the most important shift in any school that is successful in improving outcomes for students is not in its specific organizational characteristics or practices; rather, it is the intellectual shift that precedes the evolution of new characteristics (Stringfield, 1995, p. 17). When a school's vision grows out of strong, passionate feelings about the transformative power of education, it helps to sustain the interest, participation, and commitment of teachers, parents, and students (Wohlstetter & Griffin, 1997, p. 2).

One study of the long-term survival of high-quality middle grades school programs links the longevity of such programs to a heightened sense of mission and the resulting clarity of vision about the nature of the school, a vision shared by all members of the school community (George & Anderson, 1989, p. 74). The study found that exemplary programs are not established in the first place, much less sustained, "when there is no clarity about or commitment to the needs of the early adolescent age group. . . . Understanding the purpose of the middle school, and the school's commitment to the personal and educational needs of early adolescents appears to play a most important role, both prior to and following the implementation of quality middle schools."

Status Assessment. Once a vision statement has been adopted, a status assessment is the second key step in the development of a school improvement plan. A status assessment (often known as "taking stock"), accomplished through the collection and analysis of data from multiple sources, provides a point of comparison between the school's shared vision and its current circumstances (Center for Collaborative Education, 1998, p. 8). The intent is to develop a comprehensive picture of the school—its strengths and resources as well as the challenges it faces—through collaborative reflection on the existing instructional practices and their outcomes for students.

The information needed for a status assessment can be collected and analyzed by teams, inquiry groups, or study groups established specifically for that purpose. Involving students in the collection of data provides an opportunity for them to work with their teachers, parents, and others in their school community on a complex and important research project about a highly relevant topic: their school.

The type of data collected for a status assessment depends on the areas chosen for investigation and the questions that the leadership team, teacher teams, and inquiry groups pose. Clearly, student performance data provided by the local school district are essential. In most instances, much of the data will be reasonably close at hand, although sifting through it and determining what to include in the school improvement plan will take time.

The most comprehensive instrument for collecting information about critical aspects of middle grades education is the School Improvement Self-Study. The Self-Study was developed through a partnership begun in 1990 between the Center for Prevention Research and Development (CPRD) at the University of Illinois, then under the direction of Robert D. Felner, and the Association of Illinois Middle Schools. The Self-Study is an annual data collection instrument consisting of a set of surveys that are completed by teachers, principals, students, and parents in a school. The confidential and anonymous surveys cover each of the areas that *Turning Points* identified as critical to improving student performance, including classroom practices, decision-making practices, parent and community involvement, climate and attitudes, professional development needs, educational expectations, school safety, student health behaviors, and student well-being (Center for Prevention Research & Development [CPRD], 1998). Not only does the Self-Study effectively give school community members another opportunity to have a voice in school improvement, but it also produces rich and comprehensive data with minimal teacher and student disruption. Most of the data are gathered through machine-readable forms that can be analyzed and returned to schools relatively quickly.

The surveys provide reliable and systematic information on the current status of the school community that can be analyzed in relation to student performance. Over the past decade, the Self-Study has been continually updated and refined based on the information needs of practitioners engaged in Turning Points-based reform. Our sense is that further improvements in this excellent resource will be needed in the future, especially as middle grades educators place greater emphasis on improving the quality of instruction and assessment in the ways recommended in Chapters 3 and 4.

Many schools compile the results of their data collection efforts into a report, sometimes called a "school profile." An effective school profile will often contain data displayed in the form of graphs or charts, a description of how data were obtained, a concise narrative interpretation of the data indicating the school's strengths and challenges, and the implications or questions the data suggest.

Setting Priorities. By analyzing the differences between a school's vision and its status assessment, the leadership team can readily identify the areas where student learning is most in need of added support or a different approach to teaching. These areas become the school's priorities for action (Center for Collaborative Education, 1998, p. 8). Moreover, the process of identifying areas where the school is not meeting students' needs further catalyzes the school improvement process: the status quo becomes untenable (Walker, Palumbo, Nelson, & Artwell, 1998, p. 7).

Establishing priorities means just that: deciding upon a limited number of critical goals (Wagner, 1998, p. 515). Each year, a school should identify the three to five most significant issues, or "strategically consequential chunks of work" (Senge, Kleiner, Roberts, Ross, & Smith, 1994, p. 344), that are directly linked to improving student outcomes, broadly defined. In defining goals, a school may well need to align its priorities for action with mandates for improvement coming from the state or district educational agency. School staff members must consider how much can realistically be achieved within a year, and this consideration may lead instead to multiple-year goals. Also, in keeping with the notion of the Turning Points design as an interactive system (see Chapter 2), the school should design a logical sequence for tackling priorities that will enable efforts in one area to support those in another (Sarason, 1990, pp. 15–16; West, 1998, p. 781).

Each priority goal area should be stated clearly and succinctly. The problem itself may be complicated, and arriving at solutions may be difficult, but the statement of the problem should be simple and clear enough (George & Alexander, 1993, p. 512) that individuals can "put their arms around" the issues that need to be addressed (Senge et al., 1994, p. 345).

Developing Strategies for Action. Once a limited set of priorities for action have been established, school faculty members, working together in "priority area" inquiry groups, will need to investigate each one thoroughly to identify the causes of the problem that has been identified and to formulate an action plan for solving the problem. These action plans will be incorporated in the overall school improvement plan.

The key to success in this form of action research is to take a *systematic* approach; a haphazard or half-hearted effort will produce little of value and may create more confusion than clarity. Thus, understanding *why* a problem exists is critical to tailoring an effective solution, yet schools may be tempted to skip this part of the process in their haste to initiate improvements. The result can be wasted effort and frustration that can derail the school improvement process. For each priority area, staff members, with interested parents and students, should brainstorm as many potential causes for the problem as possible. Each hypothesis must then be analyzed to determine the extent to which it truly contributes to the problem (Rugen, 1998, p. 6). Rarely does a given problem have only one cause. More often, a constellation of causes exists, and potential solutions thus often need to be multifaceted to address a problem's multiple origins.

Once one or more causes of a problem are identified, the group addressing a particular priority should brainstorm alternative solutions. At this stage, the goal is to generate many ideas, to think of potential solutions that may be considered either conventional or "out of the box," without worrying a great deal about their quality (George & Alexander, 1993, pp. 513–514). External sources, such as educational research and other schools' experiences, should also be mined for good ideas.

The many alternatives for action that are generated will need to be winnowed down to one solution or a combination of solutions that the inquiry group can agree on. The strategies must clearly address the causes of the problem, and there must be clear evidence of their effectiveness; they cannot merely "sound promising."

The priority area inquiry group is then responsible for presenting an action plan to the leadership team and the school community as a whole. A main criterion for accepting an action plan or modifying it before including it in the overall school improvement plan is summarized by one middle school principal: "For every goal set, we must say how we think it will contribute to student achievement and what changes in the data we expect to see."

A good action plan is detailed, precise, and concise. A one- or two-page annotated list works well to spell out clearly what the plan's goals are and how they will be met. The plan should

- Describe specific activities, strategies, or action steps to be taken
- Identify who is responsible for implementation
- Set a timeline with target dates
- Identify financial, professional development, and other resources
- List the expected results in concrete and specific terms
- Determine how progress will be measured
- Describe how information will be shared

It is the responsibility of the leadership team to assemble all the priority-area plans into a coherent, coordinated school improvement plan. However, creating an effective school improvement plan requires more than merely collating the plans that result from the different inquiry groups. The leadership team must align the plans so that the actions they prescribe can be coordinated with demands on the school budget, the school class schedule and professional development schedule, team-level goals, and district or state mandates or initiatives. The school improvement plan must then undergo review and revision based on feedback from the school community.

Once the final plan is adopted, copies of the school improvement plan should be shared with the entire school community. The goal is for the vast majority of students, parents, and faculty to be able to describe in their own words what is expected of students and how the school plans to help students meet those expectations (Center for Collaborative Education, 1998).

Monitoring Progress

The school leadership team oversees the implementation of the school improvement plan, making necessary adjustments and developing strategies for sustaining what is working well and for changing what is not (Hopfenberg et al., 1993, pp. 55–56; Rugen, 1998, p. 6). No plan can anticipate all eventualities at the outset, and modifications will be necessary as it is implemented. Difficulties or unexpected outcomes should not be glossed over; they often provide the best opportunities to learn.

As schools build on what has been achieved and learn from mistakes, its priorities for improvement are either replaced in the school improvement plan by new priorities or revised and carried over from year to year (Shields & Knapp, 1997, p. 293). In other words, a school never "finishes" working to improve any aspect of its program.

The Self-Study is a useful tool in monitoring progress. The first time a school administers the Self-Study, the results provide baseline data. In subsequent years, the Self-Study provides concrete evidence that changes are occurring (or not occurring) at the school, grade, and classroom levels. That evidence can give positive reinforcement to those involved and information to counter critics' arguments that "nothing new is happening." The Self-Study is not used as a "high stakes" evaluation of the school for purposes of state or district accountability. Rather, it is an opportunity for schools to understand the relationship between the implementation of practices and student success in the school and thereby gauge the status of their efforts (CPRD, 1996, pp. 1, 4).

Schools have used the Self-Study to help narrow their concerns or identify new questions that are relevant to their needs and particular contexts, an essential step in creating an effective school improvement plan. Currently the Self-Study is available from the Center for Prevention Research and Development at the University of Illinois and from the National Center on Public Education and Social Policy at the University of Rhode Island.

THE SCHOOL PRINCIPAL—KEY LEADERSHIP ROLES

One of the most consistent findings in educational research is that high-achieving schools have strong, competent leaders (Useem, Christman, Gold, & Simon, 1997, p. 65; Valentine, Trimble, & Whitaker, 1997, pp. 337, 341). What is changing is our understanding of *how* a middle school principal successfully leads a school community toward improved student performance. An effective principal is not a school "manager" in the traditional sense of a lone figure controlling virtually all aspects of administrative procedure and instructional practice. Instead, he or she must take on the role of "principal change agent," setting the intellectual and interpersonal tone of the school and shaping the organizational conditions under which the school community works (Hipp, 1997, p. 45).

A middle grades school principal is no more able to increase the long-term organizational capacity of a school through a "command and control" style of leadership than a dictator is ultimately able to sustain deep and lasting increases in the economic productivity and social well-being of a nation. Authoritarianism in either context not only runs counter to our cherished sense of democracy; it simply does not work as a long-term strategy for motivating people to work harder or smarter. The drive to reach and sustain peak performance comes from within; it is intrinsically motivated and is expressed within supportive relationships. The principal's role is to cultivate teachers' intrinsic motivation—their inner voice—and to create a culture of continuous improvement by helping to define and breathe life into the structures of democratic governance (Murphy, in press).

Easier said than done. Very few principals have received training in shared leadership and decision making. Most principals have worked in settings where they were expected, if not required, to command from above and to concentrate on administrative and managerial issues rather than on teaching and learning. However, middle grades school principals can change their leadership styles. Those who do change realize that the school only stands to gain when school staff members who must carry out decisions also have a say in making those decisions (Lawler, 1992, p. 58). Also, when a controversial change is proposed, planned, and implemented within the context of shared decision making, it is the property of the broader school community. If it comes under attack, as some decisions inevitably will, the principal is not left hanging out there alone.

No single individual is more important to initiating and sustaining improvement in middle grades school students' performance than the school principal, and describing his or her role fully would require its own volume. Here, we outline some of the most important tasks faced by the principal of a high-performance middle grades school.

Mobilizing Support for Change

As noted in Chapter 6, as schools consider major shifts in practice, such as developing a schoolwide system of teams, the principal must work to mobilize a critical mass of school staff members, parents, and others to "buy in" to the proposed changes. Intensive, lasting change will not occur if the school community is opposed, or even if it is indifferent (Balfanz & Mac Iver, 1998, p. 42). Many "whole school" reform efforts, such as the Talent Development Middle School Model developed at Johns Hopkins University and the Turning Points Design Model developed by the Center for Collaborative Education in Boston, require that 80 percent of a school's faculty publicly indicate their support for adopting the new approach.

The principal's role, in conjunction with the school leadership team, is to help various constituencies within the school develop sufficient knowledge about both the need for a schoolwide improvement process and the nature of the proposed changes so that they can make an informed judgment. As the schools' educational leader, the principal "promotes the success of all students by facilitating the development, articulation, implementation, and stewardship of a vision of learning that is shared and supported by the school community" (Council of Chief State School Officers, 1996, p. 10).

Once a school elects to pursue a course of action, the school principal can strengthen the school staff's commitment both to the introduction of new practices and to the process of democratic governance itself by selecting new staff members based on their educational priorities and their willingness to collaborate (Fullan & Hargreaves, 1996, p. 96). By the same token, if a staff member stubbornly refuses to support agreed-upon changes in practice or simply cannot sufficiently improve his or her practice after intensive and prolonged professional development, we believe it is the principal's responsibility to use whatever legitimate means are available to remove that teacher from the faculty.

Maintaining a Focus on Improving Learning

The sustained improvement of middle grades school students' learning requires a relentless focus on improving the quality of teaching. It is the principal who must see that the school maintains its unwavering commitment to the goal of every student fulfilling the Turning Points vision.

An effective principal keeps a school focused on student learning by ensuring that faculty members have the professional development opportunities they need to improve their practice and that they make good use of them. Through frequent classroom visits and meetings with teams and by creating other opportunities to engage teachers in discussion about student work, a principal can closely monitor teachers' need for support (Walker et al., 1998, p. 17) and take steps to ensure that needs are met. When principals convey their own conviction that teachers can significantly influence student outcomes, they make teachers more confident in their ability to promote student growth (Hipp, 1997, pp. 42–43).

A principal cannot thoughtfully support or evaluate teachers' efforts to improve practice without immersing him- or herself in the modes of inquiry and development of knowledge unique to various subject areas (Balfanz & Mac Iver, 1998, p. 14). It is essential, therefore, for the principal to participate with teachers in targeted professional development opportunities and informational meetings related to the school's areas of instructional focus (Center for Collaborative Education, 1998, p. 6). A principal who exerts instructional and curricular leadership by learning alongside teachers is better able to create common ground within the school on what good practice looks like and what the schools' goals for improving student performance should be.

Establishing Trust

The principal also plays a pivotal role in fostering a trusting, respectful atmosphere within the school. Given the need for teachers to discuss their own and their colleagues' strengths and weaknesses openly as a basis for improving practice, a genuinely collegial climate is essential. The quality of a principal's leadership depends on the quality of his or her relationships with the entire school community (Bolman & Deal, 1993, p. 10).

Principals must model the cooperative behaviors they seek in others through genuine collaboration with teachers on important matters. An effective principal acts with integrity and fairness and is open to constructive criticism. The principal should be available to all school community members and should listen to their concerns, discuss ideas openly, and demonstrate honesty at every turn (George & Alexander, 1993, p. 510).

When cooperation and trust are well established, faculty members are more willing to take well-calculated risks and to try promising innovations in keeping with the school's vision and goals (Kilgore et al., 1997, pp. 8–10). Teachers are often more motivated to participate in all areas of decision making if they perceive their relationship with the principal as open and collaborative (Maeroff, 1993, p. 64).

Fostering trust and respect also means making school community members feel valued and important. A principal should acknowledge the responsibilities and contributions of each individual, celebrating accomplishments both big and small. A wide variety of rewards and recognition can be used, but even a note from the principal in a teacher's mailbox acknowledging good work can accomplish a great deal.

A trusting attitude on the part of the school principal nurtures teachers' development as school leaders. Within a school that shares leadership through democratic governance structures, the principal is often best positioned to identify and cultivate talents among the staff (Hopfenberg et al., 1993, p. 269) and to stimulate and celebrate examples of teacher leadership. Moreover, principals who support and are confident in their teachers' leadership tend to relinquish their need to control and, instead, empower their teachers to make collective decisions. In turn, teachers who feel empowered are more likely to be supportive of their principals (Hipp, 1997, p. 45).

Providing a caring, trusting work environment and ample opportunity for participation and shared decision making are two of the ways that organizations enlist people's commitment and involvement at all levels (Bolman & Deal, 1993, p. 2). Even skeptical and unsure teachers will be won over when they realize their views are heard and valued and when they see that they have the power to shape school policies based on what they know and discover to be best for the students (Kilgore et al., 1997, p. 6).

Advocating on the School's Behalf

As important as it is to build support for change within the school, a principal must also take the lead in communicating the school's strengths and achievements in order to build and sustain external support for improvement efforts as well as to mobilize community resources. The leadership team should invite parents, students community members, state and district officials, and the media to meet with them and to learn more about the school's goals, what the school is doing to meet them, and what the results have been. These constituents should have the opportunity to ask questions and to provide constructive criticism to help school improvement efforts.

Creating greater community access to information is itself a significant educational enterprise aimed at ensuring that all relevant groups understand the work under way and their part in making it successful. Through such communication, a principal is able to build productive alliances with diverse groups in the larger community (Fullan, 1997, p. 41) and to be responsive to the varied interests and needs of the local community (Council of Chief State School

Officers, 1996, pp. 16–17). Keeping track of appropriate outcomes and sharing those data with the community are crucial to the long-term success of middle grades school programs (George & Anderson, 1989, pp. 71–72).

DEVELOPING DISTRICT CAPACITY TO SUPPORT MIDDLE SCHOOL CHANGE

Virtually no middle school can transform itself into a high-performance middle grades school on its own, nor should it ever be forced to try. As described in greater detail in Chapter 9, educating America's adolescents is a community responsibility. It is the responsibility of parents and community members, and it is most definitely the responsibility of the local (district) education agency. The district office cannot be a silent partner in school improvement efforts, and its efforts must be aligned rather than independent, unrelated, or in the worst case, in conflict with school-based reforms. Unless the district is engaged actively in supporting school- and classroom-level change, steady and sustained improvement in students' performance will not occur (Balfanz & Mac Iver, 1998, pp. 2, 27, 43–44). Especially in schools serving high concentrations of low-income students, meaningful improvement in student learning can rarely occur without substantial assistance from the local school district.

There is no one best way for the local school district to play an instrumental role in the transformation of its middle schools. A key variable is the organizational capacity of the school to improve student performance. On the one hand, the experience of the past several decades has underscored the limits of school improvement efforts comprised *solely* of top-down reforms. Mandates to improve practice or reach higher achievement standards are futile without buy-in from teachers and others at the school level, accompanied by supportive policies and practices, along with the necessary resources, at the district level. On the other hand, there are schools, many of them in high-poverty urban areas, where the level of student performance is consistently so low that the district must take a very active and relatively prescriptive approach to improving the quality of teaching and learning, at least until the school has sufficiently improved its organizational capacity as to be able to take hold of the reins of change in the ways described in this book.

It is beyond the scope of this book to analyze how districts can best intervene in schools that are essentially dysfunctional. In this regard, we are encouraged that the Annenberg Institute for School Reform is currently spearheading an examination of the role of the local school district in the 21st century that will include a specific focus on high-poverty urban communities. Certainly, the goal of district support, whatever form it takes, to dysfunctional schools must be to vastly improve their capacity to ensure the success of every child.

When dysfunctional schools gain such capacity, or when such organizational strength already exists, the key shift that most districts must undergo is very like the shift that a school principal must make. That is, district officials must share authority with those in schools who work closely with students on a day-to-day basis. The district must shift from regulating teachers' practice to strengthening teachers' professional capacity. Effective districts, like effective principals, help educators in schools decide upon and carry out the right choices (Hatch & Hytten, 1997, p. 5), holding schools responsible "for results rather than for following set curricula, funding formulas, or other predetermined patterns and prescriptions" (Glickman, 1998, p. 65). The challenge facing a local district is to find ways to share leadership and decision making with the school community and to model, mirror, and support the kind of risk-taking and change that is expected of schools (Center for Collaborative Education, 1998, pp. 3, 11; Fullan & Hargreaves, 1996, p. 100; Hatch & Hytten, 1997, p. 67).

Currently, by limiting schools' autonomy over the use of their budget, personnel choices, performance assessment, and reporting requirements, and in other areas, the district office often prevents schools from becoming laboratories of innovation. A district's policies and practices should be part of the solution to improving school performance, and not part of the problem (Wolk, 1998, p. 45). To provide districts with greater opportunity and more incentive to remove bureaucratic barriers, state education agencies and state legislatures are being called upon to develop policies that direct districts to grant greater flexibility and autonomy to their schools (French, 1998, p. 192). In what follows, we examine more closely how districts can support innovation and improvement at the school level.

Authority over Personnel Decisions

The school principal, in collaboration with the school leadership team, should have the freedom to establish criteria for hiring new teachers based on the school's vision, to establish performance and professional development goals for all school staff members, and to hire and release personnel according to these expectations. By hiring and retaining high-quality staff members and by releasing staff members who are not competent and cannot or will not improve, or who do not buy into the school's improvement effort, a school can build a unified faculty that is committed to a common vision (Bodilly, 1998, pp. 89, 97–98; Center for Collaborative Education, 1998; Wohlstetter & Odden, 1992, pp. 542–543). By the same token, research on school improvement efforts shows that a school's lack of control over staffing is a major barrier to success (Useem et al., 1997, p. 64).

In many instances, giving schools the authority to hire and fire their own teachers will require major changes in the contract between the local teachers' unions and the district education agency. Specifically, the traditional guarantees that as teachers accrue greater seniority they also automatically gain greater influence on which school they are assigned to work in will need to be amended. However, the fundamental need for teachers to be represented by a strong local (and national) union remains, especially with regard to wages, benefits, due process, and, increasingly, the right to high-quality professional development.

Ability to Establish Working Conditions

Schools need a great deal of flexibility in the use of time and in determining work roles for school staff members in accordance with the school's vision. In particular, schools should be free to set the school day and year for both faculty and students, as long as state standards governing the overall amount of time students should be in school are met. Not only are schools best equipped to design a daily and yearly schedule that meets their students' academic and other needs, but school staff members can address their own need for substantial time for professional development (Center for Collaborative Education, 1998). For example, schools can build more continuous professional development into the school year if they are allowed to "bank time" by starting the school day earlier, by extending the number of days in the school year, or by increasing the length of the school day, although such changes may also involve renegotiation of collective bargaining agreements (Balfanz & Mac Iver, 1998, p. 36).

Budgetary Control

Adoption of the Turning Points design, or virtually any comprehensive school reform model, requires that a school receive a significant portion of its annual budget directly (80 to 90 percent or more) and that it have the authority to spend it according to its own decision-making process (Odden & Busch, 1998, pp. 42–44; Odden & Hill, 1997, p. 4). Ensuring that schools have considerable control over the resources they need to meet students' academic and other needs is crucial to holding schools accountable for educational performance (Odden & Busch, 1998, p. 202). The amount of each school's annual budget should be based on the district's average per pupil expenditures (French, 1998, p. 192; Hill, 1998, p. 21), as well as on the cost of addressing the specific needs of the schools' population of students (Odden & Busch, 1998, p. 135).

Budgetary control enables a school to focus all its resources on student learning. In fact, it becomes the school's responsibility to do so. A school would, for example, have the right to purchase certain services and goods currently provided by the district office from other vendors (French, 1998, p. 192), or to spend its money differently from year to year to support the school's own instructional priorities (Center for Collaborative Education, 1998, p. 11).

It would be highly irresponsible, however, for the district simply to enclose a check for a struggling school's annual budget inside a get-well card. To make "lump sum" budgeting work, the district will need to sponsor training, technical assistance, and follow-up support to help school community members develop the skills and knowledge needed for budgeting and resource utilization (Haslam, n.d., p. 21). A recent case study in Victoria, Australia, shows that, with appropriate training, schools can quickly learn how to manage their fiscal affairs and use their money wisely to produce higher levels of student achievement (Odden & Busch, 1998, p. 206). To facilitate effective planning, districts must provide schools with budget information early in the annual budget cycle, usually in the spring, and should announce new policies that may affect overall funding or budgetary practices at the same time.

Given the diversity of local school districts' economic circumstances across the country, any attempt to specify how much money a school needs to educate young adolescents well would be foolish. However, it is clear that schools with a high concentration of students from low-income families, students who come to school needing to learn English, or students who need other kinds of special assistance will continue to need additional resources above the "average per pupil expenditure."

At some point, our nation must face the gross discrepancies in resources between (and within) school districts that result from our continuing reliance on local property taxes as the primary means for financing public education. "Contrary to popular belief, the education system has amassed considerable financial resources throughout the twentieth century . . . however, the education dollar is neither distributed fairly, nor spent effectively. Students, by accident of place of residence, get more and others get less, regardless of their individual educational needs" (Odden & Busch, 1998, p. 203). The richest and least diverse districts have substantially more actual general revenues than districts with higher rates of poverty and more minority students. Categorical revenues such as Title I, which are designed to meet the supplemental requirements of special needs students and which are substantially higher in the poorest districts, are not enough to close the gap (Parrish & Hikido, 1998, pp. 9–10, 26). No other industrialized nation systematically concentrates its educational resources on those who are already advantaged by reason of family wealth and concentrates the least resources on those who need it most. Such *de facto* economic discrimination remains a major barrier to equality of educational opportunity for many American students.

Flexibility in Selecting Curricular Resources

A local district can provide an important service to schools by identifying textbooks and other materials that are aligned with state or district academic standards and that reflect the best approaches to inquiry and knowledge development within various academic disciplines. A school should have the right to opt out of district curriculum and instructional materials if it can demonstrate to the district's satisfaction that an alternative approach is better at improving student learning (Balfanz & Mac Iver, 1998, pp. 32–33). Such flexibility enables a school to develop its own academic standards that meet or exceed national, state, and district standards and are adapted to meet the specific needs of the school's student population. (For more on developing standards-based curriculum, see Chapter 3.)

Autonomy with Accountability

In exchange for greater freedoms afforded to schools, the district must set high standards and hold schools accountable for producing results. When held to

Box 7.1 Houston's success under the Texas Accountability System

Several years ago, if parents got involved at all at east Houston's McReynolds Middle School, it was likely to try to move their child to another school. "Historically, McReynolds was known as a place for students who couldn't get into a magnet school," recalls Principal Edward Vargas. It was also known as a school where discipline problems were frequent and where fewer than 40 percent of children passed the Texas proficiency test. Five years later, the school—which has a poverty rate pushing 80 percent—has dramatically boosted performance on the state exam, with nearly 70 percent of students meeting state standards in reading and math. But what excites Houston school officials most is that McReynolds's recent success is just one of several dozen examples in a school system that has risen to become one of the most respected urban districts in the state.

Since 1993, the 210,000-student Houston Independent School District has worked steadily to close a long-standing gap between its own performance and that of other Texas schools. Results from the Texas Assessment of Academic Skills (TAAS) test map out Houston's successes. In 1994, just 31 percent of eighth-grade students passed the test, and students in all grade levels were significantly behind their peers elsewhere. Flash forward to 1998, when at least 59 percent of students passed the exam at each grade level, with pass rates as high as 83 percent for students in the fifth grade. Houston has also seen a dramatic increase in schools that have earned the state's "exemplary" rating, going from no such schools in 1993 to 36 in 1998. Meanwhile, the number of schools that have been dubbed "low-performing" has fallen from 55 in 1993 to just 8 in 1998. The improvements, officials say, have come as the district placed an intense focus on student performance and held principals and teachers responsible for raising it. And most say those changes would not have taken place were it not for the state's highly publicized school accountability system.

Under the Texas accountability system, schools face rewards or sanctions based on a rating system. Those earning the exemplary rating could share in a pool of incentives totaling $7.5 million, while low-performing schools have faced state takeover. Houston's chief of staff for educational services Susan Sclafani said the plan found fertile ground when it was introduced to Houston seven years ago. At that time, she said, the school board and Superintendent Rod Paige were launching a district accountability model that shared many characteristics with the Texas system, with school rankings based on student performance. Sclafani said she isn't surprised that Houston as a district has been able to outpace the state in improving test scores. The district had a head start, she said, in training principals and teachers in how to use high-stakes assessments to the benefit of students.

Still, Houston administrators say the transition wasn't always easy. Initially, principals and teachers didn't always know what to make of the TAAS results, or how to use the test scores to drive instruction. The success of implementing a state accountability system, Sclafani said, hinges on having school districts that are equipped to support principals. In the Houston district, that support was targeted first at the schools that were deemed to be low-performing. Teams of central administrators visited the schools, providing extra training and, in some cases, more money.

At McReynolds Middle School, Principal Vargas said the effort started by analyzing instruction and pinpointing which concepts students were not grasping. "Now we are constantly looking at where we are," Vargas said. Sclafani said the state accountability plan works because the assessment program provides schools with far more than a single test score. Instead it tells principals exactly which skill areas need improvement for each student.

But the real genius of the accountability system, Houston officials say, is in the way it ranks schools. Under the system, schools can earn the title "exemplary" only if 90 percent of students pass the TAAS. But that 90 percent isn't a simple average. No school can be "exemplary" unless nine of ten minority students and economically disadvantaged students pass the exam. In other words, schools that have had stellar composite test scores in the past are denied state accolades if success has eluded black or Hispanic students. "Schools that were able to hide their minority performance are no longer able to," Sclafani said. "You are only as strong as your weakest link."

Still, the Texas system and the TAAS exam haven't won universal praise. Critics, including Houston Federation of Teachers President Gayle Fallon, say the district places too much pressure on principals to raise test scores. In many instances, she said, that pressure is passed on to the classroom teacher. "The problem we have had is that, to a large extent, districts have implemented the state system in a very punitive way," she said. Sclafani disagrees with Fallon's assessment. "There is never pressure for anything but good teaching," she said.

Other critics have attacked the TAAS itself, saying it is not rigorous enough, and the rising scores are not necessarily the sign of improved student performance. State officials are quick to defend the climbing TAAS scores by cross-referencing them to other forms of assessment. Specifically, Texas has boosted scores on the National Assessment of Education Progress more than almost any other state in the nation between 1990 and 1997. Last year, the U.S. Department of Education listed Texas as a model for improving performance on the NAEP scores, which is administered to a sampling of students nationwide.

Texas has launched several initiatives in the last year to fine-tune the plan—all designed to make schools accountable for the performance of every last student. The result—both in Houston and across Texas—has been a lowering of test scores and a decrease in the number of exemplary schools. Sclafani said she wouldn't have it any other way. This year, she said, Houston officials are already crafting ways to improve bilingual and special education instruction using data they have gleaned from the expanded testing. All along, she said, the Texas system and the reforms in Houston have been aimed at one thing—raising performance for all students, no matter what their description. The only way to make accountability mean something is to make schools accountable for all students. And that means testing anyone who is able. "If a child can pick up a pencil, they are taking the TAAS," she said.

high standards and supported in their efforts to achieve them, the individuals who work in, run, and send their children to a school will come up with the most effective and lasting strategies for improvement (Balfanz & Mac Iver, 1998, p. 10). They can do this best if they have real authority over day-to-day operations.

The changes in the district's role called for here are significant and would substantially alter the way the public education system is organized and managed. Nonetheless, these fundamental changes "promise to be the most successful route to greater productivity in the nation's public schools and hence higher student achievement. Such deep and fundamental change will not occur without active leadership and system redesign by the district . . . where ultimately final responsibility for school results still remains" (Odden & Busch, 1998, pp. 187–188).

District policies that couple greater autonomy with greater school accountability for student performance will, along with democratic governance structures and effective leadership practices, go far toward providing middle grades educators with the means and the motivation to improve their practice.

Middle grades schools should ensure that every student achieves higher standards and fulfills the Turning Points vision. Accountability for that result has become both carrot and stick for educators. The press, the public, and parents all clamor for better schools as a basis for a sound economy, thriving communities, and lifelong learning. In an environment of supports for and demands from schools, accountability is supposed to reveal where and with whom the buck stops.

A lot can ride on the results of the "high-stakes" accountability measures that educators and students often face. Schools can gain or lose funding, teachers and principals can polish their reputations or lose their jobs, superintendents can garner fame or notoriety, and students can be promoted or held back. High-stakes accountability is just that—high stakes—with someone reaping the benefits or paying the price.

Many states rely on standardized tests as accountability measures for schools and publish comparisons of performance in school "report cards." However, "measurement experts continue to point out that standardized tests are useful only within limits . . . when used as the sole indicator of quality, they are poor indicators of teacher quality or for comparing divergent school populations" (Gredler, 1999, p. 12). But unfortunately, according to the FairTest Study (Neill & FairTest Staff, 1997), "[S]tates continue to use outmoded, off-the-shelf, multiple-choice tests that are poorly aligned with their own standards" as the basis for their accountability systems. Such tests have no real connection with what should be happening in a standards-based classroom and thus have little to contribute to discussions of whether student performance has improved relative to the standards.

"The risk associated with all this testing," argues Michael J. Feuer, director of the National Academy of Sciences' Board on Testing and Assessment, "is that it tends to become too much of a focal point. . . . We have substantial evidence that too much reliance on testing for accountability can lead to inaccurate conclusions about student learning. It is not a rare occurrence to find test scores going up and erroneously infer from that that kids are learning more, when in fact they are just doing better on tests" (Squires, 1996).

Schools have too often felt compelled to align their curriculum and instruction with standardized tests that reward retention and regurgitation of isolated facts and skills. Such standardized tests can push teachers toward instructing students in test-taking skills, and even memorization of discrete facts and figures, both of which divert energy from the more desirable, and substantive, goal of understanding key ideas and processes (Gredler, 1999, p. 12).

In her book *Making Change*, Holly Holland (1998, p. 93) describes the impact of the Kentucky Education Reform Act (KERA) on three typical educators. Kentucky has struggled to develop or identify assessments that could be used effectively in KERA's accountability system. The experience in Kentucky "reveals the love–hate relationship that many people, locally and nationally, have with standardized tests. On one hand, the public believes that schools should be accountable for making sure students learn required material. On the other hand, few people agree about the best way to measure that achievement."

We believe that accountability should serve primarily as a tool to support the success of every student in fulfilling the Turning Points vision. When a school's performance is weak, that school should receive substantive support in improving that performance, whether the support takes the form of professional development, new staff, increased funding, intensive coaching, or opportunities to network with or visit more successful schools (see Box 7.1).

CONCLUSION

To be effective learning organizations, middle grades schools must operate as democratic, empowering institutions. The social and intellectual climate of the school depends on these characteristics of the educational environment. But just as important as being an empowering place for students and for faculty members, the middle grades school must be a healthy and safe place—a place ever mindful of the link between learning and physical and emotional health. How middle grades schools can forge this critical link is the subject of the next chapter.

8　A Safe and Healthy School Environment

Photo by Bob Durell

EW EDUCATORS WOULD DISPUTE the assertion that a young adolescent's health and fitness can affect his or her learning in school. But it is not only the health and fitness of the child that affect learning, but also the health and fitness of the school itself. A healthy school is one that provides its students and teachers with a secure and supportive environment, free from violence and discord; that promotes intergroup understanding and respect for those who differ in race, culture, gender, or religion; and that is strongly connected to the community. In this chapter, we address both these aspects of a successful middle school—the health of the students and the health of their school.

Students at any grade level who are repeatedly absent from school because of illness, who cannot participate fully in instructional activities because of health problems, or who are distracted from their school work by emotional or psychological stresses or by threats to their security are less likely to meet or exceed high academic standards. Good health does not guarantee that students will be interested in learning and able to learn, but the absence of good health makes learning all the more difficult.

Indeed, two of the core principles of a Turning Points school—that every student can and will learn, given appropriate learning opportunities; and that every adult in the school community has the responsibility to do whatever it takes to stimulate high-level learning in each and every student—compel middle grades educators to be involved actively in preventing or ameliorating health-related problems and promoting healthful lifestyles among their students. Like poverty, home language, previous achievement, or any number of other characteristics that students bring to middle school, health-related problems cannot become excuses for adults to place some students at risk of failure.

Despite the obvious links between good health and students' capacity to learn, there is no consensus among educators and the public at large about whether educators should play a primary role in preventing health-related problems or in addressing existing health problems. Moreover, many teachers and administrators have little systematic knowledge about effective, research-based practices in this arena, or about the kinds of mutually supportive partnerships that can be established with outside health and social service agencies to help students gain access to services.

Without community partners, schools cannot play an active role in ensuring students' good health and fitness to improve academic performance. The primary concern of teachers must be to teach and to learn how to teach more effectively; they cannot also be expected to assume lead responsibility for their students' health. The school should therefore be "nested" within a range of supportive professional and community relationships. Teachers and administrators need effective strategies for helping students learn about health-related risks and maintaining or developing healthful behaviors. Faculty members should also know how to create safe and supportive interpersonal environments within the school that promote positive, equitable outcomes for all students. These issues are addressed in this chapter.

Finally, while *Turning Points* argued that good health and fitness make high academic performance more likely, it is not a one-way causal relationship, but rather a mutually reinforcing "bidirectional" relationship (Battistich & Hom, 1997; Dryfoos, 1993, p. 82; Dryfoos, 1998, pp. 32–41; Jessor, Turbin, & Costa, 1998; Jessor, Van Den Bos, Vanderryn, Costa, & Turbin, 1995). A healthy lifestyle can promote academic success, and high engagement and productivity in school appear to prevent or lessen risky health and other problem behaviors.

Interview data from over 12,000 7th–12th graders collected as part of the National Longitudinal Study of Adolescent Health (Resnick et al., 1997) showed that students who feel more connected to their school or who are higher academic achievers than their peers reported significantly lower usage of cigarettes, alcohol, and marijuana and engage in their first sexual activity later than students who feel disconnected or are struggling academically. Lower academic achievement and students' feelings of being disconnected from school are also associated with greater emotional distress, including contemplation of suicide and higher levels of violent behavior. For middle grades students, health and learning are inextricably linked.

A HEALTHY LEARNING ENVIRONMENT

A safe and healthy school environment is yet another system composed of elements that interact with, and transform, each other. Critical components of a healthy learning environment include a challenging curriculum that promotes every student's learning (Chapters 3 and 4); close, personal relationships between teachers and students and among students (Chapter 6); and students' feelings of "connectedness" to the school (Chapters 6 and 7). All these components are crucial to better health outcomes for students, though we have dealt with them in chapters without the word "health" in the title. In this section, we highlight other important actions middle grades educators can take to strengthen the learning climate and support the healthy development of young adolescents.

Above all, schools must be safe places. Every middle grades student has an absolute right to guaranteed physical safety at every moment while in school. In large measure, middle schools will be safe places because of the strength of the relationships between teachers and students and among students themselves. Teams and other structures noted earlier (Chapter 6) go far toward enabling strong, caring relationships to evolve. The effective schoolwide discipline policies, thoughtful attention to interracial and interethnic relations in school, and peer mediation and conflict resolution programs described in this chapter will further strengthen the human bonds that prevent violence.

Additional measures involving the use of police or other security personnel may be needed, too, but perhaps only until all these elements of a high-performance middle grades school are in place to ensure students' safety. Some communities may have a particular need to involve law enforcement personnel, in conjunction with adult community "monitors," to ensure that students can reach school and return home safely, including returning from after-school activities. The federal Gun-Free Schools Act of 1994 requires local education agencies to expel any student found in possession of a firearm on school property for at least a year. In our view, the possession of *any* potentially life-threatening weapon on school grounds should result in immediate suspension or expulsion, and the school should notify local law enforcement authorities at once. Before being permitted to return to school, the student, and possibly other family members, should be required to receive intensive counseling about the dangers of such weapons and the student's reasons for having the weapon. Put simply, a middle grades school should be no place for violence or fear.

Classroom Management and Discipline

Many middle grades educators interviewed for this book reported that student discipline had been a significant problem in their schools. These teachers and principals also described strategies for improving student discipline that are achieving good results. Although the specifics vary, the strategies often share vital elements, including

- Developing common expectations for all students' behavior
- Clarifying the consequences of misbehavior
- Having all staff members, not just administrators, assume responsibility for maintaining or improving student discipline
- Specifying teacher and administrator roles in handling discipline problems
- Increasing consistency and follow-through in implementing schoolwide discipline policies

Schoolwide discipline policies clearly articulated and consistently enforced are crucial to the development of an orderly and safe climate for learning. However, discipline established primarily on the basis of externally imposed rewards for positive behavior and punishment for disruptive behavior will only go so far in creating the norms of cooperation and trust among students and teachers that are needed to support high-level learning. Clearly structured behavioral parameters do not necessarily provide students with an understanding of *why* it is important to follow rules governing conduct. Without understanding of or involvement in the development of rules, the drive to respect, cooperate, and collaborate with teachers and peers is fundamentally extrinsic and requires repeated reinforcement, positive or negative, from outside. In contrast, ensuring that students understand and have the opportunity to shape norms of behavior stimulates their intrinsic motivation to observe school rules because it taps into and supports students' own understanding of what is fair and just (see Box 8.1).

At the same time that they have developed more proactive school and classroom discipline policies and practices, schools have created student support teams to help prevent students' behavioral difficulties from becoming chronic problems for the students and the school. Such teams are made up of teachers, administrators, health and mental health professionals working in the school (for example, guidance counselor, school nurse, school social worker, and school psychologist), and representatives from community-based health and service agencies. The specific composition of a school's support team will vary, depending on the number and kind of professionals working in or available to the school.

The support team assembles periodically to discuss, from a variety of perspectives, students referred to the group by one or more teachers because of significant academic or behavioral problems. When the support team deems it necessary, they draft a coordinated plan of action for a student involving one or more service providers. Members of the team discuss the student's problems and the proposed plan for addressing them with the student and his or her parents. In some instances, the student support team process may result in formal procedures for providing special education services; however, this should be only one of a range of potential solutions.

Box 8.1 Involving Young Adolescents in Establishing a Climate for Learning

Each of the following approaches to managing student behavior and promoting student learning emphasizes student self-responsibility; linking the social, psychological, and cognitive dimensions of learning; the importance of students feeling connected to a caring community; and the necessity of implementing program components schoolwide if they are to be effective.

The Responsive Classroom

The Northeast Foundation for Children of Greenfield, Massachusetts, developed the Responsive Classroom, an integrated approach to school organization, teaching, and classroom management that emphasizes the development of student self-responsibility and social competence in tandem with academic achievement (Crawford & Wood, 1998). In the Responsive Classroom, respectful, caring relationships are the foundation for socially responsible action. In the middle grades, the program's approach to classroom organization and teaching methods builds upon young adolescents' desire for both freedom and responsibility by emphasizing the connection between the two. Key program components include

- Morning meetings, called the Circle of Power and Respect, that focus on strengthening relationships and improving social skills
- Collaboratively developing classroom rules and collaboratively resolving classroom conflicts through class meetings
- Applying logically related consequences to misbehavior, such as having students clean a surface they have defaced rather than simply being assigned detention
- Providing opportunities for students to exercise as much choice as possible in their academic learning throughout the regular school day

Evaluation data indicates that, when effectively implemented, Responsive Classroom strategies improve students' social skills, reduce problem behaviors, and serve as an "enabler" of improved academic achievement (Elliot, 1998).

Consistency Management and Cooperative Discipline

According to the Consistency Management and Cooperative Discipline (CMCD) program, developed by Jerome Freiberg at the University of Houston, the best classroom management and discipline policies encourage student self-discipline and shared responsibility for learning and classroom management between teachers and students. The approach assumes that classroom management practices that require unquestioning compliance with rules imposed from on high seriously undermine instructional methods designed to stimulate students' independent thinking and cooperative interaction. CMCD calls for activities such as:

- Teachers and students jointly developing classroom rules, which are written down in the form of "classroom constitutions"
- Preventing predictable conflicts between students or opportunities for misbehavior through establishing orderly routines and explicit, valued roles for students that help create an organized environment for learning
- Providing consistency in academic and behavioral expectations across classrooms
- Sharing responsibility among teachers and students for sustaining a climate of academic rigor
- Celebrating students' accomplishments and demonstrating intolerance for disparaging remarks between students
- Using various strategies for involving parents and other community members in the school to serve as positive role models for students

Evaluations show that CMCD increases student and teacher attendance, reduces disciplinary referrals, increases academic time on task by decreasing the amount of time teachers spend on discipline, and helps create a school climate that supports improved academic achievement (Freiberg, Connell, & Lorentz, 1997; Opuni, 1998).

Child Development Project

The Child Development Project (CDP), a whole-school reform program developed by the Developmental Studies Center of Oakland, California, assumes that children have basic psychological needs to belong, to have a sense of control over the environment, and to feel competent. CDP derives four key principles for effective school organization from these assumptions:

- Build warm, stable relationships between teachers and students and among students.
- Attend to the social and ethical as well as the cognitive dimensions of learning.
- Honor intrinsic motivation.
- Teach in ways that support students' active construction of meaning.

Critical components of the program derived from these principles include:

- A literature-based reading and language arts program called "Reading for Real," which strengthens students' comprehension skills while enabling them to address universal ethical issues embedded in literature selections
- Cooperative learning techniques

BOX 8.1 CONTINUED

- A "developmental" approach to discipline, which incorporates strategies such as involving students in developing classroom rules
- Parental involvement activities to encourage meaningful conversations between parents and children about their schoolwork as well as to involve parents in the life of the school
- Noncompetitive schoolwide activities designed to build a sense of community among students, parents, and teachers

Students in schools that have implemented CDP indicate increases in their level of engagement in class activities, enjoyment of class and liking for school, ability to resolve conflicts, concern for other students, and respect and trust for teachers. They also demonstrate fewer symptoms of loneliness and anxiety (Developmental Studies Center, 1998). The program is also effective in preventing violence. Evolving evidence suggests that the program's effects persist and may grow even stronger through the middle grades years (Victor Battistich, personal communication, August 9, 1999). The CDP has been named an "exemplary program" by the U.S. Center for Substance Abuse Prevention, Department of Health and Human Services because of its effectiveness in helping students resist the use of drugs, alcohol, and tobacco (Developmental Studies Center, n.d.).

A student support team's work does not end with developing an action plan. Some schools specifically require the support team to meet weekly to monitor the ongoing implementation of action plans and to discuss students' progress. Although support teams may meet less frequently, some sort of systematic follow-up is essential to ensuring that students receive the services they need.

Promoting Positive Interethnic and Interracial Relations

Children become aware of racial and ethnic differences as early as the preschool years. However, beliefs about the *meaning* of racial and ethnic differences become increasingly salient as children develop, and they reach a critical stage during the middle school years, when young people are deeply engaged in defining their own identity in relation to others. Patterns of friendliness or antipathy toward young people of different racial and ethnic backgrounds often become the foundation for lifelong attitudes that profoundly influence behavior.

Eliminating inequities for minority-group adolescents and promoting positive relations among students from different ethnic and racial backgrounds in middle grades schools will contribute to a more just world. Of more immediate importance, it will help create the kind of learning environment that will enable all students to meet or exceed high academic standards. Adolescents who see themselves as the victims of prejudice experience higher levels of emotional stress (Resnick et al., 1997), which undermines their attachment to school and their motivation to learn. As both a moral and educational imperative, no middle grades school can tolerate intolerance.

Perhaps the most critical feature of a healthy middle grades school environment is equally high expectations for all students. Yet, as argued in Chapter 4, uniformly high expectations should not lead to uniformity in instructional practices: teachers need a broad range of approaches to enable students in a heterogeneous classroom to excel. Individual students will, of course, differ in both the magnitude and kind of their intellectual achievement, but *groups* of students should not achieve differently from other groups.

Tracking students by perceived ability level or past performance is a clear manifestation of unequal expectations, as noted in Chapter 4. Tracking is easily the most formidable structural barrier to equitable learning opportunities and positive intergroup relations, given that minority-group students are disproportionately represented in the lower tracks. Tracking determines which students will have the best and most varied learning opportunities, and it denies all students the opportunity for routine and frequent interaction with other students unlike themselves (Braddock, Dawkins, & Wilson, 1995, p. 244). Likewise, tracking determines status relationships: students in higher tracks are seen as more able than students in lower tracks. The promotion of positive relations between individuals from different ethnic and racial groups requires equal status for all groups (Allport, 1954). Tracking violates this fundamental principle.

Some students for whom English is not the first language may well need separate programs if they are to learn the language and subject-area skills that will enable them to master the middle grades school curriculum, as discussed in Chapter 4. However, such tracks can lead to separate and almost inevitably unequal tracks for English-language learners if a school is not equipped to educate language-minority students *effectively* (Valdés, 1998). Tracking, however it is manifested, and whatever its motives, is anathema to equity in learning outcomes and to positive interracial and interethnic relations. In Chapter 4 we describe effective instructional methods for heterogeneously grouped middle grades students.

The middle grades curriculum can be instrumental in stimulating intergroup understanding while broadening students' knowledge. Including topics within the curriculum that make students aware of the characteristics and contributions of the world's cultures is extremely important. However, as James Banks (1995, p. 331), one of the nation's leading authorities on multicultural education, warns, it is not enough to dot the curriculum with sporadic information about "heroes and holidays," which limits ethnic content to special days, weeks, or months related to ethnic events and celebrations. When this approach is used, students learn little or nothing about ethnic groups before or after the special event or occasion. Moreover, the approach "encourages students to view ethnic groups not as an integral part of United States society and culture, rather as an addition to the curriculum and thus as an appendage to the main story of the development of the nation."

The middle grades curriculum should consistently include content related to a wide variety of ethnic groups. This content should also reflect the perspectives of the ethnic group from which it is drawn. As Banks (1995, p. 332) writes:

> For instance, in addition to stories about Thanksgiving told from the perspective of the Pilgrims, the teacher might read documents describing how the Indians perceived the occupation of their lands by the British colonists. Thus, what was a "thanksgiving" for one group was in many ways a day of mourning for another. The teacher might also ask the students to assume the roles of both the Pilgrims and the Indians in role-playing situations.

Thoughtful inclusion of content reflecting a broad array of cultures can be a springboard for substantive conversations among adolescents about issues related to race and ethnicity. The formation of a positive individual identity, including exploration of aspects of one's racial, ethnic, and gender identity, is a key developmental goal of early adolescence (Tatum, 1997, pp. 19–20). All too often, however, adults who are themselves uncomfortable discussing race and ethnicity suppress candid conversation rather than encourage it. Middle grades students need "free spaces" within which they can pursue their questions about their own and others' cultures without fear of being stereotyped, or of reprisal or intimidation (Fine, Weis, & Powell, 1997). Yet to facilitate this kind of honest dialogue, teachers themselves must first learn about their own and others' history and culture and must question their own assumptions about the ways in which race and ethnicity matter (Tatum, 1997).

Cooperative learning and other project-based approaches to instruction are another way of improving student learning and promoting tolerance and understanding among different groups. Numerous studies show that cooperative-learning groups promote cross-cultural friendships that are strong and long-lasting (Slavin, 1995, p. 309). Cooperative-learning groups seem to satisfy all the criteria identified in Gordon Allport's classic publication *The Nature of Prejudice* (1954) as needed to promote positive intergroup attitudes: equal status roles of students from different races, contact across racial lines that permits students to learn from one another as individuals, cooperation across racial lines, and communication by an authority figure of his or her unequivocal support for interracial (and intergroup) contact.

How schools acknowledge student achievement is another determinant of the intergroup climate on campus. As schools are increasingly able to help all students reach or exceed high academic standards, students from all backgrounds will naturally be honored for their achievement, indicating plainly to everyone that no one group is more able than another. Until this occurs routinely, and as long as gaps in achievement between groups persist, schools can supplement the practice of honoring students whose absolute level of achievement is outstanding by honoring students who have shown substantial improvement in their academic performance. In this way, academic values are not only reinforced, but also become more inclusive (Schofield, 1995, p. 268). This approach is standard practice in school sports, where, for example, the "most improved" member of the swim team is honored at the annual banquet, along with the swimmers with the best times, or where the "most valuable player" may not be the player with the best stats.

Peer Mediation and Conflict Resolution

To prevent interpersonal problems within the school and to promote a supportive climate for learning, middle schools can develop proactive school and classroom management policies and practices and specifically promote cooperative, equitable relationships among adolescents from different racial and ethnic groups. Such efforts will minimize but not completely eliminate conflicts between students that require intervention. Young adolescents' ability to maintain friendships in the face of conflict and to manage anger is closely related to their future psychological adjustment and school success, and indeed to success in adult life (Johnson, Johnson, Dudley, Ward, & Magnuson, 1995, pp. 838–839; Miller, 1998).

Middle grades schools have found that peer mediation and conflict resolution programs are effective in defusing conflicts between students and in teaching anger management and communication skills. Peer mediation is a structured process in which a neutral and impartial student (known as the mediator) assists two or more students in negotiating a resolution to their conflict. Students may seek mediation on their own or may be referred to it by a peer, teacher, or administrator.

A mediation typically involves the following six steps:

1. The mediator introduces himself or herself, explains the process of mediation, and asks whether both parties agree to participate and follow the rules.
2. The mediator asks each disputant in turn to explain his or her point of view while the other listens quietly. The mediator may restate the disputants' feelings or arguments to be sure they are understood by all. The mediator will stop a disputant who jumps in out of turn.
3. The mediator asks questions of each disputant in turn in order to help each party understand the other's point of view. The mediator also helps each disputant identify what it is that he or she wants from the other disputant.
4. The mediator then asks the disputants to join him or her in brainstorming possible solutions to the problem that would satisfy both of them.
5. The mediator asks the disputants to decide which possible solutions are likely to be the most feasible and effective.
6. Finally, the mediator asks each disputant to restate what they have agreed to do, writes up the agreement, and asks each of them to sign the written agreement and agree to abide by it.

The effectiveness of peer mediation programs is highly dependent on the quality of the training that mediators receive. High-quality training in mediation techniques, usually provided by an intermediary organization brought into the school by school or district officials, equips students with a broad repertoire of strategies for resolving conflicts, including the use of compromise strategies that resolve conflicts without winners and losers.

As important to successful conflict resolution as the training of mediators is the credibility of the mediator. A mediator's credibility is based on his or her ability to relate personally to the students in conflict and on the students' sense that the mediator can understand the conflict and act fairly in resolving it. Therefore, rather than encouraging only one group of students, for example, the top-achieving students, to serve as mediators, educators should draw potential mediators from throughout the student body. Among a school's mediators should be students who have themselves been involved in conflicts with other students and those who have had behavioral problems. Being entrusted with the role of mediator, a position of responsibility not often held by "difficult" students, creates a sense of self-efficacy and helps these students learn skills useful in defusing their own conflicts. In an interview with the authors, one middle school principal noted:

> Some of your key gang kids are wonderful leaders. . . . We targeted the so-called at-risk kid [for peer mediation training], the one that either has low self-esteem or is a key leader of a particular group. If they see stuff going down, they are going to have more respect when they intervene and say, "Hey, this isn't acceptable." It makes a tremendous difference in what happens, and it makes my job a lot easier too.

The Conflict Resolution Education Network (CREnet) has published a useful *Resource Guide for Selecting a Conflict Resolution Education Trainer* that helps schools locate sources of mediation training nationwide (Conflict Resolution Education Network, 1999). The guide also suggests issues that schools should consider in selecting an organization to assist them in developing peer mediation programs.

Peer Support Groups

School guidance counselors can contribute to the overall quality of a school's learning environment by helping students identify and overcome personal challenges that may be causing behavioral or academic problems. We noted in Chapter 6, however, that middle grades school counselors are often required to serve so many students that their ability to provide individualized counseling is often severely diminished. The advisory group described in Chapter 6 is one means of giving students an opportunity to discuss personal issues significant to them within a supportive environment. Peer support groups are another approach that schools have found successful in providing an outlet for students' candid conversation about personal matters.

Peer support groups are small groups of students that meet regularly to discuss an issue that is important to all of them. At all times, the groups are facilitated by a counselor or a qualified health-care practitioner, such as a school nurse or a school psychologist who has received specialized training in effectively managing sensitive group discussions. The topics of discussion reflect the issues that are most immediate and troubling in students' lives, from managing anger, drug or alcohol abuse, fear of victimization, or coping with parents' divorce, to any number of other urgent problems that are sources of stress. Groups can also be formed to provide mutual support for students facing chronic health conditions such as asthma or diabetes, or eating disorders and obesity. Peer support groups enable counselors to address systematically the concerns of a great many more students than they could through individual counseling. Many students and their families regard peer groups as less threatening than individual counseling (see Box 8.2).

A HEALTH-PROMOTING SCHOOL

How do people establish the habits and behaviors that allow them to enjoy lifelong good health? For many individuals, the period of early adolescence is the critical juncture in their lives when patterns of behavior are begun that determine the trajectory of their health, and, for some, the length and quality of their lives. What students know and are able to do to preserve and maintain good health when they leave middle school is just as vital to their ultimate happiness and well-being as their knowledge of academic subject matter.

Risky Health Behaviors

As noted in Chapter 1, young people often begin experimenting with a range of risky behaviors between the ages of 10 and 15. Just how "at-risk" are today's young adolescents? In summarizing findings from several large-scale studies of adolescent behavior, researcher and author Joy Dryfoos (1998, pp. 34–36) reports that, of more than 3.5 million 14-year-olds in 1995, 10 percent were at "very high risk" due to involvement in a wide range of high-risk behaviors, including use of illegal drugs and alcohol, and unprotected sex. The majority of these high-risk youths had been arrested at least once during the year, most had access to guns, and many routinely carried weapons, increasing the likelihood of involvement as victim or perpetrator of violence. About 40 percent were depressed, and many had attempted suicide.

Another 25 percent of all 14-year-olds are at "high risk." According to Dryfoos,

> Although they have not yet been involved with the juvenile justice system . . . they are heavily involved with drinking, smoking, and marijuana; behind modal grade in school and often truant; and frequently have unprotected intercourse. . . . These high-risk youngsters—one quarter of all 14-year-olds—are in great jeopardy unless they receive immediate, intensive interventions that will act as deterrents to further involvement in behaviors with negative consequences. (1998, p. 35)

Box 8.2 Transforming Counseling: Truman Middle School

Before she even entered the principal's office to report to work, Betty Whiton was well aware of her job description as a counselor at Truman Middle School in Albuquerque, New Mexico. Like a giant overstuffed "in-box," the school's administrative waiting room that day was crammed full of students awaiting reprimand for hall fights and bathroom brawls. "There must have been 30 kids who were sent there because of fights," she said.

Whiton's first day on the job six years ago was not unusual for the school, known as one of Albuquerque's toughest. Located on the western outskirts of town in the Westgate community, Truman draws students from transient motels, trailer parks, low-end apartment and housing developments, and the neighborhood gangs, the "Westgate Locos" and "Westgaters." During a typical lunch period, Whiton said, the school could expect as many as ten fights.

Today, administrators say Truman is tame by comparison, with conflicts much less frequent and less severe. Most credit the improvements to a gradual overhaul of the school's counseling services, which now include more than 25 support groups tackling such things as anger management, alcoholism, sexual abuse, and gang intervention. Dozens of students, meanwhile, are trained each semester as mediators, joining an army of students and staff prepared to resolve student conflicts. In all, more than a fourth of Truman's roughly 1,000 students participate in some form of weekly support group, making the school a model for student support programs at Albuquerque's 24 middle schools.

Whiton, who is now retired, says the school's transformation started with a handful of like-minded administrators. Former principal Edgar Briggs, and later principal Ellen Miller-Brown, agreed to free counselors from administrative burdens like creating the school's annual class schedule, or monitoring hallways and the cafeteria. "Oddly enough, I just believed in the concept that counselors should be counselors," said Miller-Brown, now a central administrator.

Miller-Brown said the school's needs were simply too great to spare scarce counselors on other assignments. Like all New Mexico public schools, Truman is assigned only one state-funded counselor for every 500 students. That ratio holds regardless of the school's makeup. At Truman, roughly 75 percent of the students qualify for the free- or reduced-lunch program. Eighty percent of students are Hispanic, with more than 40 percent considered monolingual Spanish speakers. A social worker is also assigned to the school, but deals only with special education students. And while Truman has attracted occasional help from interns at the University of New Mexico, nearly all of its student support programs have been designed and operated by its regular counselors.

Early on, Whiton says, administrators agreed to set up weekly gang mediation sessions, where members attempted to diffuse conflicts through diplomacy. Whiton said the meetings made gang members feel validated, while also helping them recognize that their differences were often petty. Over the course of several months, school officials say, fights began to taper off.

The concept was quickly extended to include mediation training for other students and staff. Ultimately, a "Life Skills" course was created as a for-credit elective, offering students instruction in conflict resolution. Student mediators now save counselors time by attempting to resolve minor differences between other students. Miller-Brown says that as many as 210 such student-led mediations have been conducted in a single semester, affecting more than 400 students. In nearly all cases, she says, students have held up their end of agreements and averted further conflicts.

But the backbone of Truman's student support services, counselors say, is its peer support groups. Helen Aragon Sterling, a second-year Truman counselor, says that without the peer groups she would only have time to provide intensive help for a dozen students. As it is, she oversees 13 peer groups a week, each with 5–12 students. The groups range from helping children overcome shyness to helping them cope with divorced or alcoholic parents.

Last year, Truman was able to expand the concept with the help of school district funds aimed at reducing the dropout rate. The funding has allowed the school to hire a temporary third counselor who focuses chiefly on reducing drug abuse. Pat Halama, whose background includes 16 years of therapeutic substance abuse intervention, now sponsors weekly 90-minute drug intervention classes for students and parents. The program is offered as an alternative to long-term suspension for students found possessing drugs or alcohol. Halama said that in her first year, 26 students participated. "I only had one repeat offender," she noted.

Since most of the support groups are held during regular class hours, counselors say that setting up the peer groups meant selling the idea to teachers and parents. Miller-Brown said one teacher who opposed the idea asked her how he was going to teach spelling if a student was in a support group. "My response was, 'How can they do their spelling if they need a support group?'" Over time, administrators say, teachers have gotten on board with the peer groups, largely because what happens there makes the classroom more manageable. "We have 100-percent buy-in from the staff," says current principal Ellen Moore. "There's just no conflict with it." Counselors say most of their referrals to the groups come from teachers, who they say are now more likely to look for problem behavior.

Many students refer themselves. Counselors continually promote the services that are offered, even handing fifth-graders a list of peer groups before they enter the middle school. Counselors admit that response from the community hasn't always been positive. In some cases, they say, parents initially don't want their children in a support group, particularly one dealing with sensitive issues such as sexual abuse. "Sometimes it's just a matter of easing parents' minds," Judy Burchiel, the school's current head counselor, said. Miller-Brown said she is not aware of any parent who has pulled a child out of a peer group once it has been explained to them. Now, she said, the community views the school's student support programs as a part of its instructional curriculum.

BOX 8.2   CONTINUED

Still, Burchiel and others say there is much to improve on at Truman. Counselors acknowledge that they still must take time to adjust student schedules and attend parent–teacher conferences. And school officials report they continue to feel that, even with the changes, they are understaffed with counselors. Yet they say a drop in discipline problems and a relatively peaceful office waiting room show the fruits of their progress. Replicating that success elsewhere, they say, has less to do with resources than with attitudes. "It requires student-centered people, and asking, 'What do the students on this campus need?'" Miller-Brown says.

Another 25 percent of 14-year-olds are at moderate risk because of their involvement in one or two high-risk behaviors. The remaining 40 percent of 14-year-olds are at low or no risk because of very limited or no involvement in high-risk behaviors.

Besides the more conventional definition of "at-risk," young adolescents are also vulnerable to other risk factors that affect their overall health. For example, young adolescents may begin smoking or eating poorly, two behaviors that will affect their long-term well-being. Not only are smoking-related diseases the single greatest cause of mortality in the United States (CDC, 1999), but smoking often serves as the "gateway" to other drug use (Breslau & Peterson, 1996, p. 214; Hamburg, 1997, p. 124; Lindsay & Rainey, 1997, p. 123). The younger the age of onset of smoking, the harder it is to quit and the greater the potential for permanent negative health consequences. Smokers who start smoking by age 13 are significantly less likely to quit than those who start even a few years later (Breslau & Peterson, 1996).

Preventing or at least delaying the onset of smoking among middle grades school students through education must be a high priority. The middle grades school should provide a model for healthful lifestyles for both students and adults. It should go without saying that schools should be tobacco-free for both students and adults. Teachers must model nonsmoking behavior, and, obviously, eliminating or reducing adults' tobacco dependency will improve their health as well.

Proper diet is a key factor in a healthy lifestyle. Obesity, poor nutrition, and other dietary problems are implicated in numerous long-term health problems such as diabetes, heart disease, cancer, and stroke. Obesity has doubled among children and adolescents over the past 30 years, children and adolescents eat far more fat and far fewer fruits and vegetables than are recommended, and harmful weight loss practices such as vomiting or taking diet pills have been reported among girls as young as nine (CDC, 1997b).

Health and Physical Education

Health Education. To prevent or at least minimize the onset of risky behaviors, and to enable students to make appropriate choices to safeguard their health generally, health education must be a part of the middle grades curriculum. Health education provides students with the information they need to make informed choices. Young people are willing to study and discuss health education issues because they see the obvious relevance to their lives. Perhaps most crucial, health education helps young people develop skills in communication, goal-setting, and decision making that enable them to resist peer pressure to begin risky behaviors. Having multiple structured opportunities to practice and role-play health-related skills before encountering actual opportunities to engage in risky behaviors enables students to translate knowledge about health into health-promoting behavior (Dusenbury & Falco, 1995; Kane, 1993, pp. 18–21; Lohrmann & Wooley, 1998, pp. 46–47). Research on the effectiveness of health education shows that students' gains in health knowledge and skills last into adulthood (Dusenbury & Falco, 1995, pp. 420–421).

As with any element of the middle grades curriculum, the content and instructional approaches used in health education are critical determinants of its effectiveness for students. Middle grades health education should reflect high standards that clearly indicate what students should know and be able to do. The Joint Committee on National Health Education Standards has recently published national health education standards (American Cancer Society, 1997). The Joint Committee included representatives from such major national health-related organizations as the Association for the Advancement of Health Education, the American Public Health Association, the American School Health Association, and the Society of State Directors of Health, Physical Education, and Recreation. The Joint Committee defines the goal of "health literacy" as "the capacity of an individual to obtain, interpret, and understand basic health information and services, and the competence to use such information and services in ways which enhance health" (p. 5) and calls for all students to be able to

- Comprehend concepts related to health promotion and disease prevention
- Demonstrate the ability to access valid health information and health-promoting products and services
- Demonstrate the ability to practice health-enhancing behaviors and reduce health risks
- Analyze the influence of culture, media, technology, and other factors on health
- Demonstrate the ability to use interpersonal communication skills to enhance health
- Demonstrate the ability to use goal-setting and decision-making skills to enhance health
- Demonstrate the ability to advocate for personal, family, and community health

In the context of these standards, greatest emphasis should be placed on providing students with knowledge and skills related to six key areas of potential harm: smoking, alcohol and other drug use, early and unprotected sexual activity, poor nutrition, insufficient exercise, and aggressive or reckless behavior that can result in injury and death.

The health curriculum must also provide students with sufficient knowledge to support desirable behaviors, offer them opportunities to practice applying health knowledge and skills, and develop their decision-making and communication skills so that they can avoid or escape health-threatening situations. Young adolescents need help, for example, in identifying options and assessing the likely consequences of various behaviors; developing refusal skills, including the ability to resist subtle and overt pressure to conform; advocating for their own rights and the rights of others to health information and services; recognizing unhealthy stresses; and reaching out for help when needed (Dusenbury & Falco, 1995; Kane, 1993, 28–31). A well-designed and effectively implemented health curriculum will enhance students' ability to use the information they acquire to avoid risks and to make health-enhancing choices.

For example, the middle grades health education curriculum should provide sound, up-to-date information on nutrition and diet. Yet if a school does not provide students with food choices that are consistent with this information, the strength of the message is severely compromised (CDC, 1996). As noted in *Turning Points* (p. 64):

> Food services should eliminate items that are high in animal fat, salt, or sugar, and should substitute healthful snacks such as fruit and fruit juice for candy and soft drinks. Given their rapid growth, young adolescents need foods containing sufficient calcium and iron. Where appropriate, schools can offer special diets for obese children or those on dietary regimens. Schools can add variety and promote awareness of and appreciation for different foods by offering those from many cultures.

Physical Education. Regular exercise is also critical to adolescents' immediate and future physical and mental health, yet nearly half of 12- to 21-year-olds are not vigorously active on a regular basis (CDC, 1997a). Moreover, exercise rates drop sharply with age among adolescents. Physical education should be provided regularly to all middle grades students as a matter of course within the curriculum. As in the case of health education, the content and pedagogy of physical education should reflect standards established by reputable national organizations such as the National Association for Sport and Physical Education (NASPE), which has produced both overall physical education standards (NASPE, 1995) and specific *Guidelines for Middle School Physical Education* (NASPE, 1992). Also, the CDC has produced *Guidelines for School and Community Programs to Promote Lifelong Physical Activity Among Young People* (1997a).

Physical education is especially important in early adolescence, when young people are increasingly concerned with body image, physical development, and attractiveness. Involvement in sports and noncompetitive physical activities provides opportunities for students to gain strength, coordination, and endurance and to explore ways of using their bodies in healthful ways that can be a source of pride and self-confidence. A wide variety of activities should enable every student to find some sort of physical activity they enjoy or in which they can excel. All students can thus learn that physical prowess can be acquired, like intellectual capacity, when physical education activities relate to students' interests and when students and educators invest their work with sufficient effort to reach critical goals. Under no circumstances should opportunities for regular physical exercise be limited to competitive or interscholastic sports.

Some schools have shown great creativity in finding ways to draw students into physical activity. One middle school found that their female students were very worried about body image but were hesitant to engage in physical education or after-school sports. When the school began offering a "health club" in the gym two nights a week, providing aerobics and weight-training classes and equipment such as exercise bicycles, many girls "joined the club," and so did some of their parents!

Health and Physical Education Teachers

Whenever possible, health education should be provided by professional health educators. Even if health education is not taught by professional health educators, those who do teach the subject, often physical education teachers, should be well grounded in the theoretical and practical knowledge that undergirds the curriculum and teaching methods appropriate to the discipline (Dusenbury & Falco, 1995; Kane, 1993, pp. 32–33; Lohrmann & Wooley, 1998, p. 54).

Difficult questions will arise in health education that teachers must both anticipate and enable young people to ask without fear of embarrassment; students must have confidence that they will receive an honest, straightforward response. Health education teachers, therefore, require ongoing professional development in the interactive teaching strategies, such as skills demonstration, role playing, cooperative learning, facilitated discussions, and student-led instruction, that support effective health education (Dusenbury & Falco, 1995; Lohrmann & Wooley, 1998, p. 55; Price, Gioci, Penner, & Trautlein, 1993, p. 45).

Physical education teachers also need to be well trained to teach young adolescents effectively about the necessity of regular, active participation in physical activities throughout their lives. One unfortunate consequence of the recent emphasis on improving children's cognitive capacities is a de-emphasis on physical education—a kind of swapping of time spent in gym class and other organized opportunities for play, movement, and the like, for more time in instruction in the "core" subject areas. This trade-off brings a real danger for young people's development that can lead to serious health consequences as they become adults. Many children become seriously overweight during adolescence, in part due to lack of proper exercise. These youth are at risk of diabetes, heart disease, and other preventable health complications.

Organizing for Effective Health Education

The effectiveness of health education increases with the amount of time spent on instruction. William Kane, a nationally recognized expert on adolescent health, recommends that middle grades students receive two to three hours a week of instruction in health education (Kane, 1993, p. 32). The national health education standards make a similar recommendation (American Cancer Society, 1997, p. 69). Unfortunately, numerous studies show that the amount of health education received by students is typically far less than the recommended levels and too little to effect much change in behavior (American Cancer Society, 1997, p. 69). Moreover, health education appears to be more effective when it is taught as a separate discipline rather than having health topics covered in the context of other subject areas (Kane, 1993, p. 32; Lohrmann & Wooley, 1998, p. 54). The instruction and support services students receive in earlier years heavily influence the attitudes and beliefs that shape their health-related behavior in adolescence. Thus, the middle grades school health curriculum will be most effective when it is part of a comprehensive K–12 health education curriculum developed or adopted by the local school district (Hamburg, 1997, p. 115; Kane, 1993, p. 28).

Finally, implementing a health education curriculum requires great sensitivity to the concerns of parents and other community members. Perhaps even more than with other aspects of the middle grades curriculum, educators will need to explain clearly the purposes and goals of health education and its importance in the lives of developing adolescents. As with health services, discussed below, educators will need to listen carefully to and work closely with members of the community to ensure that health education is provided to students in a manner that respects community and cultural values.

HEALTH SERVICES

Given the basic public health standards in the United States, the vast majority of 10- to 15-year-olds do not have debilitating diseases or chronic conditions that would affect their ability to learn. Yet what millions of American young adolescents need but do not have is ready access to preventive health and mental health services or to services for acute or sporadic health-related problems that, if left untreated, could severely affect their success in school and in their adult lives.

Access to appropriate health care services is the major problem in adolescent health (Dryfoos, 1993, p. 84; Hamburg, 1997, p. 108; Hurrelmann & Klocke, 1997, p. 102). Adolescents' concerns about confidentiality; their discomfort over discussing personal, medical, or psychological problems; and their lack of independent transportation often discourage them from seeking care. Transportation and insurance problems are, of course, even more of a barrier for young people from poor families and rural communities. Moreover, even middle-class communities have very few adolescent health specialists, who are trained to recognize and treat the problems of adolescents, especially the psychosocial problems such as depression or anxiety that are increasingly common in this age group (Dryfoos, 1993, p. 84; Dryfoos, 1995, p. 149; Hurrelmann & Klocke, 1997, p. 102; Millstein & Litt, 1990, p. 446).

The cost of health care contributes greatly to its inaccessibility for young adolescents. Many adolescents are not covered by private health insurance, and many adolescents in low-income families are not enrolled in the Medicaid system (Dryfoos, 1993, p. 84; 1995, p. 149). Overall, according to Millstein and Litt (1990, p. 446),

> Although adolescents experience a greater number of acute conditions than do adults, their utilization of private physician services is lower than for any other age group. Given their level of need, adolescents also underutilize other health care systems. Differences in utilization patterns as a function of sociodemographic factors point to pockets of underserved adolescents, with more unmet needs among younger adolescents, minority group members, and those living in poverty.

The largest category of unmet needs is mental health. Mild to severe mental health problems, particularly depression, are widespread among young adolescents, yet adolescents often do not receive the services they need. About one in five adolescents aged 10–18 suffers from a diagnosable mental disorder (Jackson, 1997, p. 23). Suicide is now a major cause of death among adolescents: in 1997 16.3 percent of ninth-grade students reported having made a suicide plan within the previous year and 10.5 percent reported actually attempting to kill themselves (Kann et al., 1998, Table 10).

Given the link between the health of young adolescents and their success in school, and given the glaring lack of access to health services faced by many young adolescents, middle grades schools must accept significant responsibility to ensure that health services are accessible to students. How schools ensure such access will vary from school to school, or at least from school district to school district, depending on students' needs, the mix of available health-related resources, and community values regarding the appropriate way to meet the needs of young adolescents. What no middle grades school can afford to do, however, is to turn a blind eye toward young adolescents' need for health services and hope that no children fall through the cracks, because inevitably some will.

Developing a Health Services Plan

The student support team described earlier in this chapter in relation to students' behavioral problems has a role to play here, too. The team can systematically coordinate the school's response to students' needs for health services, follow up with students and parents to see that services were utilized, and monitor results. At times, the support team may need to intervene on behalf of students in difficult situations involving abuse, neglect, or child endangerment, or to ensure that students have adequate food and housing.

An equally important role for the student support team is to serve as the core of an inquiry or planning committee within the school's governance structure. In this capacity, the support team becomes a health planning committee, with the addition of parents and community providers of health services. The health planning committee is responsible for identifying health-related challenges affecting all or a broad range of students in the school; recommending schoolwide policies and programs that generally enhance the quality of the school as a learning environment; and enabling students to seek out and utilize health and counseling services on their own before problems become crises.

A health planning committee's initial task is to conduct a thorough assessment of student health needs, which should be periodically updated to monitor trends and ensure its accuracy. Besides identifying health needs, this assessment should address the kinds of health-related services the community would and would not like offered. (To develop a comprehensive health survey, schools may wish to adapt one of several existing surveys that can be accessed through George Washington University's "Making The Grade" website at http://www.gwu.edu/~mtg.) Schools can also collect community public health data and information from informal conversations with parents and community members to develop a broad picture of the community's health needs.

The health planning committee will also need to assess existing community health resources that could be linked to the school. Committee members can list all the different agencies that provide (or are believed to provide) health-related services to adolescents. The committee should then systematically contact all these organizations to find out whether they serve young adolescents, what kinds of services they provide, their capacity and willingness to provide services to additional numbers of adolescents, hours of operation, fees and funding sources, and whatever other information is needed to develop a comprehensive community profile of health resources. Universities are often excellent potential resources, as they may be able to provide high-quality health-related personnel in need of training placements.

By comparing students' health needs with available health resources, the planning committee can draft short- and long-range plans for ensuring student access to health services. These plans must consider potential sources of funding for services. The committee's plans should be discussed within the school, like the work of any other school governance committee. However, given both the involvement of community organizations in developing the health plan and the need for sensitivity to community values, the committee's draft plan should also be discussed at community forums such as local school board meetings or meetings of parents and community members at the school. At the end of the process, a strategic plan should be in place that

- Outlines goals to address student health needs
- Identifies the responsibilities of school personnel and external agencies for meeting the goals
- Delineates a process for continually monitoring the effect on students' access to and use of high-quality health services

- Establishes a method for assessing the impact of services on students' health

School-Based and School-Linked Services

To create access to health services, a school community will need to decide whether such services are best provided by referring students and families to health organizations scattered within the community or by centralizing service delivery through the establishment of a school-based or school-linked health center. School-based health centers or clinics are located on school grounds, while school-linked centers are located off school grounds and serve the school and perhaps other area schools.

Students are more likely to use services regularly if they are centrally located in or near the school. With school-based or school-linked health centers, service providers can integrate services more effectively, consult with teachers and other school officials for help in identifying and addressing students' problems, maintain records of students' use of services more easily, and effectively coordinate follow-up care. Moreover, once a student has received permission from a parent or guardian to enroll at a school-based or school-linked clinic, he or she can use its services confidentially, which may increase the likelihood that services will be used when needed. There are potential disadvantages to developing school-based or school-linked centers: acquiring an appropriate facility to house the center, developing and coordinating adequate funding mechanisms to support the clinic and to ensure the quality of services, and creating a viable system of service integration between providers who may have had little previous contact with each other.

As of 1996, the United States had 1,040 school-based or school-linked health centers. Surveys of these centers show that 42 percent serve middle grades students, although typically only about half the centers provide complete data (Fothergill, 1998). When school-based health centers are available, students make good use of them. Using information on center enrollment and rates of use, Dryfoos (1995, pp. 162–163) writes, "In most schools, about 70% of the students register for the clinic (to register means to receive written parental consent to visit the clinic if necessary). Clinic users are more likely to be female, African-American, or Hispanic, and disadvantaged. Many of the clinic users have no other source of routine medical care and no health insurance."

With regard to the kinds of services typically provided, Dryfoos (1995, pp. 154–155) adds,

> In schools with school-based health clinics, the most heavily utilized services are for acute illnesses and injuries, mental health counseling, and physical examinations and screenings. However, clinics may also provide medical and therapeutic services such as: family planning; treatment for sexually transmitted diseases; dental care; counseling regarding nutrition, substance abuse, and chronic disease management; and immunizations. A survey of school-based and school-linked health centers showed that 70%

offer on-site individual counseling, over 30% provide group counseling, and more than half offer health information and prevention education within the classroom.

Although students may come in reporting other complaints, in some clinics 30–40 percent of the primary diagnoses are mental health related (Dryfoos, 1993, pp. 88–89).

Students, parents, teachers, and school personnel generally report a high level of satisfaction with school-based clinics and health centers. They appreciate their accessibility, convenience, and caring attitudes. Students particularly value confidentiality. A survey of state health officials conducted by the Office of the Inspector General reports "overwhelming" agreement that school-based health centers improved access to health care by going "to where the kids are" (Dryfoos, 1995, p. 163).

A number of key lessons have emerged from schools that have developed successful school-based or school-linked centers. To plan a center, a school can create an ad hoc subcommittee of the standing student support team. This center planning committee should include broad representation from community and health-related organizations, including individuals or groups that have expressed concerns about establishing a health center (see Box 8.3). Welcoming potential critics during the planning stages should make it possible to resolve differences amicably while still ensuring that students have access to services. Meetings of the health center planning committee should be open to anyone wishing to observe, and representatives of local media organizations should be invited to attend meetings, or to be on the committee itself, so that the group's deliberations and plans can be accurately reported to the public. The health center committee's plan should carefully consider the community's and the school's needs for health services, as well as local politics that may affect support for the center. In Bridgeport, Connecticut, for example, Dunbar Middle School opted to locate its health clinic in a separate facility near the school and to make services available to all families in the community, not just Dunbar families. The clinic is open during nonschool hours, allowing working parents to use its services for their children and themselves. As a community facility, the clinic receives funds from the city of Bridgeport to support its operation, giving it a sounder financial base than school district funding.

Once a health center is up and running, a school should require students to provide written permission from parents or legal guardians to access services. Successful centers also need computerized information management systems to maintain and update student health records, to facilitate billing (if applicable), and to maintain information on center usage for future planning and provide evidence that the center is meeting students' needs.

School health centers are intended to ensure student access to health services, but an important by-product is their effect on school–community relations. School-based and school-linked centers are tangible evidence of a school's concern for the total well-being of its students and its commitment to their intellectual and personal development.

Box 8.3   Picacho Middle School—A Healthy Approach to School-Based Clinics

It is likely that little can be known about opening a school-based health clinic that the people at Picacho Middle School haven't learned in the boot camp of experience. Six years ago, administrators, parents, and teachers at the Las Cruces, New Mexico, school spent the greater part of nine months opening such a clinic, while convincing a conservative community that condoms would not become a required school supply as a result. Thanks to an innovative planning process that sought to include, rather than defeat, the clinic's critics, Picacho's efforts were rewarded. In recent years, the school has not only housed a free physician-staffed clinic, but has transformed the way the school community views health—down to which side dish appears on the cafeteria lunch plate.

As fate would have it, however, just as administrators were sure they had cracked the code behind merging health and educational services on campus, sweeping health care reforms suddenly changed the combination. A recent overhaul of Medicaid procedures in New Mexico has, as an indirect result, severed Picacho's ties with physicians. The health clinic, which once bustled with two dozen patients a week, now looks the same as it did six years ago—like an ordinary nurse's office.

It's all familiar territory for Las Cruces Assistant Superintendent Erlinda Martinez. As Picacho's principal in 1993, Martinez was the one who first saw a need for extensive health services at the school. Today, she is confident that those services will be restored, provided the community follows the same process that opened the clinic in the first place. The only thing that has changed, she said, is the nature of the opposition. What once was a divisive fight over reproductive health issues has shifted to a battle to stay ahead of a changing health care environment. "I'd much rather be where we are now, than where we first started," she said.

Martinez recalls some of the circumstances that first inspired her and other school officials to first push for a clinic. Located less than an hour from Mexico, Picacho has a student body where 60 percent of students participate in the federal lunch program and more than 15 percent are immigrant children. Limited access to health care would manifest itself almost daily, Martinez said. One student, she recalls, reported to school on Monday complaining of pain that turned out to be due to a broken arm that had gone untreated over the weekend.

Teacher Dorothy Weiser remembers how faculty members first gathered to discuss the possibility of using available grant money to offer health services at the school. From the start, she said, Martinez had insisted that the planning process involve as many members of the community as possible. "We wanted to make sure that we represented the wishes of our clientele," Weiser said. An 18-member advisory group—which included parents, physicians, teachers, business leaders, and school staff—soon confirmed what faculty had suspected about the clinic. It would not have the backing of the community if it even offered a hint of reproductive health services. Immediately, the prospect of offering such services was off the table. But that didn't

BOX 8.3 CONTINUED

mean the clinic was free and clear of the issue. In fact, it would be months before most of the community was convinced that the clinic wasn't a wedge that would lead to wide-scale condom distribution. "At that time, whenever you said health clinic, that was synonymous with reproductive health," Weiser said.

The key to changing that mentality, officials said, was the advisory committee. And no one proved a more valuable member than parent and fundamentalist pastor Jim Dixon. Weiser said Dixon not only made sure that family planning was not a part of the clinic, but worked to make sure the community believed him. "He got to be a real convert of the clinic, and he had a lot of credibility with the community," she said. Martinez recalls how members of the planning committee would travel en masse to speak to conservative and religious groups to defend the clinic. Weiser's husband, a veteran journalist, was also brought on board to handle media relations. Weiser said having even an informal public relations representative required the group to be more focused. As a result, she said, the clinic's advocates were speaking with one voice to the school board, the media, and the community. Martinez said the process worked because it was so open that even the most fervent opponent would be unable to unearth an ulterior motive. "We didn't want anyone to think we were using the clinic to bring condoms in the back door of the school," she said.

In 1994, the clinic opened, thanks to funding from private grants and the state department of health. A nurse-practitioner saw patients the first year, with her services paid directly from the grant money. In subsequent years, two doctors were brought in on contract to work a half day each week. A nonprofit group was set up in Las Cruces to handle the financial end of the clinic and help support two other school clinics that opened after Picacho. Doctors were paid both from Medicaid and the state's Healthier Kids Fund, designed to cover New Mexico's uninsured children.

Martha Riemenschneider, Picacho's current nurse, recalls how, at its peak, the clinic buzzed. Services ranged from immunizations to the diagnosis and treatment of sprains, broken bones, ear infections, and the flu. Referrals were also made to dental and mental health services, with occasional visits by therapists. "For many of these immigrant families, this was the only health care they could find," Riemenschneider said. "The fear of deportation would keep many out of a hospital, but for some reason they felt they could trust a school."

Kathy Vigil, the school's current principal, said the clinic helped reduce absenteeism. Faculty members point to several instances where a student's perfor-mance improved as a result of better health. Riemenschneider said one boy was missing two or three days of school a week because of depression, but after referral to therapy "he missed only one day a month and his grades doubled." But for Vigil, perhaps the clinic's greatest dividend was that it brought in parents who might otherwise never set foot in the school. "The best thing that came out of it was the parent contact and the fact that the community was able to look at the issues facing the whole child for the first time," she said.

With parental support for the on-campus health clinic established, Weiser said, the school was able to add a long list of additional services. Curriculum was overhauled to integrate wellness into most every subject area. More peer mediators have also been trained, giving several dozen students conflict resolution skills each semester. Other additions include parent health fairs, vaccination awareness programs, and even a change in the menus at the school cafeteria.

And, as was the case from the start, behind all the added services is a steering committee comprised of parents and faculty. The "Wellness Team" meets regularly to discuss which services are needed and to act as a liaison to the community in health issues.

But with the recent closing of the health clinic, Berger said, the Wellness Team has faced a challenge it cannot overcome alone. The slow demise of the clinic started two years ago when New Mexico opted to place many Medicaid services under managed care. The clinic and the nonprofit organization that oversaw it were unable to bill Medicaid to pay doctor contracts for the 1998–1999 school year. And while the school attempted to bring in a health care provider who could bill Medicaid directly, the provider withdrew his application at the last minute, before the board had a chance to approve it. Riemenschneider was forced to close the clinic's doors last September.

And that's where Martinez has found herself coming full circle. Only now, it's not just one clinic she finds herself trying to open, but several across Las Cruces. But while her problem is a new one, she said, her solution has already been tested. Success, she said, will come by inviting all the city's health community to the table and using community support to forge the more lasting relationships with the health providers that are essential to the clinics' survival.

A principal whose school had had a poor relationship with its parents and students said of its health clinic, "The clinic has changed the relationship of parents to our school. Thirty of our kids got eyeglasses who wouldn't have. The parents now know we want to help their kids." Another school reported a decline in their previously high rate of student mobility after starting a school health clinic because parents did not want to move away from the supportive atmosphere and the health and social services provided through the school (Tyson, 1999, p. K6).

CONCLUSION

School-based and school-linked health centers and other approaches to providing students with access to health services, along with a school's efforts to provide high-quality health education and a healthy, supportive learning environment, together constitute a powerful, integrated approach to ensuring that students' health needs do not interfere with their ability to learn. These efforts build on a long-standing American tradition of using schools to maintain and improve students' health; they place the school in the center of a web of community supports. In the next chapter, we look further at how parents and community organizations can be effectively involved in the life of the school and how this involvement enhances young adolescents' learning and development.

9 Involving Parents and Communities

Photo by Doug Martin

IT WOULD BE AMAZING if a book like this one did *not* advocate parent and community involvement in the life of middle grades schools. Given our nation's tradition of local control of education and our deep-seated beliefs about parents' rights to control the way their children are raised, including choices about their education, parent and community involvement, at some level, is considered axiomatic. Moreover, as a "mom and apple pie" political issue, it would be damaging to the entire Turning Points model if *Turning Points 2000* did not strongly advocate parent and community participation in middle grades schools. Politics aside, as a way of supporting student learning and healthy development, does evidence demonstrate such involvement is worth the effort? If so, why, and are some forms of involvement more beneficial than others? These are the central issues that we explore in this chapter.

PARENT INVOLVEMENT TO IMPROVE STUDENT LEARNING

In fact, it is no mystery that parents' participation in the life of the school and in their children's schoolwork has a positive impact on student outcomes. Anne Henderson and Nancy Berla (1994, p. 1) summarized findings from 66 studies of the relationship between parent behaviors, including parent involvement in schools, and children's learning:

> The evidence is now beyond dispute. When schools work together with families to support learning, children tend to succeed not just in school, but throughout life. In fact, the most accurate predictor of a student's achievement in school is not income or social status, but the extent to which that student's family is able to:
>
> 1. create a home environment that encourages learning
> 2. express high (but not unrealistic) expectations for their children's achievement and future careers
> 3. become involved in their children's education at school and in the community
>
> Encouraging parental involvement is particularly important in facilitating a smooth transition to U.S. schools for recent immigrant children, bridging cultural gaps that may exist between the home and school lives of all language minority students, regardless of the length of time they have been in the U.S.
>
> When schools support families to develop these three conditions, children from low-income families and diverse cultural backgrounds approach the grades and test scores expected for middle-class children. They are also more likely to take advantage of a full range of educational opportunities after graduating from high school. . . . The studies have documented these benefits for students:
>
> - Higher grades and test scores
> - Better attendance and more homework done
> - Fewer placements in special education
> - More positive attitudes and behavior
> - Higher graduation rates
> - Greater enrollment in postsecondary education
>
> Schools and communities also profit. Schools that work well with families have:
>
> - improved teacher morale
> - higher ratings of teachers by parents
> - more support from families
> - higher student achievement
> - better reputations in their communities

[Reprinted with permission from Henderson & Berla, 1994, p. 1.]

More recently, Karen Mapp (1997, p. 1) concludes that "studies conducted over the last 30 years have identified a relationship between parent involvement and increased student achievement, enhanced self-esteem, improved behavior, and better student attendance."

The importance of parent involvement is also apparent when it is absent. In a long-term study of literacy achievement, for example, formal parent–school involvement was associated with good student performance among elementary school students. However, a dramatic drop in student gains occurred once the students entered junior high and high school. The drop appears to be directly related to the decline in family-related supports the researchers identified as key to achievement, including formal contact between home and school, out-of-school literacy experiences, and cooperative relationships between parents and teachers (Snow, Barnes, Chandler, Goodman, & Hemphill, 1991). Lawrence Steinberg and his colleagues (Steinberg, Brown, & Dornbusch, 1996) indicate that adolescents whose parents have "checked out" (that is, significantly reduced monitoring of their children's behavior and schoolwork) are less self-reliant, have lower self-esteem and social competence, and are less engaged and less successful in school.

Despite the evidence that parent involvement continues to be an important determinant of student outcomes throughout their children's academic careers, many parents do "check out" as their children make the transition from elementary to middle school. For example, in one study conducted by the U.S. Department of Education, the parents of 39 percent of children in grades 3–5 could be classified as "highly involved" in their children's school based on the number of activities they had participated in at the school. The parents of only 24 percent of children in grades 6–8 were classified as highly involved (U.S. Department of Health and Human Services, n.d., p. 410).

Similar trends are evident in other research on parents who are highly or moderately involved in their children's schools. About three-fourths of American parents of 8- to 10-year-old children report high or moderate involvement in their children's schools. By the time their children reach age 16, only 50 percent of parents report high or moderate involvement (Carnegie Council on Adolescent Development [CCAD], 1995, p. 65). Clearly, family–school relations tend to weaken as students move into the higher grades (Eccles & Harold, 1996; Epstein, 1996b).

Outreach to Parents

Will finger-wagging at middle grades parents stem the ebb tide of declining involvement in their children's education? Not in this world. Like it or not, if schools want to reap the benefits of parent support to improve student learning, they will need to understand why the relationship between families and schools often weakens as children grow older and take steps to prevent it from occurring.

Many parents genuinely believe that distancing themselves from their children's schoolwork is necessary to promote maturity, though they may not believe that they should distance themselves from the school in other ways. In a recent survey of American parents (Farkas, Johnson, & Duffett, 1999, p. 30), more than 90 percent of parents agreed with the statement that "as children get older, it's important that they increasingly handle schoolwork on their own." Over 60 percent of parents believe that "less parental involvement in later grades is natural and a sign that the student is learning to be independent and to manage school on their own, rather than a sign of trouble."

Many parents also feel intimidated as their children's course work becomes more challenging. Parents who are uncomfortable with their level of English proficiency, who themselves did poorly in school, or who dropped out may lack the confidence to participate in school life, or may harbor anger and resentment from their own sense of being shortchanged. These issues may be particularly close to the surface in low-income and racial and ethnic minority communities, given our nation's history of systematically excluding poor and minority people from the benefits of high-quality education.

Immigrant families or those who are not proficient in English may be similarly reluctant to approach their children's school because of difficulty in communicating and because the culture of the school is unknown to them. Some immigrant parents may not realize that parents are expected to have direct contact with their children's teachers and may see questioning teachers about their children's progress as a sign of disrespect. Others may assume that such involvement is unnecessary and that they can simply trust their children's school to provide a high-quality education to all children. While this separation of home and school responsibilities is common to some cultures, teachers unfamiliar with the culture of their students may incorrectly take this "hands-off" attitude of the parents to mean they are uninterested in their child's education. Still other immigrant parents may worry that becoming known in their children's school may negatively affect their own status in the country.

Finding the time for involvement in their children's school life is, of course, a major barrier for many parents, regardless of their background. This is especially true when school events or conferences are scheduled during the workday. When the school is far away from the family's home or parents' workplace or parents do not have access to a car or public transportation, transportation problems can make involvement even more difficult.

Schools and families may also have differences of opinion or misunderstandings about what constitutes desirable parent involvement in children's education. In one middle school, for example, a survey of parents and students indicated high levels of parental involvement and high parental expectations, whereas teachers taking the survey reported very low levels of both. When school officials looked into this apparent contradiction, they found that students and parents, on the one hand, and teachers, on the other, defined parent involvement differently. To teachers, parent involvement meant coming to school for meetings and conferences and volunteering to help out in the school. To parents and students, it meant encouraging students to study hard and to respect the teachers, or checking over report cards. The school found that the key to building a better relationship between the school and its parents was to hold meetings to discuss and clarify the expectations each held for the other.

To involve parents meaningfully in middle grades school life, and in their own children's education, requires constant outreach by the school. This in turn requires a school to regard parent involvement as a high priority and to develop structures and practices that will enable it to reach its goal.

A first step in improving parent–school relations is an honest self-appraisal of the school's openness to parents (Mapp, 1997). A school's self-appraisal should be done in much the same way as a school conducts inquiries into other critical aspects of its instructional program and its supports for healthy development (see Chapters 7 and 8).

Joyce Epstein (1997), one of the nation's leading experts on school–family relations and director of the Center on School, Family, and Community Partnerships at Johns Hopkins University, recommends, on the basis of more than two decades of research, that a school should establish an Action Team for School–Family–Community Partnerships. The action/partnerships team consists of 6–12 members, including parents, teachers, administrators, other school staff (such as nurses, counselors, parent liaisons, and community police officers assigned to the school), community representatives, and students. In the democratic governance system we described in Chapter 7, this action team might be a standing subcommittee of the school leadership team or the student support team (described in Chapter 8), or it might be a separate group, with the appropriate connections and lines of communication with other parts of the school's governance system.

Action/partnership teams are responsible for finding out through surveys and other means of communication where the school's strengths and weaknesses are with regard to parent–school communication and involvement and for developing a plan for strengthening each of six core elements of effective school–family–community relations:

- *Parenting*—helping all families establish home environments that support children's learning
- *Communicating*—designing and conducting effective forms of communication about school programs and children's progress
- *Volunteering*—recruiting and organizing help and support for school functions and activities
- *Learning at home*—providing information and ideas to families about how to help students at home with schoolwork and related activities
- *Decision making*—including parents in school decisions
- *Collaborating with the community*—identifying and integrating resources and services from the community to strengthen and support schools, students and their families.

To support schools' efforts to improve parent–school–community relations, the Center on School, Family, and Community Partnerships sponsors the National Network of Partnership Schools, a nationwide alliance of schools, local school districts, and state education agencies (Epstein, Coates, Salinas, Sanders, & Simon, 1997; see also the network's website, http://www.csos.jhu.edu/p2000).

Schools must be both persistent and flexible in their approach to increasing parent involvement. It may be necessary to schedule parent meetings or workshops, school orientations, and other events in locations that are less intimidating and more accessible to parents, such as churches or community centers. It may also be necessary to prepare parent materials in several languages or to have translators present at parent meetings.

One principal reported that through various types of involvement strategies such as those described later in this chapter, the school was able to increase parent involvement significantly. However, a small group remained of extremely disengaged parents of students who were performing very poorly. In a last-ditch effort to try to reach these parents, the principal wrote on their children's report cards, "These grades are totally unacceptable. The team teachers have been contacting you, and we really need to see you. Please call me on my private line." He included his private phone number. About 40 percent of the parents responded. The principal noted, "Anytime you personalize the process, you're going to get another hit. . . . The key, and several parents mentioned it to me, is the private line. . . ."

As noted in Chapter 6, one reason for reorganizing traditional junior highs into team-based middle grades schools is to enable teachers to improve parent communication. In Chapter 6, we noted that some middle grades teams have found it useful to designate one teacher as the parent liaison. When a team of teachers is responsible for the same relatively small number of students, however, the team members can divide up the work of communicating with those students' families, enabling each teacher to get to know a group of families well and to be in regular contact with them. Either arrangement lessens the strain and confusion for parents as they attempt to keep in regular contact with their child's teachers. Research in Michigan middle schools (Mertens et al., 1998, p. 59) has shown that schools that are teaming "are able to capitalize on their coordinated efforts to divide up the contacts with parents among all teacher members of the team. So, for example, if a team has 125 students and 5 teachers, each teacher may be assigned 25 students for parent contact purposes. If this school were not teaming, one teacher may have been responsible for the parent contacts for all 125 students." The Michigan middle grades schools that were not teaming reported the least contact with parents.

Contact with parents should start before the school year begins, if possible. Conference time should produce no surprises: conversations and communications about children's performance should be ongoing throughout the year, and formal conferences should allow students to share with their teachers and parents the results of their learning and of their analysis of their own strengths and needs for improvement (Cromwell, 1999; Hackmann, 1996; Hayden, 1998; Le Countryman & Schroeder, 1996; Santa, 1995). (See Box 9.1 for an account of the successful use of student-led conferences at a California middle school.)

Finally, to reach out to families facing cultural or language barriers between home and school, some schools have found that paraprofessionals, after-

Box 9.1   Student-Led Conferences at Southridge Middle School

When Kelli Panattoni, age 14, was in elementary school, she used to stand in the hallway wondering what went on behind the closed doors of a parent–teacher conference. "It was kind of nerve-racking because you don't know what's being said," she said. When Panattoni moved on to middle school, she found that the teachers there disliked the conferences as much as she did. Over the past seven years, Southridge Middle School in Fontana, California, has eliminated all traditional parent–teacher conferences, replacing them with conferences that are planned and conducted almost entirely by students. Originally brought to Southridge by Kit Marshall of Action Learning, the conferences have been modified to meet the needs of Southridge students. In the process, school officials say, Southridge has not only reduced tensions that used to exist between parents and teachers but has increasingly seen students take command of the conferences and of their own education.

For Susan Miller, who has driven much of the school's switch to the new approach, a dislike of traditional parent–teacher conferences has roots in what she calls their unavoidably antagonistic setup. Teachers, she said, often wind up telling parents what to do, while parents often fight back by defending their children or blaming the teacher for problems. "It has a tendency to put things in terms of an 'us-versus-them' situation," she said. All the while, Miller added, the most important player in the process—the student—is locked out.

Of course, overturning years of tradition wasn't always easy. And Miller said the endeavor would have failed miserably had it not first been tried as a small pilot, and then gradually extended to the entire school. Former Southridge principal Gary Soto encouraged staff members to try them out. An ardent supporter of student-led conferences, Soto believes that they are "the most powerful delivery of information that schools have today." The current Southridge principal, David Linzey, concurs, saying he now has no doubts about the effectiveness of the approach. "They are the most powerful conferences I've seen. They simply blow traditional conferences out of the water." Miller, who now trains teachers from schools other than Southridge on student led-conferences, said she used to "tiptoe" around teachers who were hesitant about handing control of the conferences over to students. "Now I just tell them to let go," she said.

Letting go at Southridge has also meant creating a lot of work. And Miller doesn't pretend that student-led conferences aren't more difficult in many respects. For starters, preparing for the conferences is a task that, in itself, requires several hours of class time and one-on-one work with students. Overall, teachers feel that the time spent is well worth it, since the preparation tends to make students more accountable, better organized and more likely to communicate with their parents. Before each twice-yearly conference, students at Southridge produce portfolios that contain not only samples of their work and test scores but essays on such things as

BOX 9.1 CONTINUED

citizenship, goals, and areas in which the student sees need for improvement. In addition, students handle scheduling and even produce and take home invitations to the conference. Finally, teachers and students work together to role-play, so students can practice ways of presenting their work to their parents. Panattoni recalls how nervous she was as a sixth grader facing the prospect of taking over the role once occupied by her teacher. "I was afraid because it felt a little uncomfortable," she said.

But Panattoni's mother, Sheila, said her daughter's fear was apparently shed easily when she launched into the conference. An hour later, Kelli was still presenting her portfolio to her mother. Four years later, Sheila Panattoni—who also works as a teachers aide at Southridge—has been entirely won over by the conferences. "I like the fact that the student has to take ownership of their education," she said. As a parent, Panattoni has had more experience with the conferences than most others at Southridge. Her son Chad was among the first students to participate in the pilot program six years ago. She credits the conferences with helping to transform her shy son's attitudes about education and his own role at school. "It taught my son, who used to think that teachers gave him grades, to understand that he earns grades," she said. As her son moved into the seventh and eighth grades, Panattoni said, he took more and more control of the conferences. "Initially he didn't want anyone but me to hear his presentation, but by the eighth grade he didn't care who heard him," she said.

Miller said the student-led conferences work if all involved understand their roles. In a typical conference session, four groups of parents and students will be in the room at the same time. From the start, it's clear that students have the floor as parents are asked to keep all their questions until the end. As students present their portfolios, teachers roam from table to table to answer questions and listen in. Miller said the process saves time, but more important, makes it clear that students—and not teachers—control the information. The teachers, Miller said, serve more as facilitators of the discussion and find themselves on the same team as the parent.

Miller said the dividends of the approach are often noted by the students themselves. She recalls how one student couldn't get over the fact that his father would turn off his pager and cellular phone to listen to him. Parents, meanwhile, often end the conference by committing themselves to increase communication with their children. "I've heard parents say over and over again that 'We need to talk like this more,'" Miller said. Linzey said the conferences often mark the first time a student has had an extended conversation about school with a parent. "Some of them haven't spoken to their parents about academics ever," he said.

However, even Miller once doubted that the conferences could run as smoothly as they have. The most common concern among Southridge teachers was that the student-led events would be merely a masquerade of a true conference, with parents demanding a separate private meeting with teachers to discuss "the real situation." But that hasn't happened as often as some would have expected. Miller said she's only been approached a handful of times by skeptical parents after a conference. More times than not, she said, she simply assures parents as they are leaving the conference that there is nothing more for them to know. There are exceptions, however, as teachers and parents continue to meet in private to discuss serious behavioral problems, but for the most part students are responsible for articulating what goes on in the classroom.

Miller said she also wondered how low-performing students might fare in the conferences. Over time, she said teachers have come to recognize that the conference benefits struggling students the most. "For the high-performing students these conferences are more of a show, but the low-performing students generally have a much more powerful conference," she said. Carole Lee, department chair of special education at Southridge, said the conferences are especially valuable to underachieving students because they give these students a chance for self-evaluation. "It's not a stress-inducing thing for them," she noted. Miller said that teachers help students prepare their portfolios but will not doctor them to make things seem rosier than they are. "It's important for parents to know how things really stand," she said.

Teachers say Southridge's success with the conferences is partially due to their willingness to adapt the format over time. Initially, portfolios were focused more on essays and goals. But as the Fontana district has demanded greater accountability, standardized test scores as well as results from reading and math assessments have found their way in the portfolios as well. The shift toward standards has meant that students are even more keenly aware of where they stand academically. That often leads to a desire on the part of students to set goals to increase their proficiency. "My children would see the reading score and work at improving it by the next conference," Panattoni said. The consensus among the staff is that classroom instruction has improved because teachers are constantly thinking about the contents of the portfolios. Rather than focusing on "drill-and-kill" exercises, teachers often shift to performance-based exercises that can be measured and included in portfolios.

Miller said that schools will fail with student-led conferences if they see them solely as a way of avoiding the ugly confrontations they've come to hate in traditional conferences. In fact, she added, focusing on the conference itself isn't the point. The approach is working at Southridge, she said, because it has been accompanied by a sweeping new philosophy of encouraging students to navigate their own learning. And that happens all year, as students take more pride in their work and set goals because they have a clearer picture of what the process is all about. For that to happen, she said, teachers at a school have to have the courage simply to step aside and remember who is most important. The school must be focused on the needs of the students.

school program group leaders, a parent outreach worker, or mentors from programs like Big Brother/Big Sister can be helpful in enabling parents and teachers to connect. These individuals, whose backgrounds are often similar to those of the student and who may even live in the immediate community, yet who also "speak the language" of the school and are familiar with its workings, can serve as a bridge between parents and teachers.

Key Aspects of Effective Parent–School Relations

The relationship between schools and parents is multifaceted. Scholars and practitioners have organized efforts to link home and school in a number of ways (for example, Epstein's six core elements noted above). Our approach focuses on four key areas where collaboration between parents and school staff members is essential: establishing continuity and communication between home and school; monitoring students' schoolwork and their school "careers"; creating opportunities outside the school for safe, engaging exploration; and improving the school through on-site parental involvement.

Establishing Continuity Between Home and School. Cultural, linguistic, and socioeconomic differences between school staff members and families of middle grades students can cause confusion among young adolescents that is detrimental to their academic achievement. If they perceive different expectations for their schoolwork between home and school, or if they perceive a lack of respect between the two, the result is a stressful sense of divided loyalty. The message that schoolwork and academic achievement are important, whether coming from school or home, becomes muddled.

In contrast, if students do not perceive home and school as being in competition, but rather as being mutually reinforcing, then the effect of each is multiplied. For example, the role that a Hispanic child may play at home, where often the focus is on the collective good of the family, can stand in stark contrast to the highly defined sense of individualism and personal accomplishment that is the focus in many U.S. classrooms. However, by having a family member or mentor from the same background involved in their schooling, language minority students also see that participating and succeeding in a primarily "Anglo" school does not mean they are forsaking their own culture. Partnership between home and school helps to create complementary—rather than competing—worlds for language minority students. James Comer was one of the first to identify the malign psychological effects of fractured home–school relations. Summarizing his work in this area, Henderson and Berla wrote: "If children know that their parents and teachers understand and respect each other, that they share similar expectations and stay in touch, children feel comfortable with who they are and can more easily reconcile their experiences at home and school" (Henderson & Berla, 1994, p. 11).

For many parents, the first and only contact they have with their child's school occurs when their child is having an academic or behavioral problem. Thus the school–home relationship is instantly adversarial. Starting off the year with positive communication and following up with "good news" throughout the year makes parents more receptive and cooperative if teachers must report some "bad news." If a student is having significant difficulty, even celebrating a single day's improvement can build trust with the child and his or her parents.

The efforts that schools make to communicate with parents—surveys, telephone calls, written messages, meetings—and their efforts to bring parents fully into the life of the school through various opportunities for direct involvement should extend as much as possible to the school community at large. The goal is to create within the community a kind of "force field" of support and high expectations for all young adolescents that they simply cannot ignore.

Monitoring Students' Work. One of the primary ways in which parents make the importance of school clear to middle grades students is by continuously monitoring their schoolwork and working with them when appropriate. A key focus here is students' homework, but as with much else about middle grades education, it is not a simple issue.

Surprisingly, in 1996, almost one-fourth of eighth-grade students reported receiving no daily homework, a figure virtually unchanged since 1984. Thirty-six percent reported spending less than an hour a day on homework, identical to the 1984 statistic. Slightly more students reported spending more than two hours a day on homework in 1996 than in 1984, but in both years the number was under 10 percent. Research provides no evidence that schools serving high concentrations of low-income students tend to assign less homework than schools in more affluent areas (Snyder & Wirt, 1998, indicator 37).

If not homework, what are students doing after school? Apparently they are watching a great deal of television. Eleven- to twelve-year-olds spend more time watching television than any other group of children aged 3 to 17, with 11- to 12-year-old boys watching the most—an average of 26 hours a week (Miller, 1998, pp. 19–21). Another study found that nearly 20 percent of middle grades students spent four hours or more a day watching television or playing video games; 43 percent reported spending only 30 minutes to an hour a day on homework (Center for Prevention Research & Development, 1997).

Middle grades schools need to think seriously about whether it is really possible to enable all students to reach high academic standards if so little of students' after-school time is being used to support classroom learning. We recognize that some parents view homework as a burden because getting adolescents to complete the work leads to almost nightly battles. Other parents question the amount of homework their children receive, the usefulness of assignments, and the fact that it is sometimes simply too hard for students to complete on their own. One in five parents indicate that they have done their children's homework because it was too difficult for them or the child was too tired (Farkas, Johnson, & Duffett, 1999).

These problems notwithstanding, it seems that middle grades schools would be well advised to work on improving the quality of homework assignments rather than de-emphasizing this important opportunity to help students learn. As one veteran middle grades principal noted, homework should never be a time when new material is introduced, with parents expected to teach it, but it is a golden opportunity to reinforce and extend classroom learning, and to draw parents and other adults into students' academic life.

Janet Alleman and Jere Brophy (1996) recommend reconceptualizing homework so that it more directly supports classroom learning. They offer the following guidelines:

- Assign students homework activities that will help them learn powerful curriculum ideas.
- Give homework assignments that are at the appropriate level of difficulty for each individual so that students will be challenged without being confused or frustrated. In contrast to this suggestion, Rogers (1992) found that more than 50 percent of classroom teachers give every student the same homework assignment.
- Provide students with the information and resources to do their homework successfully.
- Determine whether the benefit of the homework justifies the time and effort required of students. The U.S. Department of Education recommends 20–40 minutes of homework each school day for fourth to sixth graders and up to two hours each school day for seventh through ninth graders (Paulu, n.d.).

In a team structure like the one we advocate (see Chapter 6), teachers on a team will communicate with each other about homework expectations, specific assignments, and deadlines; they should remember that teachers often underestimate the amount of time homework assignments will require. Finally, research has found that "spending more time on homework does not automatically raise achievement. For elementary and junior high school students especially, long assignments . . . do not raise achievement" (Black, 1996, p. 50).

The Teachers Involve Parents in Schoolwork (TIPS) program, developed by researchers at the Center on School, Family, and Community Partnerships at Johns Hopkins University, is a good model for homework. It both reinforces learning and supports high-quality parent–child–teacher interaction and communication around children's learning. Center director Joyce Epstein (n.d.) writes,

> TIPS activities (which supplement the curriculum) are homework assignments that require students to talk to someone at home about something interesting that they are learning in class. . . . TIPS enables all families to become involved, not just those who already know how to discuss math, science, or other subjects. The homework is the students' responsibility; parents are not asked to "teach" subjects or skills. TIPS requires students to share their work, ideas, and progress with their families. It asks families to comment on their children's work and to request other information from teachers in a section for home-to-school communications.

Schools that have had particular success with TIPS activities have provided time and compensation to groups of teachers to work together in the summer to select and adapt TIPS activities in order to align them with the curricula they will be teaching.

Middle grades teachers can help parents monitor their children's work by helping parents keep track of their children's homework assignments, giving them specific advice about ways to help their children with homework, and listening to what they have to say about the quantity and quality of students' homework assignments. Monitoring students' schoolwork has other important dimensions as well.

By keeping track of their children's educational career, parents act as both coaches and advocates. As coaches, they offer homework assistance and encouragement and discuss with their children issues the children find important and interesting (Riera, 1995; Schurr, 1996). They also dream about the future with their children, helping them to set goals. Schiamberg and Chun (1986) found that parents' expectations have a powerful effect on students' educational and occupational attainment, more than any other single variable.

As advocates, parents also play a critical role. They try to ensure that their children enroll in challenging courses, help their children overcome any problems that arise, and get their children the extra help they may need to do well. By playing an active part in their children's educational career and thus demonstrating their deep concern for their children's success, parents become known in the school. Research strongly suggests that teachers are more responsive to families with whom they have regular contact and that they hold higher expectations of those families' children (Baker & Stevenson, 1986; Stevenson & Baker, 1987).

Out-of-school Learning. A third important area of school–home collaboration is in the creation of safe out-of-school opportunities for learning. By directing their children toward constructive learning activities outside the school, parents give them access to new areas of knowledge and to knowledgeable adults, such as coaches, employers, youth workers, and other parents. Such activities permit adolescents to acquire and test new ideas, explore social issues, develop strategies for solving their own problems, and be exposed to a variety of role models that will help them shape their own identity. Research has shown that high-achieving students tend to spend at least 20 hours a week outside school engaged in constructive formal and informal learning. Parents play a critical role in brokering such opportunities and supervising their children's participation (Clark, 1990).

On-site Involvement. Finally, parents can play a crucial role by assisting directly in a school's effort to improve. Noted throughout the book are instances when parents' input is deemed essential—the assessment of needs, the analysis of research on promising approaches, and the development and implementation of a plan of action. The role of parents in defining goals and supporting the school complements the school staff's role in developing the academic program. As noted in *Turning Points* (p. 67), "Parents involved in planning the work of the school feel powerful, develop confidence, and are more likely to attend school activities, which signals the importance of school to their young adolescents. Parents on school-wide governance committees who work effectively and cooperatively with school staff become models of such behavior for their young adolescents and other students."

Parent volunteers can also provide vitally important support in middle grades schools. Joyce Epstein describes two examples that illustrate parents' contribution. One school had significant problems with children walking out of class and roaming the halls. Parents were asked by the principal and the parent liaison to volunteer to monitor the halls, and more than 25 signed up. The parent liaison said, "When the kids found out that their parents were coming to school volunteering, there was a big turnaround. And it wasn't just fear; some of the students were proud that their parents were part of the school" (Sanders & Epstein, 1998, p. 9). Another school had problems with rowdiness and bullying at the bus stops. After parents and school staff met to discuss the problem and possible solutions, a group of parents agreed to monitor the bus stops in the morning until the children boarded the bus (Sanders & Epstein, 1998, p. 10).

Parent volunteers may play many roles:

- Enriching students' classroom instruction by sharing their relevant experiences or skills with the class
- Sharing their career experiences in advisory or other settings where career exploration and planning are being discussed
- Chaperoning field trips
- Tutoring students
- Serving as translators for meetings or conferences
- Monitoring attendance and phoning families of absent students
- Doing outreach to hard-to-reach parents
- Planning and leading parent education sessions
- Working on "parent patrols" in or around the school for safety
- Organizing community service or school fund-raising activities such as fairs, clothing drives, and sales
- Enriching out-of-school learning opportunities for students by organizing or participating in clubs
- Serving in advisory or decision-making capacities
- Providing child care during school events or conferences
- Helping in the school office or library

Parent volunteers from language-minority groups may also serve as community recruiters for other parents of similar background. Emphasis should be placed on the value of all parents' contributions, regardless of their English-speaking abilities. Mapp (1997) draws some lessons from research on ways to encourage parents to become volunteers:

- Be specific in defining what you want parents to do.
- Define helpful volunteer activities that can be done both at home or outside school and in school.

- Follow up immediately with parents who indicate a willingness to help.
- Reach out to new parents through home visits, breakfasts, and evening gatherings where the parent coordinator or liaison can discuss volunteering and the school's need for help and can show parents that they can be of help in many ways, even when the parents themselves may be initially unaware of how they might contribute.
- Honor and recognize every voluntary contribution of time or materials through thank-you notes and regular celebrations to honor volunteers.
- Provide a comfortable place for volunteers to meet and work together, such as a parent center or lounge.
- Provide any training necessary to volunteers, such as in how to tutor effectively.

Working together, parents and schools can strengthen the ties between home and school and, in doing so, can promote higher academic achievement for every student.

LINKING ADOLESCENT LEARNING TO COMMUNITY RESOURCES

It doesn't take a rocket scientist to realize that the middle grades school experience is only one of a myriad of influences on the trajectory of an adolescent's development. What happens to young people within their families, neighborhoods, peer groups, religious institutions, out-of-school programs, and a wide range of other formal and informal relationships and settings can easily have as much or more impact on how young people "turn out" as the middle grades school. Many middle grades schools acknowledge these other influences and "do the best we can while we have them," assuming that relatively little can or should be done to link what happens inside the school with what happens outside. Yet many others realize that to achieve their goals for students, they simply cannot get there from here without forging strong relationships with community partners.

For some schools, the need to reach out to community agencies for help in providing services to young people and their families is painfully obvious. Educators in schools serving high concentrations of low-income families are faced daily with the barriers to teaching and learning caused by their students' poor nutrition, health problems, emotional distress, and other stresses linked to poverty and poor access to services. These problems become less prevalent in middle- and upper-income communities, but even in the most affluent communities, coordinating access through the school to outside support for students in times of extraordinary stress or crisis can be extremely important in preventing a negative impact on their learning and healthy development.

For all middle grades schools, including those serving predominantly low-income families, the surrounding community is an enormous potential resource for educating young adolescents. We strongly agree with Anne Lewis and Anne Henderson (1998, p. 45) when they write that middle grades school leaders should think of "the entire community as an extension of the classroom, filled with skilled and knowledgeable residents with teaching and learning agendas and capacities of their own." What middle grades schools need are strategies for systematically "mining" this resource, while simultaneously helping to build the capacity of the community itself to support its children and families.

Partnerships with community organizations also provide middle grades schools with valuable opportunities to enhance and extend classroom learning in the out-of-school hours, especially since so many young people have significant discretionary time but little to do with it. Children spend only about 25 percent of their waking hours in school, and "[e]ach school day, America's 19 million young adolescents decide how they will spend at least 5 of their waking hours when they are not in school" (CCAD, 1995, p. 105).

Some adolescents, particularly in affluent communities, have a wide range of enriching activities to engage in during the nonschool hours. Still, gaining access to constructive, positive activities during the "witching hours" of 3:00–8:00 p.m. is a very real problem for many kids, not only the poorest, though they may have the greatest need. Parents of children in all socioeconomic brackets often are not home during those after-school hours to provide transportation or supervise activities at home. Overall, research shows that 40 percent of adolescents' discretionary time is spent socializing, 20 percent watching television, and very little on reading, arts involvement, sports, or hobbies (Zill, Nord, & Loomis, 1995). Zill et al. (1995, pp. 24–25) conclude that "American adolescents are spending very little time on activities that strengthen their ties to society or provide them with the necessary skills to succeed in school or in the labor force."

Besides providing connections to needed services and learning opportunities for young adolescents, strong ties with local community organizations help build essential political support and goodwill toward the school as it continuously seeks to improve itself. School improvement often requires changing time-honored practices within a school, and change, no matter how potentially beneficial to students, will almost always be met with resistance both within and outside the school. It is crucial, therefore, to create a constituency of supporters among key community leaders and organizations that are knowledgeable about the school's goals, have had an opportunity to contribute to them through open, candid discussions with school officials, and are fully "on board" and ready to contribute whatever additional resources they can to help achieve common objectives. One observer (Partee, 1996, pp. 38–39) writes:

> Getting to a common understanding about the available resources from the combined sources of school, home, and community and their most successful use for the benefit of the young adolescent requires ample give and take plus a willingness to openly communicate motives, strategies, and barriers. This is a level of frank conversation that rarely exists in public dialogue, but that is especially necessary in successful school reform. . . . It is essential that reform is grounded in a common knowledge of what is being done and why among all stakeholders.

Some of the paths that schools can follow to establish solid ties to their communities are described in the following pages. At the outset, it is important to note that, as with virtually all aspects of middle grades reform, establishing links to community organizations requires time and opportunities for educators to be trained in the new skills needed to create effective partnerships. Schools can do a great deal on their own to reach out to their communities, but local school districts have a responsibility to assist them in doing so, especially by providing teachers and administrators with opportunities to learn from the successes and failures of others.

Integrating the Community Within the Curriculum

The notion of linking schools to their communities almost inevitably conjures up an image of activities that may support, but are not truly a part of, the core instructional program. In contrast to this image, we advocate integrating community-based learning opportunities firmly within the curriculum.

Service Learning. Service learning is "curriculum-based community service that integrates classroom instruction with community service activities" (National Center for Education Statistics, 1999, p. 3). In *Turning Points*, the Task Force on Education of Young Adolescents wrote (p. 45), "Early adolescence offers a superb opportunity to learn values, skills, and a sense of social responsibility important for citizenship in the United States. Every middle grades school should include youth service—supervised activity helping others in the community or in school—in its core instructional program."

Currently, some 38 percent of all middle grades schools are engaged in service learning (National Center for Education Statistics, 1999, p. 5). This represents a substantial increase during the 1990s (Scales, 1999, p. 40). Although much of what we know about the impact of service learning in the middle grades is based on anecdotal or self-reported data, the available evidence suggests significant positive effects.

A study of more than a thousand sixth through eighth graders conducted by the Search Institute (Scales, 1999, pp. 40–42) found that, compared with other students, students who had more than 31 hours of service learning per year and significant time for reflection on their experience, and who thought service learning had motivated them to be more interested in their other classes, had significantly improved their sense of duty to others and substantially increased their sense that they could make a difference when helping others. These students improved to some degree in pursuing good grades and in their commitment to class work (even though increasing student achievement is not usually a major goal of service-learning programs) and felt more empowered at school because of their sense of having decision-making opportunities and recognition from adults. For students who performed fewer than 31 hours of service learning, and did only "some" reflection about it, similar findings were not obtained. Twenty-six percent of the students in the study said service learning made them more interested in their other classes. As studies show that 40–50 percent of students are bored with school (Scales, 1996), a strategy that can increase self-reported interest in other classes is a potentially powerful tool for increasing overall engagement, motivation, and achievement (Scales, 1999, pp. 41–43).

David Hornbeck (1999), then superintendent of Philadelphia's public schools and former chair of the task force that produced the original *Turning Points*, recently commented on Philadelphia's efforts to "imbed quality service learning into the culture of all 259 public schools":

> We clearly understand that a one-shot service experience will transform nothing—not the student, the community, or the larger society. That is why the school board adopted service learning as a central component of the district's new promotion and graduation standards for all students—elementary, middle, and high school.
>
> The project-based requirement . . . is also quite different from any hourly "volunteerism requirement." Service learning in Philadelphia engages students in the real-world problem solving of genuine community needs, through inquiry, research, reflection and direct service or advocacy. Further, the majority of the projects are tied to academic curriculum.
>
> For example, . . . middle-school students in the Mill Creek section of West Philadelphia have studied and mapped a flood plain and are now presenting land-use solutions to policy makers. . . . Several teachers have reported that when their classrooms are extended into the community, students become intellectually engaged and personally empowered. Teachers speak of feeling inspired, creative and passionate. (p. D6)

The service learning projects that Hornbeck describes could be woven into a place-based curriculum, described in Chapter 3, which embeds schoolwork in a local setting, connects the community to other related contexts, and adds value to others in the school and in the community (Haas & Nachtigal, 1998).

If young adolescents are to reap the benefits of service learning, programs must be well designed. Results from the Search Institute study mentioned above suggest that, to have a significant impact on academic attitudes, behaviors, and outcomes, service learning programs should (Scales, 1999, pp. 43–44):

- Provide more than 30 hours of service and connected learning, with substantial time for preparation and reflection
- Be staffed with teachers who have formal training in service learning beyond a one-day workshop
- Be truly integrated in all subjects rather than piecemeal across the curriculum
- Explicitly name academic achievement as a desired outcome of student participation in service learning
- Explicitly incorporate more intentional student–parent activities into the service learning program

The opportunity for students to reflect on their service learning activities is especially important as a means of integrating these "outside" learning experiences within the middle grades curriculum. Young people are able to think, write, and talk about their service, to consider how it relates to the classroom, how it benefits them personally, and how it benefits others. Receiving feedback from supervisors, those served, and peers allows young people to share their thoughts with others while considering different perspectives on service. This further promotes the "learning" aspect of service learning by helping young people analyze the broad array of skills and knowledge that they have gained from their experience. "Sufficient reflection time has consistently been shown to be an important contributor to the positive effects of service-learning" (Scales, 1999, p. 43).

Career Education. In Chapter 1, we noted that today's young adolescents will be entering a sophisticated, technology-driven workplace where many of the jobs available to them will be ones that did not even exist a generation ago. Middle grades students need to know what the demands of the workplace will be in order to guide their choices in school and to give them a clear sense of the level of effort required to participate fully in the 21st-century economy. This is especially true for students in low-income communities. "Many high-risk youth do not know anyone in the labor force. They lack role models—family members or friends who have prepared for a career and found gainful employment. The young people themselves have no idea how to enter the labor force, have unrealistic dreams about the future, and have no access to career options" (Dryfoos, 1998, p. 39). Mentor programs, particularly for language minority students, are greatly needed. Career education and guidance are therefore critical elements in the education of young adolescents.

In the middle grades, emphasis should be placed on exposing young people to a wide variety of work roles through written and visual media and through direct observation and contact with adults in these roles. By the end of their middle grades career, students should have had extensive opportunities for career exploration through job shadowing, field trips, youth-run enterprises, visits to workplaces, project-based research on career fields, and school visits from employers and employees (Council of Chief State School Officers, 1995, pp. 4, 14). Schools must ensure that the opportunities that are available are appropriate for a diverse population of students, including those with disabilities. English-language learners should also be made aware that unique opportunities open to those who are bilingual or multilingual.

After-School Programs

The mere fact of being without supervision seems to have malignant effects on young adolescents, and all too many children find themselves home alone after school every day. Results from research on the Michigan Middle Start initiative (Mertens & Flowers, 1998) reveal significant differences in student outcomes— depression, self-esteem, behavior problems, and academic success—depending on the "latchkey" status of the 46,000 young adolescents included in the research sample. Students were asked how many days a week they took care of themselves after school without an adult present, and how many hours a day they usually took care of themselves.

Students home alone each week for three or more consecutive hours, even if only on one to two days, reported significantly worse results on all the student outcomes than those students who were home alone for less than three consecutive hours. On average, students who were home alone for less than three hours at a stretch reported adjustment scores similar to those of students who spent no days alone. Steven Mertens, senior researcher at the Center for Prevention Research and Development for Michigan Middle Start, remarked that the policy implications seem pretty obvious: "We found a full standard deviation of difference in adjustment scores for kids home alone three or more hours. Kids are just better off with an adult supervising them, even if the kids are just standing around and shooting basketball with an adult present, than they are at home alone" (personal communication, March 8, 2000). High-quality after-school programs can provide many other options besides shooting basketball, of course.

Middle grades educators, along with their counterparts in elementary and high school, are fast recognizing the immense benefits of well-designed after-school programs. After-school programs are increasingly looked upon as a way of preventing young people from engaging in unhealthy or dangerous behaviors, as a way to reinforce and extend classroom learning, and as a rich opportunity for young people to explore their own creativity.

After-school programs for adolescents can be operated on the school grounds or elsewhere in the community. In recent years, the number of offerings at schools has risen dramatically, although primarily in elementary schools. Programs housed in schools can be run by the schools themselves, either under the direction of the principal or through another unit within the local school district such as a community education department. These programs may also be administered by other organizations and agencies within the community and simply be located at the school under a partnership or even a rental agreement (Miller, 1998, p. 34). Common sponsors include churches, community centers, youth service organizations, parent organizations, and national organizations with local affiliates, such as the National Urban League, 4H, YMCA, YWCA, Boys and Girls Clubs, and Girls, Inc. (Miller, 1998, p. 16). Coalitions of parents and other community members may also set up and administer after-school programs (Miller, 1998, p. 34).

Nationally, more than 17,000 organizations offer community-based youth programs after school, on weekends, or during vacation periods, yet only about 29 percent of all young adolescents are reached by these programs (CCAD, 1995, p. 106). Participation in existing after-school programs is markedly lower among those most in need: youth from low-income families. "Youth from higher socioeconomic backgrounds are more likely to take advantage of the opportunities available in their community" and to participate in fine arts activities and music lessons (Miller, 1998, p. 24). Programs that do serve low-income children often face difficult structural and operational problems, including high turnover of children; lack of staff training in child development, activity planning, and group process; competitive, aggressive interactions between children; low staff–child ratios; lack of opportunities to work with parents and social workers; and lack of time for planning, team-building, training, and orientation for staff (Halpern, 1992). Other problems that may befall programs serving low-income or language minority students include a lack of community support and a lack of reliable personnel who are able to speak the native language(s) of the students.

What are the key components of an effective after-school program? All high-quality programs aim to provide three major components: positive relationships with adults and peers, enriching activities, and a safe place. Before creating a new after-school program, the principal and the school support team should conduct a thorough assessment of students' needs and existing services (see Chapter 8). Often the most effective after-school programs have both academic and recreational content. To enhance students' learning, effective programs are often linked to the school-day curriculum, staffed by well-qualified and well-trained personnel, and offer one-to-one tutoring (Fashola, 1999). High-quality programs also allow young people to explore topics, skills, or projects that interest them deeply but that may not be explicitly tied to the school curriculum; such exploration will enhance their capacity for creative thinking and problem solving. After-school programs should not primarily be "more school, after school," but rather an opportunity to learn for the sheer joy of learning.

The recreational components of after-school programs can help middle grades students develop important skills that are not always or explicitly taught in the classroom, such as good sportsmanship. Promoting social competence is often a major goal of after-school programs. "The informal setting of after-school programs can be an optimal setting to help students develop positive peer relations and social skills, and a sense of group belonging" (Miller, 1998, p. 5).

Full-Service Community Schools

In Chapter 8, we described a process that schools can use to assess the health needs of students and their families and then to develop, implement, and evaluate a plan for addressing those needs. School-based or school-linked clinics, which provide primary health care, emergency care, and counseling, are one aspect of a broader trend in community–school partnerships that is called full-service community schools. As Joy Dryfoos (1998, p. 72) writes, "A full-service community school integrates the delivery of quality education with whatever health and social services are required in that community . . . [drawing] on both school resources and outside community agencies that come into the schools and join forces to provide seamless programs. . . ."

Full-service community schools are created through collaboration among the school principal, other faculty members, community leaders, and service agency officials. A "full-service community school is a home-grown product with many variants, developed at the local level by committed individuals who come together from diverse parts of the community to build more responsive institutions" (Dryfoos, 1998, pp. 88–89).

In addition to health services, some full-service community schools have developed family resource centers, located at the school or in a nearby community site, where parents come for parenting education classes; help in learning English and in employment; legal assistance; immigration information; help with housing, food, and clothing; and child care. Others have developed youth service centers, usually operated by outside agencies within the school building, to provide after-school academic and recreational programs, mentoring programs, and individual and group counseling.

Overall, we have found no one ideal model for full-service community schools. Instead, each community seeks to develop a well-planned, multifaceted, coordinated array of programs directly responsive to the needs of students and families in that community. According to Dryfoos (1998, p. 83), full-service community schools strive in different ways to "become a village hub, with joint efforts from school and community agencies to create as rich an environment as possible for the children and their families."

To create a full-service school, the principal often must take a strong leadership role. He or she may first convene the relevant stakeholders within the community, who might include school staff members, the parent association, the local health department, the local social service agency, the probation office, community police, the mental health agency, the local Urban League chapter, youth organizations (for example, Girls Inc., Boys and Girls Clubs), and students. Once a plan of action is developed, the principal must work with other stakeholders to secure the resources and training needed for effective implementation. Virtually all successful full-service community schools have a full-time coordinator who facilitates the participation of community agencies. Currently, school districts pay for only a few programs. Funding comes from outside sources, primarily states, that contract with one or more community agencies to work in partnership with the school (CCAD, 1995, p. 84).

In attempting to create full-service community schools, educators take on the daunting task of mobilizing a community's resources to support students and families not solely because the needs exist, but rather because these needs directly affect the schools' core mission: ensuring that every student fulfills the Turning Points vision. In an interview with the authors, a teacher at a middle school serving a low-income Southern California neighborhood said:

> As a classroom teacher, it was apparent to me and to my colleagues that if we could help deal with the health and welfare issues being faced by our students and their families, we would be able to reach kids in the classroom more effectively. Now when I have a student who has a problem, whether it is a need to go to the dentist, or get eyeglasses, or talk to a psychologist, we can take care of that. Not only does the problem get taken care of, it helps build a trust relationship between the teacher and the student that then allows the student to be more involved in the activities in the classroom.

The school's principal wanted to create "a trusted place in the community where parents could come and find answers to the problems that they had

. . . [a school where] every child and adult knows that every adult in the school takes responsibility for the welfare, not just the educational welfare but the total welfare, of every child on the campus."

Full-service community schools are a promising approach to establishing the kind of school–community partnerships that markedly increase the odds of student success, especially in low-income communities. Recently, an impressive array of education, health, social service, youth development, and other organizations have formed the Coalition for Community Schools, an advocacy organization housed at the Institute for Educational Leadership in Washington, D.C., to support the growing full-service school movement. Yet the essential idea of full-service community schools is not new—in fact, it is an ancient one: family members and citizens acting, as individuals and through the local community institutions they have created, to support the healthy development of their children.

SCHOOLS, FAMILY, AND COMMUNITY: A STRONG FOUNDATION

In this chapter we have described many ways in which parents and communities can join in common cause with middle grades schools to prepare young adolescents, regardless of their language or socioeconomic backgrounds, for the daunting challenges and the enormous opportunities that lie ahead of them. In partnership, schools, families, and community organizations can provide the strong foundation that all middle grades students need to succeed in the 21st century.

10 Taking Action: Challenges and Opportunities

Photo by Doug Martin

THERE IS AN INHERENT DANGER in writing a book like this, one that is essentially the sequel to a highly influential earlier work. Many middle grades educators quite unabashedly told us that the original *Turning Points* was their Bible. Their dog-eared, marked-up copies of the report gave evidence of its frequent use. What need is there, really, for a further iteration of a work that has already found its way deeply into the culture of middle grades education?

As we noted in Chapter 1, this book attempts to take up where we believe *Turning Points* left off by providing detailed information on how *Turning Points'* broad recommendations can be made to work in practice, the kind of information that educators need if we are to strengthen middle grades education for every young adolescent in the 21st century. *Turning Points* was an extraordinary call that rallied thousands of educators to respond. We have attempted—by synthesizing our observations of their efforts over the past ten years and combining our learning with the wealth of education research that so rarely reaches practitioners—to provide a new call to action that is anchored in a deeper understanding of what it takes to create high-performance middle grades schools.

This book should also stand as an affirmation of the enormous progress in improving middle grades education that has been made not only in the past decade but also since the "movement" began many years earlier. It is also a statement—not *to* the community of middle grades educators, but *from* that community—that we are not satisfied with the quality of middle grades education today and we know there is a great deal of difficult work ahead. And that we accept and are capable of meeting the challenges we face.

We have also written this book to reaffirm and to some extent make more explicit the core values of *Turning Points* that we believe resonate so loudly within the middle grades community because they are its core values as well. The *Turning Points 2000* approach to middle grades education emphasizes excellence and equity equally and seeks to clarify what "excellence" means. We define excellence as all students learning to use their minds well, manifested in their ability to reach or exceed higher academic standards and in their strong ability to communicate and work collaboratively with others, to identify and solve "real world" problems, and to think creatively. Finally, we spotlight what to us is a glaring and obvious need to dramatically intensify efforts to improve middle grades education in the lowest-performing schools, which are often struggling in areas of urban and rural poverty.

Our approach has been to build on a seminal idea in *Turning Points*: that its major recommendations are, in effect, the design elements of a system for educating young adolescents. Our revision of the *Turning Points* system now has seven key design elements, and we note, as the original report did, that the goals of excellence and equity can be reached only through comprehensive, ongoing change involving all the design elements (although, from a practical perspective, not all at once).

The middle grades school as a system of design elements is a useful way of characterizing the complexities inherent in improving education for young adolescents. In truth, however, a middle grades school is not a system so much as it is a community. From the most affluent suburbs to the poorest barrios, design elements do not interact in middle grades schools; people do. It follows that making the kind of changes recommended in *Turning Points* and in this book involves countless interactions between a great many people, each of whom brings to bear his or her own firmly held beliefs, often reflecting broader social values and norms, about the way things "ought to be."

Nevertheless, communities *are* like systems in that they naturally seek some manner of equilibrium and will strive, sometimes unknowingly, to resist or co-opt threats to that equilibrium. Thus, changing middle grades schools is inherently a complex process and one that predictably will meet with resistance, from within and outside the school. Nothing worth fighting for comes easily. In this final chapter, we review some of the key themes raised in the book and illuminate both some of the challenges that are likely to arise as changes are implemented and some ideas on how educators can respond to these challenges effectively.

TEACHING AND LEARNING

The *Turning Points 2000* approach to middle grades education embraces academic content standards as an essential component of a school's instructional program. Standards define what students should know and be able to do and thereby serve as the starting point for teachers' development, through a backward-design process, of curriculum, assessments, and instructional activities. Standards make the goals of middle grades education "transparent" so that students, faculty members, parents, and the community know precisely what students are expected to learn and that success is expected of all of them.

It is our observation that middle grades schools have generally embraced content standards as a useful way of clarifying the purposes of instruction. Some educators and parents complain that standards focus too narrowly on academic outcomes for students. They believe an overemphasis on meeting standards causes the school to neglect or retreat from helping students develop the interpersonal skills or "habits of the heart" such as caring, empathy, tolerance, and patriotism, that are equally important if a child is to become a productive, happy adult and responsible citizen.

To maintain a healthy balance in the school's overall mission, we have emphasized that schools should not merely accept state or national standards as a guide to their own practice. Instead, they must use these standards as the basis for thoughtful consideration of what the school's overall goals are. For example, a school community may believe that young adolescents should become actively involved in improving their local community. Thus, state standards that specify what students should know about how government and other civic institutions operate may be augmented by school standards that call for students to become engaged in projects of their own design to improve local conditions.

A significant challenge facing schools is to prevent standards-based instruction from becoming synonymous with instruction meant solely to improve students' scores on high-stakes tests. Currently, middle grades educators, like their counterparts in elementary and high schools, are caught in what psychologists call a classic "double bind." On the one hand, states and local districts demand adherence to academic standards as the basis for curriculum development, yet on the other hand they hold schools accountable for student performance on standardized state tests that are poorly aligned with academic standards. Given the rewards and sanctions schools face in relation to students' test performance, educators predictably elect to focus the curriculum and instruction on what state tests will cover. They feel compelled to sacrifice attention to the essential concepts and "enduring understandings" within and across academic disciplines that are crucial to developing students' thinking abilities, in favor of teaching students to memorize seemingly unrelated factual information and blindly apply mathematical algorithms or scientific formulas.

The solution to this challenge will come in part from greater alignment between state tests and academic standards. However, what state and local policymakers must ultimately realize is that no one test, however well aligned with academic standards, provides an accurate reflection of students' capacities.

Holding schools accountable on the basis of students' performance on a single test is like judging the quality of a theatrical company on the basis of the actors' ability to remember their lines. It is an important but unidimensional perspective on a multidimensional phenomenon.

We also believe that state and local policymakers should strive to create multiple performance-based measures of student achievement that will produce a more balanced public understanding of how well schools are doing and where they need to improve. If state and district tests are going to shape educators' decisions about curriculum and instruction, as they will for the foreseeable future, these tests must provide the kind of multifaceted feedback on student performance that we have stressed teachers must acquire from the assessments they themselves design.

Of course, the fly in the ointment here is that more "authentic" state and local tests would be significantly more expensive to develop and score than the current standardized tests. That is simply the way things are, and we call on policymakers to stop hiding behind the rhetoric of accountability and to deal honestly with the real costs and complexity of accurately assessing student performance in middle grades schools, as well as in elementary and high schools. In their own right, educators must continue their advocacy for more accurate and just assessments even in the face of today's tremendous pressures for "getting the scores up."

Improvements in district and state testing systems for public accountability are critically needed, but middle grades schools themselves can take steps to resolve the conundrum that academic standards and high-stakes tests create. They can do this by fully utilizing structures such as the team and inquiry groups—structures that are hardwired into the *Turning Points 2000* model—that promote teacher collaboration and problem solving.

In their book *Tinkering Toward Utopia*, David Tyack and Larry Cuban (1995) analyze the way American educators have historically dealt with sweeping reforms decreed by state and district offices that are impractical or inadequately supported by new materials and training. Left essentially on their own to implement broad mandates, teachers rarely have the capacity to "reinvent" their practice as the new policies would require. Rather than fundamentally change the instructional program, teachers and administrators shape the implementation of new policies to support current practice, although they often will draw upon the new reforms to do what they do better.

In contrast, we believe that teams, leadership committees, inquiry groups, and other structures that shape the collaborative culture of *Turning Points 2000*–based schools at least offer the opportunity for teachers to solve the kinds of problems inevitably brought on by policy shifts, such as the press for greater accountability, and to do so in powerfully creative ways that can actually produce *different* modes of practice. Certainly, if state standards and tests are totally out of alignment, there is no amount of creativity that can bridge the gap. Where standards and tests are not so poorly aligned, however, schools can best help students learn effectively by providing teachers with opportunities for ongoing, focused conversations about student work; high-quality professional development and curricular materials; and the freedom to identify, evaluate, and implement the changes in teaching that are needed in order to improve student performance. As we discuss below, educators differ in their capacity to engage in this kind of creative problem solving. Yet without the opportunity to customize mandates for change creatively, middle grades schools will forever be tinkers of mediocrity rather than tailors of excellence.

RELATIONSHIPS, COLLABORATION, AND DECISION MAKING

As we noted in Chapter 6, the quality of relationships between school staff members and adolescents, and among all the adults within the school community, makes an enormous difference in the ability of the school to mount an effective instructional program. Positive relationships based on trust and respect, nurtured over time by supportive organizational structures and norms of interaction, are the human infrastructure within a school that enables effective teaching and learning to occur.

It has become increasingly apparent over the past decade that the size of the school plays a crucial role in establishing and maintaining a positive interpersonal environment. It is not impossible within a large school for every adolescent to be known well by the adults there, but the greater frequency of formal and informal interaction in small schools between teachers and students makes it all the more likely. It therefore becomes essential to divide large schools into houses or schools-within-schools, and especially into teams, to create the interpersonal and intellectual climate needed in a high-performance middle grades school.

The team is also the critical organizational structure supporting relationships and interactions between teachers. It is primarily within the team structure that the ongoing conversations about how to improve student performance occur. We have described how teachers on a team, given sufficient time and support, can collaboratively construct effective, developmentally appropriate curriculum, assessment, and instruction capable of responding to adolescents' varied needs and interests. We have also noted how the team, through its team leader, can connect meaningfully to the school's leadership committee and related inquiry groups charged with continuously monitoring students' performance throughout the school. The team can identify key areas in need of improvement and effective ways of addressing them and evaluate the effect of changes in practice against the bottom line: student learning.

The *Turning Points 2000* approach is obviously dependent on teachers and administrators being engaged in ongoing, focused discussion about student performance and how it can be improved. The model therefore makes a fundamental assumption about the capacity of teachers in schools to continuously assess and improve their own practice. Moreover, it assumes that teachers are *interested* in engaging in ongoing dialogue and are willing to leave behind the notion that teaching is essentially a matter of "private practice." In implementing the original *Turning Points*' recommendations, both of these assumptions have been challenged from within and outside the school walls.

The primary thrust of the challenge is that teachers of middle and other grades rarely have the training and experience needed to develop curriculum, assessments, and instructional activities that are sufficiently rigorous to promote effective student learning. Very little of teachers' undergraduate and graduate training prepared them for this role, it is argued, nor do they have the in-depth knowledge of their own primary academic discipline needed for the task.

Developing the kind of integrated curriculum deemed essential in middle grades education is even more problematic. Left on their own, middle grades teachers may produce curriculum that is thematically linked and entertaining to young adolescents, but shallow in its treatment of important concepts within and across academic disciplines. The result is a trivialization of integrated curriculum that encourages students to produce the kind of "sugar cube Alamo" projects, noted in Chapter 3, that tenuously link history, social studies, and mathematics. Finally, critics of teacher-developed curriculum say that while early adolescence is a period of developmental upheaval, young adolescents are ultimately more similar than different in their patterns of intellectual development, so the kind of creative customization of curriculum we call for is really unnecessary. One size— in the form of externally designed and highly prescriptive curriculum, assessment, and instructional materials—can be made to fit all, or so they say.

To those who believe passionately in teacher empowerment as a prerequisite to developing effective schools, these are fighting words! Their instinct may well be to decry yet another example of "teacher bashing," and they may be tempted to shout down the opposition on the grounds of the integrity of teachers and the humanity of their students. In the everyday lives of schools, however, we believe that a more balanced response is one that first considers what will best promote student learning and then determines teachers' appropriate roles.

We have observed in schools attempting to develop appropriate, powerful middle grades instructional programs that teachers are capable of doing this work well, but it does not come "naturally" or solely as a function of being empowered to do so. Teachers and administrators generally do not have much experience in working collaboratively on teams or in leadership and inquiry groups. If they are to function productively within these structures, we cannot overemphasize the importance of providing sufficient time for school faculty to engage in the focused discussions of student work that are at the heart of such efforts.

Even with sufficient time, however, school staff members need guidance to learn how to make these collaborative structures function effectively, and especially how to maintain a laserlike focus on improving student performance amid so many distractions. For many schools, such guidance will need to come from outside, from well-trained district personnel or from educational development organizations. Providing such expert guidance is a centerpiece of the work of the Center for Collaborative Education, for example, which as noted in Chapter 1 has developed a Turning Points-based approach for supporting middle grades improvement that was recently approved as a New American Schools design-based model for school improvement.

We must recognize, however, that providing high-quality professional development to help teachers realize their capacities for curriculum development and creative problem solving presumes at least some organizational capacity to begin with. Moreover, it presumes a foundation of communication and trust among faculty members and between the school and surrounding communities upon which a collaborative culture can be built. And it presumes a real interest in engaging in the challenging work of collaborating with colleagues, which some teachers may truly believe is not "what they signed up for." Finally, and perhaps most important, there are some schools, particularly those serving high-poverty urban and rural communities, where student performance and teacher morale is so low that what is needed is what basketball fans call a "stop." As when the opposing team is raining down basket after basket, these schools need something *now* to stop the poor student performance that is rapidly draining young adolescents of any chance of a successful future.

Especially in high-poverty, low-performing schools, we believe more prescriptive approaches to middle grades improvement can play a useful role. However, at no time should such approaches be foisted on a school faculty without their informed and uncoerced consent. Essential to this belief is our observation that more prescriptive approaches need not be less engaging to students or less "constructivist" in intellectual orientation than curriculum, assessment, and instructional strategies developed by teachers.

One of the best of the more prescriptive middle grades "whole school" designs is the Talent Development Middle School Model, developed at John Hopkins' and Howard University's Center for Research on the Education of Students Placed At Risk. It meshes some of the best research-based approaches to "teaching for understanding" into a coherent curriculum and includes high-quality professional development and excellent materials. The Talent Development Middle School Model has mounted an impressive early record in promoting achievement among low-income, low-performing students (Balfanz & Mac Iver, 2000).

Though only in its pilot phase, another promising whole school design is the Success for All (SFA) Middle School project. Grounded in the effective practices of the Success for All and Roots and Wings programs for elementary schools, the SFA Middle School builds on an impressive track record in schools in disadvantaged communities (Daniels, Madden, & Slavin, 2000). (For more on this pilot project, see Chapter 4.) The SFA Middle School has three goals:

- To create a positive school climate built around small communities of learners
- To promote literacy for all children
- To engage both teachers and students in a demanding, standards-based curriculum

Such efforts at "packaging" curriculum materials and professional development have been harshly criticized by some as new attempts to create a "teacher-proof" instructional program. This strikes us as too harsh, given the lack of organizational capacity in some schools, the thoughtfulness of the program developers, and the need across the range of all middle grades schools for more than one strategy to improve student performance. Even schools able and willing to take on the challenge of designing their own instructional program need not start from scratch and may learn much from externally designed efforts.

Prescriptive approaches to improving student performance have a useful role to play in middle grades education. There should be a point in any middle grades school's development, however, when it should be capable of responding through its own internal collaborative processes to the fundamental question: How do we get better? Ultimately, no one-size educational program can possibly fully capitalize on the diversity of student and faculty interests and talents, and community resources, that define each and every middle grades school.

One of the true paradoxes of middle grades education, or any form of education, is that to enable all students to reach high, common standards of excellence requires maximizing the diversity of approaches to learning, not reducing their variability. As any actor will say, the same play brilliantly performed will produce a different response in different audiences. An equivalent phenomenon occurs in schools because each student varies in personality, interests, and experiences, and each school varies in terms of the shared history and culture of those present. Each middle grades school must, therefore, find a differentiated set of solutions to the specific problems and points of leverage of its own school community—not a reinvention of the wheel, but a unique mosaic of effective approaches to learning that builds on students' and educators' diversity and strengths.

COMMUNITY CONNECTIONS

Transforming existing middle grades schools into high-performance learning communities is an enormous undertaking. This is especially true of low-performing schools in high-poverty communities. In the school improvement literature, the analogy is often made of turning an ocean liner around and heading in the opposite direction. This is a compelling image, but one we find incomplete. Transforming dysfunctional or even moderately successful middle grades schools into high-functioning institutions is like turning a big boat around *and* changing the direction of the current that speeds the boat to its destination. Without parent and community support, comprehensive school improvement efforts are dead in the water.

In Chapters 8 and 9, we described how schools can reach out to parents, community members, and local service agencies to form a kind of force field of caring people and institutions to support healthy adolescent development. Over the past ten years, we have seen many schools mount concentrated efforts to engage their local communities. In most instances these schools have significantly strengthened their capacity to educate all students well. In no instance, however, have broad networks of support been established without some challenges.

The important work of forming parent and community collaborations is challenging because it takes time for teachers and administrators to reach out beyond the school walls, and there are so many other aspects of teaching and learning that, according to conventional wisdom, are more critical to student learning. We have not discovered an easy solution to the "time problem" in school improvement efforts. However, we have seen schools make better use of existing time by incorporating parent and community outreach into their every-day business, instead treating it as an "if we have time" add-on. The most successful schools are those that realize that they simply cannot get to where they want to go without parent and community support.

Forming strong community connections is also difficult because both teachers and administrators generally lack formal training in how to build and sustain these bridges. Just as "internal" collaboration within a school does not come naturally and so requires support and practice, collaboration with parents, community members, and agency representatives will flow more smoothly when supported by guidance and training from individuals experienced in bringing divergent groups together. It is for this reason that we have noted the importance of intermediary organizations like the National Network of Partnership Schools established at Johns Hopkins University and the Texas-based Interfaith Education Fund's Alliance Schools network, which provides schools with well-substantiated methods for systematically connecting with their local community.

Effective school–community collaborations in low-income communities face a particular kind of challenge. What should be collaborative work among equals toward a common purpose of adolescents' intellectual and healthy development may become charitable work on the part of schools to "serve" impoverished local families and children. Oakes and her colleagues (Oakes, Quartz, Ryan, & Lipton, 2000, pp. 161–162) describe vividly how schools' well-intentioned efforts to address the "extra baggage" that students from low-income families in violent, crime-ridden neighborhoods bring to the learning environment can thwart the essential purposes of middle grades education:

> Dealing with the "extra baggage" had become one of the school's main jobs, often outweighing academic instruction. . . . Despite [the school principal's] deeply held belief that Mann [middle school] needed to envision itself as a caring community, Mann's care generally amounted to distributing services, many of which interrupted students' academic growth and communicated a clear message that they needed to be "fixed." To be sure, Mann's students faced enormous challenges. Family, neighborhood, and societal circumstances placed many of them at risk; doing nothing would have been far worse. However, the school's approach rested on making up for students' inadequacies, relying on authoritarian standards of correct behavior and doing *for* rather than doing *with* or showing how. Mann's approach, as well intentioned as it was, echoes a long-standing cultural view that assumes nonmainstream populations are damaged and need to be "repaired."

In reaching out to their local communities, middle grades educators must recognize that the essence of this work is in creating relationships. And just as relationships between faculty members must be based on a respect for what each person can contribute to the relationship, so it must be with relationships between school officials, parents, and community members.

FINAL REFLECTIONS: ON EXCELLENCE AND EQUITY

Perhaps the biggest challenge stemming from the approach to middle grades education described in this book is inherent in the very notion of a school that is equally dedicated to excellence and equity. By embracing high expectations and high performance standards for every student, teachers and administrators in a *Turning Points 2000*–based school are saying, publicly, that they *believe* every student has the capacity for high-level intellectual development and that their actions will be guided by that belief. In effect, they take a moral and a political stand that takes seriously the fundamental ideals of American education, so rarely realized.

Imagine a group of middle grades educators going on local public television and stating, "We believe that every young adolescent, black or white, rich or poor, English-speaking or otherwise, has the same intellectual potential that any affluent white adolescent does. Our goal is to create a school where there are no observable differences in performance by race, class, or any other group characteristic, so that upon leaving the middle grades school, all groups of adolescents are equally likely to succeed as adults." That is, in effect, what the *Turning Points 2000* approach to middle grades education espouses. One can further imagine that this broadcast would be better received in some communities than in others.

As Oakes and her colleagues (2000) masterfully document, the Turning Points concept challenges deeply rooted and structurally reinforced norms in American education that support existing social and economic inequities between different groups of people. Put differently, some Americans are vastly more privileged than others, and differences in educational expectations and resource allocation serve to keep it that way. Schools operating based on the Turning Points principles, which believe in high academic standards for all students and act accordingly, represent a threat to established social and economic hierarchies. This threat does not go unnoticed by the parents of children who stand to gain the most from more traditional and less equitable approaches to middle grades education. It is not surprising, then, that the implementation of Turning Points practices, especially heterogeneous grouping for instruction, has met with considerable and often vitriolic opposition within some communities, and, because they represent the society in microcosm, from within school faculties themselves.

As Tyack and Cuban point out (1995, p. 29), "In the abstract, people may favor giving all children a fair chance, but at the same time they want their children to succeed in the competition for economic and social advantage. . . . When secondary schools succeed in retaining and graduating minorities and the poor, for example, they appear to lessen the advantage once enjoyed by middle-class whites." At the heart of some parents' and educators' concerns is that the "smart kids" will be less well educated in schools that strive for high, equitable outcomes. Undergirding these concerns are beliefs rooted deeply within our society about group differences in intelligence, and an unspoken but nearly palpable ambiguity about the worthiness of some groups of children to receive the best education has to offer.

We have not found an easy way to address concerns that run so close to the heart of the American condition. It is important, however, to be as broadly inclusive and open as possible in communicating the value of a standards-based approach to learning and the kinds of engaging teaching practices research suggests are most effective in enabling students to reach or exceed higher academic standards. Conversations with the school community should include the presentation of data that graphically depict both the challenges the school faces in eliminating performance gaps between groups and its goals for raising the absolute level of achievement for every student. As when schools seek to address students' health needs through what some consider controversial means such as school-based clinics (see Chapter 8), educators attempting to implement the *Turning Points 2000* approach to teaching and learning should anticipate stirring up what may be a hornet's nest of concern. To proactively address such concerns, we recommend that, early in the process, schools engage in dialogue representatives of those groups most likely to perceive a threat. The school should show these skeptics what their children are likely to gain from the changes rather than what they will lose, and then encourage them to communicate on behalf of the school to others who share their initial skepticism.

As we noted in Chapter 1, however, *talk* only goes so far in changing beliefs about the purposes of education and the potential of every student to learn at much higher levels. Ultimately, seeing is believing. Parents and educators may well be convinced to try a new, more equitable approach to learning on the basis of a deeper understanding of its potential. But they will not be "won over" until they see convincing evidence of the power of that approach to improve the achievement of every student at the expense of none. While we hold no illusions that implementing *Turning Points 2000*'s recommendations will ever be easy, we strongly believe that the approach to educating adolescents described in this book has that power. In that respect, we are greatly encouraged by the emerging evidence of the power of the Turning Points model noted in Chapter 1.

We further believe that as educators are increasingly successful in realizing that power, in raising all boats, they have an enormous opportunity to prove the fallacy of one of this country's most pernicious myths: that all children really cannot learn. Thus we see the work of middle grades educators implementing Turning Points reforms as much more than "school reform." It is nothing less than a heroic attempt to realize the American ideal that all men (and women) are truly created equal and that every one of us has an unalienable right to the pursuit of happiness, for which an excellent education is essential. At its heart, the middle grades movement is a movement in the service of social justice. In their hearts, middle grades educators are determined that the dream of high achievement for every young adolescent will become a reality.

Ten years ago, *Turning Points* argued that the middle grades schools "are potentially society's most powerful force to recapture millions of youth adrift" (p. 32). In effect, the report provided a vision of a possible future and asked parents, community members, policymakers, educators, and students to translate that vision into a better reality for young adolescents. To the framework of ideas developed in the original report, innumerable courageous individuals have added layer upon layer of knowledge and experience. They have added not only flesh on the bone, but muscle, heart, and soul. *Turning Points 2000* builds on these efforts, coupling them to the best in current education research, to provide firmer footing for the next phases of the journey to educate every middle grades student to his or her fullest potential. As we enter the 21st century, we see no more important goal in American education.

References

Achieve, Inc. (1998). *Aiming higher: 1998 annual report* [Brochure]. Washington, DC: Author.

Ainscow, M., Hopkins, D., Southworth, G., & West, M. (1994). *Creating the conditions for school improvement: A handbook of staff development activities.* London: David Fulton Publishers.

Alan Guttmacher Institute. (1998). *Facts in brief—Teen sex and pregnancy* [Online]. Available: www.agi-usa.org/pubs/fb_teen_sex.html [1999, April 1].

Alan Guttmacher Institute. (April 29, 1999). *U.S. teenage pregnancy rate drops another 4% between 1995 and 1996: Teenage pregnancy declines in all states* [Press release]. New York: Author.

Alleman, J., & Brophy, J. (1996). *Reconceptualizing homework as out-of-school learning opportunities.* East Lansing: Michigan State University Institute for Research on Teaching.

Allen, L. E., & Hallett, A. C. (1999). *Beyond finger-pointing and test scores.* Chicago: Cross City Campaign for Urban School Reform.

Allington, R. L. (1990). What have we done in the middle? In G. G. Duffy (Ed.), *Reading in the middle school* (2nd ed.). Newark, DE: International Reading Association.

Allport, G. W. (1954). *The nature of prejudice.* Garden City, NY: Doubleday.

American Cancer Society. (1997). *National health education standards: Achieving health literacy.* Atlanta: Author.

American Federation of Teachers. (1999). *Making standards matter, 1999: An annual fifty-state report on efforts to raise academic standards.* Washington, DC: Author.

Ames, N., & Miller, E. (1994). *Changing middle schools: How to make schools work for young adolescents.* San Francisco: Jossey-Bass.

Angelo, T. A., & Cross, K. P. (1993). *Classroom assessment techniques: A handbook for college teachers* (2nd ed.). San Francisco: Jossey-Bass.

Anglin, J. (1997). Teaming beyond the core four. In T. S. Dickinson & T. O. Erb (Eds.), *We gain more than we give: Teaming in middle schools* (pp. 387–401). Columbus, OH: National Middle School Association.

Annie E. Casey Foundation. (1998). *When teens have sex: Issues and trends—KIDS COUNT special report.* Baltimore, MD: Author.

Araki, C. T. (1990). Dispute management in the schools. *Mediation Quarterly, 8*(1), 51–62.

Archer, J. (1999, March 17). New teachers abandon field at high rate. *Education Week, 1,* 20–21.

Arhar, J. M. (1992). Interdisciplinary teaming and the social bonding of middle level students. In J. L. Irvin (Ed.), *Transforming middle level education: Perspectives and possibilities* (pp. 139–161). Boston: Allyn & Bacon.

Arhar, J. M. (1997). The effects of interdisciplinary teaming on teachers and students. In J. L. Irvin (Ed.), *What current research says to the middle level practitioner* (pp. 49–55). Columbus, OH: National Middle School Association.

Arnold, J. (1997). Teams and curriculum. In T. S. Dickinson & T. O. Erb (Eds.), *We gain more than we give: Teaming in middle schools* (pp. 443–463). Columbus, OH: National Middle School Association.

Arnold, J., & Stevenson, C. (1998). *Teachers' teaming handbook: A middle level planning guide.* Orlando, FL: Harcourt Brace & Company.

Ashton, P., & Webb, R. (1986). *Making a difference: Teachers' sense of efficacy and student achievement.* New York: Longman.

Baker, D. P., & Stevenson, D. L. (1986). Mothers' strategies for children's school achievement: Managing the transition to high school. *Sociology of Education, 59,* 156–166.

Balfanz, R., & Mac Iver, D. J. (with assistance from Merritt, J. C.). (1998, December 1). *The school district's role in creating high performing urban middle schools.* Johns Hopkins University. Unpublished paper commissioned by Carnegie Corporation of New York for the Turning Points 2000 book project.

Balfanz, R., & Mac Iver, D. J. (2000). *Journal of Education for Students Placed At Risk, 5*(1&2).

Banks, J. A. (1995). Multicultural education and the modification of students' racial attitudes. In W. D. Hawley & A. W. Jackson (Eds.), *Toward a common destiny: Improving race and ethnic relations in America* (pp. 315–339). San Francisco: Jossey-Bass.

Barbe, W. B., & Swassing, R. H. (1994). *Teaching through modality strengths: Concepts and practices.* Columbus, OH: Zaner-Bloser, Inc.

Bargar, J. R., Bargar, R. R., & Cano, J. M. (1994). *Discovering learning preferences and learning differences in the classroom.* Columbus, OH: Ohio Agricultural Education Curriculum Materials Service. (The Ohio State University, 2120 Fyffe Road, Columbus, OH 43210.)

Barton, P. E., & Coley, R. J. (1998). *Growth in school: Achievement gains from the fourth to the eighth grades.* Princeton, NJ: Educational Testing Service.

Battistich, V., & Hom, A. (1997). The relationship between students' sense of their school as a community and their involvement in problem behaviors. *American Journal of Public Health, 87,* 1997–2001.

Beane, J. A. (1997). *Curriculum integration: Designing the core of democratic education.* New York: Teachers College Press.

Bergman, S. (1992). Exploratory programs in the middle level school: A responsive idea. In J. L. Irvin (Ed.), *Transforming middle level education: Perspectives and possibilities* (pp. 179–192). Boston: Allyn & Bacon.

Black, S. (1996, October). The truth about homework. *The American School Board Journal, 183*(10), 48–51.

Bloom, B. (Ed.). (1956). *Taxonomy of educational objectives: The classification of educational goals: Handbook I: Cognitive domain.* New York: David McKay Company, Inc.

Bodilly, S. J., with Keltner, B., Purnell, S., Reichardt, R., & Schuyler, G. (1998). *Lessons from New American Schools' scale-up phase: Prospects for bringing designs to multiple schools.* Santa Monica, CA: RAND.

Bolman, L. G., & Deal, T. E. (1993). *The path to school leadership: A portable mentor.* Newbury Park, CA: Corwin Press, Inc.

Braddock, J. H. (1989). *Tracking of Black, Hispanic, Asian, Native American, and white students: National patterns and trends.* Baltimore, MD: Center for Research on Effective Schooling for Disadvantaged Students.

Braddock, J. H., II, & Slavin, R. E. (1992, September). *Why ability grouping must end: Achieving excellence and equity in American education.* Center for Research on Effective Schooling for Disadvantaged Students, Johns Hopkins University. Paper presented at the Common Destiny Conference, Washington, DC.

Braddock, J. H., II, Dawkins, M. P., & Wilson, G. (1995). Intercultural contact and race relations among American youth. In W. D. Hawley & A. W. Jackson (Eds.), *Toward a common destiny: Improving race and ethnic relations in America* (pp. 237–256). San Francisco: Jossey-Bass.

Bransford, J. D., Brown, A. L., & Cocking, R. R. (Eds.). (1999). *How people learn: Brain, mind, experience, and school.* Washington, DC: National Academy Press.

Breslau, N., & Peterson, E. L. (1996). Smoking cessation in young adults: Age at initiation of cigarette smoking and other suspected influences. *American Journal of Public Health, 86,* 214–220.

Brooks, J. G., & Brooks, M. G. (1993). *In search of understanding: The case for constructivist classrooms.* Alexandria, VA: Association for Supervision and Curriculum Development.

Burkhardt, R. M. (1997). Teaming: Sharing the experience. In T. S. Dickinson & T. O. Erb (Eds.), *We gain more than we give: Teaming in middle schools* (pp. 163–184). Columbus, OH: National Middle School Association.

Callahan, J. S. & Clark, L. H. (1988). *Teaching in middle and secondary schools: Planning for competence.* New York: Macmillan.

Carnegie Council on Adolescent Development. (1989, June). *Turning points: Preparing American youth for the 21st century.* The Report of the Task Force on Education of Young Adolescents. New York: Carnegie Corporation of New York.

Carnegie Council on Adolescent Development. (1992, December). *A matter of time: Risk and opportunity in the nonschool hours.* Report of the Task Force on Youth Development and Community Programs. New York: Carnegie Corporation of New York.

Carnegie Council on Adolescent Development. (1994, September). *Consultation on afterschool programs.* New York: Carnegie Corporation of New York.

Carnegie Council on Adolescent Development. (1995, October). *Great transitions: Preparing adolescents for a new century.* Concluding Report. New York: Carnegie Corporation of New York.

Catterall, J. S., Chapleau, R., & Iwanaga, J. (1999). Involvement in the arts and human development: General involvement and intensive involvement in music and theater arts. In Fiske, E. B. (Ed.), *Champions of change: The impact of the arts on learning.* Washington, DC: The Arts Education Partnership and the President's Committee on the Arts and the Humanities.

Center for Collaborative Education. (December 3, 1998). *Turning points design model* (Draft). Boston, MA: Author.

Center for Prevention Research & Development. (1996). *The self-study overview* [Brochure]. University of Illinois, Institute of Government & Public Affairs. Urbana, IL: Author.

Center for Prevention Research & Development. (1997). *Michigan Middle Start aggregate data analysis: 1994–1995, 1996–1997.* University of Illinois, Institute of Government & Public Affairs. Urbana, IL: Author.

Center for Prevention Research & Development. (1998). *The school improvement self-study: A data-driven approach to school reform* [Pamphlet]. University of Illinois, Institute of Government & Public Affairs. Urbana, IL: Author.

Centers for Disease Control and Prevention. (1996). Guidelines for school health programs to promote lifelong healthy eating. *Morbidity and Mortality Weekly Report (MMWR), 45*(No. RR-9), 1–41.

Centers for Disease Control and Prevention. (1997a). Guidelines for school and community programs to promote lifelong physical activity among young people. *Morbidity and Mortality Weekly Report (MMWR), 46*(No. RR-6), 1–36.

Centers for Disease Control and Prevention. (1997b). *Nutrition and the health of young people: Fact sheet.* Washington, DC: U.S. Department of Health and Human Services, National Center for Chronic Disease Prevention and Health Promotion.

Centers for Disease Control and Prevention. (1997c). *Physical activity and the health of young people: Fact sheet.* Washington, DC: U.S. Department of Health and Human Services, National Center for Chronic Disease Prevention and Health Promotion.

Centers for Disease Control and Prevention. (1999). *Targeting tobacco use: The nation's leading cause of death* [Online]. Available: www.cdc.gov/nccdphp/osh/oshaag.htm [1999, April 14].

Centers for Disease Control and Prevention. (n.d.). *Fact sheet: Youth risk behavior trends—From CDC's 1991, 1993, 1995, and 1997 Youth Risk Behavior Surveys.* Available: www.cdc.gov/nccdphp/dash/yrbs/trend.htm [1999, June 1].

Chase, W. G., & Simon, H. A. (1973). Perception in chess. *Cognitive Psychology, 4,* 55–81.

Chi, M. T. H., Feltovich, P. J., & Glaser, R. (1981). Categorization and representation of physics problems by experts and novices. *Cognitive Science, 5,* 121–152.

Clark, R. M. (Spring, 1990). Why disadvantaged students succeed: What happens outside school is critical. *Public Welfare,* 17–23.

Commission on Adolescent Literacy of the International Reading Association (1999, March 18). Adolescent literacy: A position statement. *Journal of Adolescent & Adult Literacy, 43*(1), 97–109.

Cone, J. (1993, Fall). Learning to teach an untracked class. *The College Board Review, 169,* 20–31.

Conflict Resolution Education Network. (1999). *Resource guide for selecting a conflict resolution education trainer* (4th ed.). Washington, DC: Author.

Cooney, S. (1998). *Improving teaching in the middle grades: Higher standards for students aren't enough.* Atlanta: Southern Regional Education Board.

Cooney, S. (1999). *Leading the way: State actions to improve student achievement in the middle grades.* Atlanta: Southern Regional Education Board.

Corcoran, T. B. (1998). *Professional development for K-12 educators: Issues and opportunities.* Consortium for Policy Research in Education (CPRE), the University of Pennsylvania. Unpublished commissioned paper for Carnegie Corporation of New York.

Corporation for National Service and National Institute on Out-of-School Time. (n.d.). *Service as a strategy in out-of-school time: A how-to manual* [Online]. Available: www.siu.edu/~aftersch/scho_morefacts.html [1999, June 16].

Cotton, Kathleen. (1996). *School size, school climate, and student performance,* Close-Up #20 [Online]. Available: www.nwrel.org/scpd/sirs/10/c020.html [1998, July 8].

Council of Chief State School Officers. (1995). *Youth preparation for employment 1995.* Washington, DC: Author.

Council of Chief State School Officers. (1996). *Interstate school leaders licensure consortium: Standards for school leaders.* Washington, DC: Author.

Council of Chief State School Officers. (1998). *State education accountability reports and indicator reports: Status of reports across the states.* Washington, DC: Author.

Crawford, L., & Wood, C. (1998). *Guidelines for the responsive classroom in middle schools.* Greenfield, MA: Northeast Foundation for Children.

Cromwell, S. (1999, April 26). Student-led conferences: A growing trend. *Education World* [Online], 4 pages. Available: www.education-world.com/a_admin/admin112.shtml [1999, May 18].

Cuban, L. (1992). What happens to reforms that last? The case of the junior high school. *American Educational Research Journal, 29,* 227–251.

Dalin, P. (1998). Developing the twenty-first century school: A challenge to reformers. In A. Hargreaves, A. Lieberman, M. Fullan, & D. Hopkins (Eds.), *International handbook of educational change* (pp. 1059–1073). Dordrecht, The Netherlands: Kluwer Academic Publishers.

Daniels, C., Madden, N. A., & Slavin, R. E. (2000). *Success for All Middle School project design.* Baltimore, MD: Success for All Foundation.

Darling-Hammond, L. (1997a). *Doing what matters most: Investing in quality teaching.* New York: National Commission on Teaching & America's Future.

Darling-Hammond, L. (1997b). *The right to learn: A blueprint for creating schools that work.* San Francisco: Jossey-Bass.

Darling-Hammond, L., Ancess, J., & Falk, B. (1995). *Authentic assessment in action: Studies of schools and students at work.* New York: Teachers College Press.

Davidson, J., & Koppenhaver, D. (1993). *Adolescent literacy: What works and why* (2nd ed.). New York: Garland Publishing.

DePascale, C. A. (1997, April). *Education reform restructuring network: Impact documentation report.* Data Analysis & Testing Associates, Inc. Prepared for Massachusetts Department of Education.

Developmental Studies Center. (1998, September). *The Child Development Project: A brief summary of the project and findings from three evaluation studies.* Oakland, CA: Author.

Developmental Studies Center, Child Development Project. (n.d.). *Helping students resist drugs, alcohol, and tobacco* [Brochure]. Oakland, CA: Author.

Devlin, B. (1997). The heredity of IQ. *Nature, 388,* 468.

Dickinson, D. K., & DiGisi, L. L. (1998). The many rewards of a literacy-rich classroom. *Educational Leadership, 55*(6), 23–26.

Dickinson, T. S., & Erb, T. O. (Eds.). (1997). *We gain more than we give: Teaming in middle schools.* Columbus, OH: National Middle School Association.

Donahue, P. L., Voelkl, K. E., Campbell, J. R., & Mazzeo, J. (1999). *The NAEP 1998 reading report card for the nation and the states* (NCES 1999–500). Washington, DC: U.S. Department of Education, Office of Educational Research and Improvement, National Center for Education Statistics.

Dornbusch, S. M., & Glasgow, K. L. (1996). The structural context of family-school relations. In A. Booth & J. F. Dunn (Eds.), *Family-school links: How do they affect educational outcomes?* (pp. 35–44). Mahwah, NJ: Lawrence Erlbaum Associates.

Dryfoos, J. G. (1993). Schools as places for health, mental health, and social services. In R. Takanishi (Ed.), *Adolescence in the 1990s: Risk and opportunity* (pp. 82–109). New York: Teachers College Press.

Dryfoos, J. G. (1995). Full service schools: Revolution or fad? *Journal of Research on Adolescence, 5*(2), 147–172.

Dryfoos, J. G. (1998). *Safe passage: Making it through adolescence in a risky society.* New York: Oxford University Press.

Dusenbury, L., & Falco, M. (1995). Eleven components of effective drug abuse prevention curricula. *Journal of School Health, 65*, 420–425.

Eccles, J. S., & Harold, R. H. (1996). Family involvement in children's and adolescents' schooling. In A. Booth & J. F. Dunn (Eds.), *Family-school links: How do they affect educational outcomes?* (pp. 3–34). Mahwah, NJ: Lawrence Erlbaum Associates.

Eccles, J. S., & Midgley, C. (1989). Stage—Environment fit: Developmentally appropriate classrooms for young adolescents. In R. Ames & C. Ames (Eds.), *Research on motivation in education, volume 3: Goals and cognitions* (pp. 139–186). Orlando: Academic Press.

Eccles, J. S., & Wigfield, A. (1997). Young adolescent development. In J. L. Irvin (Ed.), *What current research says to the middle level practitioner* (pp. 15–29). Columbus, OH: National Middle School Association.

Edelsky, C., Altmeyer, B., & Flores, B. (1991). *Whole language: What's the difference?* Portsmouth, NH: Heinemann.

Edmonds, R. (1979). Effective schools for the urban poor. *Educational Leadership, 37*(1), 15–24.

Education Commission of the States. (1999). *Education accountability systems in 50 states.* Denver, CO: Author.

Education Development Center. (1999, October). *Improving teacher preparation programs: A briefing paper for funders.* Prepared for the W. K. Kellogg Foundation. Newton, MA: Author.

Education Development Center, National Forum to Accelerate Middle-Grades Reform. (n.d.). *Vision statement* [Online]. Available: www.edc.org/FSC/MGF/Resources/vision.html [1999, July 26].

Edwards, V. B. (Ed.). (1998, January 8). Quality Counts '98. The urban challenge: Public education in the 50 states [Special issue]. *Education Week, XVII*(17). [Published in Collaboration with Pew Charitable Trusts].

Elliot, S. N. (1998). *The Responsive Classroom approach: Its effectiveness and acceptability in promoting social and academic competence.* University of Wisconsin-Madison. Summary available from the Northeast Foundation for Children.

Elmore, R. F. (1995). Structural reform and educational practice. *Educational Researcher, 24*(9), 23–26.

Elmore, R. F., with the assistance of Burney, D. (1997, August). *Investing in teacher learning: Staff development and instructional improvement in community district #2, New York City.* New York: National Commission on Teaching & America's Future, Teachers College, Columbia University, and Consortium for Policy Research in Education.

English, F. (1992). *Deciding what to teach and test: Developing, aligning, and auditing the curriculum.* Thousand Oaks, CA: Sage Publications.

Epstein, J. L. (1996a). Improving school-family-community partnerships in the middle grades. *Middle School Journal, 28*(2), 43–48.

Epstein, J. L. (1996b). Perspectives and previews on research and policy for school, family and community partnerships. In A. Booth & J. F. Dunn (Eds.), *Family-school links: How do they affect educational outcomes?* (pp. 209–246). Mahwah, NJ: Lawrence Erlbaum Associates.

Epstein, J. L. (1997). A comprehensive framework for school, family, and community partnerships. In J. L. Epstein, L. Coates, K. C. Salinas, M. G. Sanders, & B. S. Simon (Eds.), *School, family, and community partnerships: Your handbook for action* (pp. 1–25). Thousand Oaks, CA: Corwin Press.

Epstein, J. L. (n.d.). *Teachers Involve Parents in Schoolwork (TIPS)—Interactive homework in math, science/health, and language arts* [Online]. Available: www.csos.jhu.edu/p2000/tips.htm [1999, June 16].

Epstein, J. L., Coates, L., Salinas, K. C., Sanders, M. G., & Simon, B. S. (1997). *School, family, and community partnerships: Your handbook for action.* Thousand Oaks, CA: Corwin Press.

Epstein, J. L., & Mac Iver, D. (1990). *Education in the middle grades: National practices and trends.* Columbus, OH: National Middle School Association.

Erb, T. O. (1997). Thirty years of attempting to fathom teaming: Battling potholes and hairpin curves along the way. In T. S. Dickinson & T. O. Erb (Eds.), *We gain more than we give: Teaming in middle schools* (pp. 19–59). Columbus, OH: National Middle School Association.

Erb, T. O. (1999). Interdisciplinary: One word, two meanings. *Middle School Journal, 31*(2), 2.

Erb, T. O., & Doda, N. M. (1989). *Team organization: Promise—Practices and possibilities.* Washington, DC: National Education Association.

Erb, T. O., & Stevenson, C. (1999a). From faith to facts: *Turning Points* in action—What difference does teaming make? *Middle School Journal, 30*(3), 47–50.

Erb, T. O., & Stevenson, C. (1999b). From faith to facts: *Turning Points* in action—Fostering growth inducing environments for student success. *Middle School Journal, 30*(4), 63–67.

Erickson, H. L. (1998). *Concept-based curriculum and instruction: Teaching beyond the facts.* Thousand Oaks, CA: Corwin Press.

Evans, D. L. (1999, February 3). Assistance for underqualified teachers: Differentiated responsibilities. *Education Week,* 35–36.

Farber, P. (1998, March/April). Small schools work best for disadvantaged students. *The Harvard Education Letter,* 6–8.

Farkas, S., Johnson, J., & Duffett, A. (1999). *Playing their parts: Parents and teachers talk about parental involvement in public schools.* New York: Public Agenda.

Fashola, O. S. (1999). *Report no. 24: Review of extended-day and after-school programs and their effectiveness* [Online]. Available: www.csos.jhu.edu/crespar/CRESPAR%20Reports/report24entire.htm [1999, June 14].

Felner, R. D., Jackson, A. W., Kasak, D., Mulhall, P., Brand, S., & Flowers, N. (1997). The impact of school reform for the middle years: Longitudinal study of a network engaged in *Turning Points*-based comprehensive school transformation. *Phi Delta Kappan, 78,* 528–532, 541–550.

Fenwick, J. J. (1996). *Creating communities for learning.* San Diego, CA: Fenwick and Associates. Unpublished paper commissioned by Carnegie Corporation of New York.

Ferguson, R. (1991, Summer). Paying for public education: New evidence on how and why money matters. *Harvard Journal on Legislation, 28,* 465–498.

Fideler, E. F., & Haselkorn, D. (1999). *Learning the ropes: Urban teacher induction programs and practices in the United States.* Belmont, MA: Recruiting New Teachers.

Fine, M., Weis, L., & Powell, L. C. (1997). Communities of difference: A critical look at desegregated spaces created for and by youth. *Harvard Educational Review, 67,* 247–284.

Finley, M. K. (1984). Teachers and tracking in a comprehensive high school. *Sociology of Education, 57,* 233–243.

Fischer, C. F., & King, R. M. (1995). *Authentic assessment: A guide to implementation.* Thousand Oaks: Corwin Press.

Flowers, N., Mertens, S., & Mulhall, P. (2000). What makes interdisciplinary teams effective? *Middle School Journal, 31*(6), 53–56.

Fogarty, R. (1991). *The mindful school: How to integrate the curricula.* Arlington Heights, IL: Skylight Training and Publishing.

Fothergill, K. (1998). *Update 1997: School-based health centers*. Washington, DC: Advocates for Youth, Support Center for School-Based and School-Linked Health Care.

Freiberg, H. J., Connell, M., & Lorentz, J. (1997, March). *The effects of socially constructed classroom management on student mathematics achievement in seven elementary schools*. Paper presented at the annual meeting of the American Educational Research Association, Chicago.

French, D. (1998). The state's role in shaping a progressive vision of public education. *Phi Delta Kappan, 80*, 185–194.

Fried, R. L. (1998, December). Parent anxiety and school reform: When interests collide, whose needs come first? *Phi Delta Kappan, 80*, 264–271.

Fuhrman, S. H. (1999). The new accountability. *Consortium for Policy Research in Education: Policy Briefs*. University of Pennsylvania, Graduate School of Education, RB-27.

Fullan, M. (1993). *Change forces: Probing the depths of educational reform*. London: The Falmer Press.

Fullan, M. (1997). *What's worth fighting for in the principalship*. New York: Teachers College Press.

Fullan, M. (1998). Leadership for the 21st century—breaking the bonds of dependency. *Educational Leadership, 55*(7), 6–10.

Fullan, M., & Hargreaves, A. (1996). *What's worth fighting for in your school?* New York: Teachers College Press.

Fullan, M. G., & Miles, M. B. (1992). Getting reform right: What works and what doesn't. *Phi Delta Kappan, 73*, 745–752.

Galassi, J. P., Gulledge, S. A., & Cox, N. D. (1997). Middle school advisories: Retrospect and prospect. *Review of Educational Research, 67*, 301–338.

Gamoran, A., & Mare, R. D. (1989). Secondary school tracking and educational inequality: Reinforcement, compensation, or neutrality? *American Journal of Sociology, 94*, 1146–1183.

Gamoran, A., Nystrand, M., Berends, M., & LePorte, P. (1995). An organizational analysis of the effects of ability grouping. *American Educational Research Association Journal, 32*(4), 687–715.

Gardner, H. (1991). *The unschooled mind: How children think and how schools should teach*. New York: Basic Books.

Gatewood, T. E., & Mills, R. C. (1973). *Preparing teachers for the middle/junior high school: A survey and a model*. Research Report. Mount Pleasant, MI: Central Michigan University.

Gelb, M. J. (1998). *How to think like Leonardo da Vinci: Seven steps to genius every day*. New York: Delacorte Press.

George, P. S. (1999, Fall). *A middle school—If you can keep it: Part II*. Midpoints Occasional Papers, National Middle School Association.

George, P. S., & Alexander, W. M. (1993). *The exemplary middle school* (2nd ed.). Orlando, FL: Harcourt Brace & Co.

George, P. S., & Anderson, W. G. (1989). Maintaining the middle school: A national survey. *NASSP Bulletin, 73*, 67–74.

Gladden, R. (1998). The small school movement: A review of the literature. In M. Fine & G. I. Somerville (Eds.), *Small schools, big imaginations: A creative look at urban public schools* (pp. 113–137). Chicago: Cross City Campaign for Urban School Reform.

Glickman, C. D. (1993). *Renewing America's schools: A guide for site-based action*. San Francisco: Jossey-Bass.

Glickman, C. D. (1998). *Revolutionizing America's schools*. San Francisco: Jossey-Bass.

Goodenow, C. (1993). Classroom belonging among early adolescent students: Relationships to motivation and achievement. *Journal of Early Adolescence, 13*(1), 21–43.

Grady, D. (1999, April 7). Genetic damage in young smokers is linked to lung cancer. *The New York Times*, p. A17(L).

Gredler, M. E. (1999). *Classroom assessment and learning*. New York: Longman.

Greeno, J. (1991). Number sense as situated knowing in a conceptual domain. *Journal for Research in Mathematics Education, 22*(3), 170–218.

Greenwald, E. A., Persky, H. R., Campbell, J. R., & Mazzeo, J. (1999). *The NAEP 1998 writing report card for the nation and the states*, NCES 1999–462. Washington, DC: U.S. Department of Education. Office of Educational Research and Improvement. National Center for Education Statistics.

Greenwald, R., Hedges, L. V., & Laine, R. D. (1996). The effect of school resources on student achievement. *Review of Educational Research, 66*(3), 361–396.

Gregorc, A. F. (1987). *Inside styles: Beyond the basics.* Maynard, MA: Gabriel Systems, Inc. (P.O. Box 357, Maynard, MA 01754).

Guild, P. B., & Garger, S. (1998). *Marching to different drummers* (2nd ed.). Alexandria, VA: Association for Supervision and Curriculum Development.

Guiton, G., Oakes, J., Gong, J., Quartz, K. H., Lipton, M., & Balisok, J. (1995). Teaming: Creating small communities of learners in the middle grades. In J. Oakes & K. H. Quartz (Eds.), *Creating new educational communities. 94th yearbook of the National Society for the Study of Education* (pp. 87–107). Chicago: University of Chicago Press.

Guskey, T. R. (1994). Results-oriented professional development: In search of an optimal mix of effective practices. *Journal of Staff Development, 15*(4), 42–50.

Haas, T., & Nachtigal, P. (1998). *Place value: An educator's guide to good literature on rural lifeways, environments, and purposes of education.* Charleston, WV: ERIC Clearinghouse on Rural Education and Small Schools.

Hackmann, D. G. (1996). Student-led conferences at the middle level: Promoting student responsibility. *NASSP Bulletin, 80*(578), 31–36.

Halpern, R. (1992). The role of after-school programs in the lives of inner-city children: A study of the "Urban Youth Network." *Child Welfare League of America, LXXI,* No. 3, 215–230.

Hamburg, B. A. (1997). Education for healthy futures: Health promotion and life skills training. In R. Takanishi & D. A. Hamburg (Eds.), *Preparing adolescents for the twenty-first century: Challenges facing Europe and the United States* (pp. 108–135). Cambridge, United Kingdom: Cambridge University Press.

Harris, D., & Carr, J. F. (1996). *How to use standards in the classroom.* Alexandria, VA: Association for Supervision and Curriculum Development.

Haslam, M. B. (n.d.). *How to rebuild a local professional development infrastructure.* Arlington, VA: New American Schools.

Hatch, H., & Hytten, K. (1997). *Mobilizing resources for district-wide middle-grades reform.* Columbus, OH: National Middle School Association.

Hayden, L. (1998, Fall). Letting students lead parent conferences. *Middle Matters* [Online], 2 pages. Available: www.naesp.org/comm/mmf98b.htm [1999, May 18].

Henderson, A. T., & Berla, N. (Eds.). (1994). *A new generation of evidence: The family is critical to student achievement.* Washington, DC: Center for Law and Education.

Henderson, A. T., & Wilcox, S. (1998, August). *Now more than ever: Parent involvement in middle school education.* Unpublished paper prepared for Carnegie Corporation of New York for the Turning Points 2000 book project.

Herman, R. (1999). *An educators' guide to schoolwide reform.* Arlington, VA: Educational Research Service.

Hill, P. T. (1998). *Supplying effective public schools in big cities.* Unpublished manuscript, The Brookings Institution and the University of Washington.

Hipp, K. A. (1997). The impact of principals in sustaining middle school change. *Middle School Journal, 28*(5), 42–45.

Holland, H. (1997). The challenge of teaching: New report suggests major changes in training, organization and practice. *High Strides, 9*(4), 12–13.

Holland, H. (1998). *Making change: Three educators join the battle for better schools.* Portsmouth, NH: Heinemann.

Hopfenberg, W. S., Levin, H. M., Chase, C., Christensen, S. G., Moore, M., Soler, P., Brunner, I., Keller, B., & Rodriguez, G. (1993). *The Accelerated Schools: Resource guide.* San Francisco: Jossey-Bass.

Hornbeck, D. W. (1999, October 17). Philly schools and service learning. Letter to the editor. *Philadelphia Inquirer*, p. D6.

Hough, D. (1997). A bona fide middle school: Programs, policy, practice, and grade span configurations. In J. L. Irvin (Ed.), *What current research says to the middle level practitioner* (pp. 285–294). Columbus, OH: National Middle School Association.

Hough, D., & Irvin, J. L. (1997). Setting a research agenda. In J. L. Irvin (Ed.), *What current research says to the middle level practitioner* (pp. 351–356). Columbus, OH: National Middle School Association.

Huberman, M., & Miles, M. (1984). *Innovation up close*. New York: Plenum.

Huling-Austin, L. (1989). Beginning teacher assistance programs: An overview. In L. Huling-Austin, S. J. Odell, P. Ishler, R. S. Kay, & R. A. Edelfelt (Eds.), *Assisting the Beginning Teacher* (pp. 5–18). Reston, VA: Association of Teacher Educators.

Hurrelmann, K., & Klocke, A. (1997). The role of the school in comprehensive health promotion. In R. Takanishi & D. A. Hamburg (Eds.), *Preparing adolescents for the twenty-first century: Challenges facing Europe and the United States* (pp. 82–107). Cambridge, United Kingdom: Cambridge University Press.

Irvin, J. L. (1998). *Reading and the middle school student: Strategies to enhance literacy* (2nd ed.). Needham Heights, MA: Allyn & Bacon.

Jackson, A. W. (1997). Adapting educational systems to young adolescents and new conditions. In R. Takanishi & D. A. Hamburg (Eds.), *Preparing adolescents for the twenty-first century: Challenges facing Europe and the United States* (pp. 13–37). Cambridge, United Kingdom: Cambridge University Press.

Jacobs, H. H. (Ed.). (1989). *Interdisciplinary curriculum: Design and implementation*. Alexandria, VA: Association for Supervision and Curriculum Development.

Jenkins, D. M., & Jenkins, K. D. (1991). The NMSA Delphi report: Roadmap to the future. *Middle School Journal, 22*(4), 27–36.

Jessor, R., Turbin, M. S., & Costa, F. M. (1998). Protective factors in adolescent health behavior. *Journal of Personality and Social Psychology, 75*, 788–800.

Jessor, R., Van Den Bos, J., Vanderryn, J., Costa, F. M., & Turbin, M. S. (1995). Protective factors in adolescent problem behavior: Moderator effects and developmental change. *Developmental Psychology, 31*, 923–933.

Johns Hopkins University & Abt Associates, Inc. (1997). *Urban and suburban/rural special strategies for educating disadvantaged children: Final report*. Washington, DC: U.S. Department of Education, Planning and Evaluation Service.

Johnson, D. W., Johnson, R., Dudley, B., Ward, M., & Magnuson, D. (1995). The impact of peer mediation training on the management of school and home conflicts. *American Educational Research Journal, 32*, 829–844.

Johnston, L. D., O'Malley, P. M., & Bachman, J. G. (1999). Drug use by American young people begins to turn downward. In L. D. Johnston, P. M. O'Malley, & J. G. Bachman (Eds.), *National survey results on drug use from the Monitoring the Future study, 1975–1998. Volume I: Secondary school students*. NIH Publication No. 99-4660. Rockville, MD: National Institute on Drug Abuse.

Jones, J. P. (1997). Mature teams at work: Benchmarks and obstacles. In T. S. Dickinson & T. O. Erb (Eds.), *We gain more than we give: Teaming in middle schools* (pp. 205–228). Columbus, OH: National Middle School Association.

Joyce, B., & Showers, B. (1995). *Student achievement through staff development: Fundamentals of school renewal* (2nd ed.). White Plains, NY: Longman.

Joyce, B., & Weil, M. (in press). *Models of teaching* (6th ed.). Needham Heights, MA: Allyn & Bacon.

Kain, D. L. (1997). Misplaced camels, crowded captains, and achieving greatness: Leadership of interdisciplinary teams. In T. S. Dickinson & T. O. Erb (Eds.), *We gain more than we give: Teaming in middle schools* (pp. 403–424). Columbus, OH: National Middle School Association.

Kane, W. M. (1993). *Step by step to comprehensive school health: The program planning guide*. Santa Cruz, CA: ETR Associates.

Kann, L., Kinchen, S. A., Williams, B. I., Ross, J. G., Lowry, R., Hill, C. V., Grunbaum, J. A., Blumson, P. S., Collins, J. L., Kolbe, L. J., & State and Local YRBSS Coordinators. (1998, August 14). *Youth Risk Behavior Surveillance—United States, 1997, 47*(SS-3), 1–89. Washington, DC: U. S. Department of Health and Human Services, Centers for Disease Control and Prevention. [Available online at: www.cdc.gov/nccdphp/dash/MMWRFile/ss4703.htm.

Keene, E. O., & Zimmermann, S. (1997). *Mosaic of thought: Teaching comprehension in a reader's workshop.* Portsmouth, NH: Heinemann.

Kilgore, K., Webb, R. B., & the Faculty and Staff of Coral Springs Middle School, Broward County, Florida. (1997). Making shared decision making work. *Middle School Journal, 28*(5), 3–13.

Killion, J. (1999). *What works in the middle: Results-based staff development.* Oxford, Ohio: National Staff Development Council.

Klemp, R., & Special Guests. (1998, February). *The teaming process—A school wide process: Creating successful interdisciplinary small communities for learning.* Presentation at MGSSPI State Leaders' and Principals' National Conference, Anaheim, CA.

Knapp, M. S., Shields, P. M., & Turnbull, B. J. (1992). *Academic challenge for the children of poverty: Summary report.* Washington, DC: U.S. Department of Education, Office of Policy and Planning.

Koppich, J. E., & Knapp, M. (1998). *Federal research investment and the improvement of teaching, 1980–1997.* Washington DC: U.S. Department of Education.

Kramer, L. R. (1992). Young adolescents' perceptions of school. In J. L. Irvin (Ed.), *Transforming middle level education: Perspectives and possibilities* (pp. 28–45). Boston: Allyn & Bacon.

Kruse, S. D., & Louis, K. S. (1995). Teacher teaming: Opportunities and dilemmas. *Brief to Principals,* No. 11. Madison, WI: University of Wisconsin-Madison School of Education, Center on Organization and Restructuring of Schools.

Kruse, S. D., & Louis, K. S. (1997). Teacher teaming in middle schools: Dilemmas for a schoolwide community. *Educational Administration Quarterly, 33*(3), 261–289.

Lamme, J., & Hysmith, C. (1991). One school's adventure into portfolio assessment. *Language Arts, 68*(8), 620–629.

Larkin, J. H. (1981). Enriching formal knowledge: A model for learning to solve problems in physics. In J. R. Anderson (Ed.), *Cognitive skills and their acquisition* (pp. 311–334). Hillsdale, NJ: Lawrence Erlbaum Associates.

Larkin, J. H. (1983). The role of problem representation in physics. In D. Gentner, & A. L. Stevens (Eds.), *Mental models* (pp. 75–98). Hillsdale, NJ: Lawrence Erlbaum Associates.

Lawler, E. E., III. (1992). *The ultimate advantage: Creating the high-involvement organization.* San Francisco: Jossey-Bass.

Le Countryman, L., & Schroeder, M. (1996). When students lead parent-teacher conferences. *Educational Leadership, 53*(7), 64–68.

Lee, V. E., & Smith, J. B. (1993, July). Effects of school restructuring on the achievement and engagement of middle-grade students. *Sociology of Education, 66,* 164–187.

Leithwood, K., Jantzi, D., & Steinbach, R. (1995). An organisational learning perspective on school responses to central policy initiatives. *School Organisation, 15*(3), 229–252.

Lewis, A. C. (1991, Fall). *Gaining ground: The highs and lows of urban middle school reform, 1989–91.* New York: Edna McConnell Clark Foundation.

Lewis, A. C. (1992, September). *Urban youth in community service: Becoming part of the solution. ERIC/CUE Digest,* Number 81 [Online]. Available: ericae.net/db/digs/ed351425.htm [1999, June 25].

Lewis, A. C. (1993, Fall). *Changing the odds: Middle school reform in progress, 1991–93.* New York: Edna McConnell Clark Foundation.

Lewis, A. C. (1995, November). *Believing in ourselves: Progress and struggle in urban middle school reform.* New York: Edna McConnell Clark Foundation.

Lewis, A. C. (1999, Summer). *Figuring it out: Standards-based reforms in urban middle grades.* New York: Edna McConnell Clark Foundation.

Lewis, A. C., & Henderson, A. T. (1998). *Building bridges—Across schools and communities: Across streams of funding.* Chicago: Cross City Campaign for Urban School Reform.

Lindsay, G. B., & Rainey, J. (1997). Psychosocial and pharmacologic explanations of nicotine's "gateway drug" function. *Journal of School Health, 67,* 123–126.

Lipsitz, J. (1980). *Growing up forgotten.* New Brunswick, NJ: Transaction Books.

Lipsitz, J., Mizell, M. H., Jackson, A. W., & Austin, L. M. (1997). Speaking with one voice: A manifesto for middle-grades reform. *Phi Delta Kappan, 78,* 533–540.

Little, J. W. (1997, March). *Excellence in professional development and professional community.* Office of Educational Research and Improvement Working Paper. Benchmarks for Schools. Washington, DC: U.S. Department of Education, National Institute on Educational Governance, Finance, Policy Making, and Management.

Lohrmann, D. K., & Wooley, S. F. (1998). Comprehensive school health education. In E. Marx & S. F. Wooley with D. Northrop (Eds.), *Health is academic: A guide to coordinated school health programs* (pp. 43–66). New York: Teachers College Press.

Lounsbury, J., & Clark, D. C. (1990). *Inside grade eight: From apathy to excitement.* Reston, VA: National Association of Secondary School Principals.

Lyman, F. (1992). Think-pair-share, thinktrix, and weird facts. In N. Davidson & T. Worsham (Eds.), *Enhancing thinking through cooperative learning* (pp. 169–181). New York: Teachers College Press.

Lynn, L., & Wheelock, A. (1997a). Making Detracking Work. *The Harvard Education Newsletter, 13*(1), 1–5.

Lynn, L., & Wheelock, A. (1997b). Successful detracking: Navigating the political waters. *The Harvard Education Newsletter, 13*(1), 7–10.

Lyon, G. R. (1998). Why reading is not a natural process. *Educational Leadership, 55*(6), 14–18.

Mac Iver, D. J., & Epstein, J. L. (1993). Middle grades research: Not yet mature, but no longer a child. *The Elementary School Journal, 93,* 519–533.

Mac Iver, D. J., Mac Iver, M. A., Balfanz, R., Blank, S. B., & Ruby, A. (in press). Talent development middle schools: Blueprint and results for a comprehensive whole-school model. In W. Jordan & M. Sanders (Eds.), *Schooling students placed at risk: Research, policy, and practice in the education of poor and minority students.* Mahwah, NJ: Lawrence Erlbaum Associates.

Maeroff, G. I. (1993). *Team building for school change: Equipping teachers for new roles.* New York: Teachers College Press.

Many, J. E., Fyfe, R., Lewis, G., & Mitchell, E. (1996). Traversing the topical landscape: Exploring students' self-directed reading-writing-research processes. *Reading Research Quarterly, 31*(1), 12–35.

Manzo, K. K. (1998, November 18). NAEP paints poor picture of arts savvy. *Education Week,* pp. 1, 9.

Mapp, K. (1997). Making the connection between families and schools. *The Harvard Education Letter, XIII*(5), 1–3.

Marsh, R. S., & Raywid, M. A. (1994). How to make detracking work. *Phi Delta Kappan, 76,* 314–317.

Marshall, R., & Tucker, M. (1992). *Thinking for a living: Education and the wealth of nations.* New York: Basic Books.

Marzano, R. J. & Kendall, J. S. (1996). *A comprehensive guide to designing standards-based districts, schools, and classrooms.* Alexandria, VA: Association for Supervision and Curriculum Development and Aurora, CO: Mid-Continent Regional Educational Laboratory.

Marzano, R. J., & Pickering, D. J. (1997). *Dimensions of learning: Teacher's manual* (2nd ed.). Alexandria, VA & Aurora, CO: Association for Supervision and Curriculum Development and Mid-continent Regional Educational Laboratory.

Masten, A. S. (1994). Resilience in individual development: Successful adaptation despite risk and adversity. In M. C. Wang & E. W. Gordon (Eds.), *Educational resilience in inner city America: Challenges and prospects* (pp. 3–25). Hillsdale, NJ: Lawrence Erlbaum Associates.

McCarthy, B. (1987). *The 4MAT system: Teaching to learning styles with right/left mode techniques.* Barrington, IL: Excel, Inc. (200 West Station St., Barrington, IL 60010).

McDiarmid, G. W. (1995, April). Realizing new learning for all students: A framework for the professional development of Kentucky teachers. *NCRTL Special Report.* East Lansing, MI: Michigan State University, College of Education, National Center for Research on Teacher Learning.

McDonald, J. P., & Naso, P. (1986). *Teacher as learner: The impact of technology.* Cambridge, MA: Educational Technology Center, Graduate School of Education, Harvard University.

McEwin, C. K., & Dickinson, T. S. (1995). *The professional preparation of middle level teachers: Profiles of successful programs.* Columbus, OH: National Middle School Association.

McEwin, C. K., & Dickinson, T. S. (1996). *Forgotten youth, forgotten teachers: Transformation of the professional preparation of teachers of young adolescents.* Middle Grades School State Policy Initiative, Carnegie Corporation of New York.

McEwin, C. K., Dickinson, T. S., Erb, T. O., & Scales, P. C. (1995). *A vision of excellence: Organizing principles for middle grades teacher preparation.* Columbus, OH: National Middle School Association.

McEwin, C. K., Dickinson, T. S., & Hamilton, H. (2000). National board certified teachers' views regarding specialized middle level teacher preparation. *The Clearing House, 73*(4), 211–213.

McEwin, C. K., Dickinson, T. S., & Jenkins, D. M. (1996). *America's middle schools: Practices and progress—A 25 year perspective.* Columbus, OH: National Middle School Association.

McEwin, C. K., Dickinson, T. S., & Swaim, J. H. (1997). *Specialized middle level teacher preparation in the United States: A status report.* Boone, NC: Appalachian State University.

McLaughlin, M. J. (2000). *Reform for EVERY learner: Teacher's views on standards and students with disabilities.* Alexandria, VA: The Center for Policy Research on the Impact of General and Special Education Reform on Students with Disabilities.

Mendel, E. (1999, March 20). Education reformers study Texas. *The San Diego Union-Tribune,* pp. A–1, A–16.

Merritt, J. C. (1998, July). *Targeted review: The role of the school district in promoting high performance middle schools.* Unpublished paper commissioned by Carnegie Corporation of New York for the Turning Points 2000 book project.

Mertens, S. B., & Flowers, N. (1998, November). *The effects of latchkey status on middle-grades students: New research findings.* Paper presented at the annual conference of the National Middle School Association, Denver, CO.

Mertens, S. B., Flowers, N., & Mulhall, P. F. (1998, August). *The Middle Start Initiative, Phase I: A longitudinal analysis of Michigan middle-level schools.* University of Illinois, Center for Prevention Research & Development.

Midgley, C., & Edelin, K. C. (1998). Middle school reform and early adolescent well-being: The good news and the bad. *Educational Psychologist, 33*(4), 195–206.

Miller, B. M. (1998, November). *Border zones: Out-of-school time and young adolescents.* Unpublished paper commissioned by Carnegie Corporation of New York for the Turning Points 2000 book project. Wellesley, MA: National Institute on Out-of-School Time, Center for Research on Women, Wellesley College.

Millstein, S. G., & Litt, I. F. (1990). Adolescent health. In S. S. Feldman & G. R. Elliott (Eds.), *At the threshold: The developing adolescent* (pp. 431–456). Cambridge: Harvard University Press.

Mitchell, R. (1992). *Testing for learning: How new approaches to evaluation can improve American schools.* New York: The Free Press.

Mitchell, R. (1996). *Front-end alignment: Using standards to steer educational change: A manual for developing standards.* Washington, DC: The Education Trust.

Mitchell, R., Willis, M., & the Chicago Teachers Union Quest Center. (1995). *Learning in overdrive: Designing curriculum, instruction, and assessment from standards.* Golden, CO: North American Press.

Mohrman, S. A., Cohen, S. G., & Mohrman, A. M., Jr. (1995). *Designing team-based organizations: New forms for knowledge work.* San Francisco: Jossey-Bass.

Morrow, C. (1999, April). Remarks during Middle Grade School State Policy Initiative training session, Moving toward interdisciplinary curriculum, Chicago.

Murphy, J. (in press). *Leadership for tomorrow's schools.* A report to the U.S. Department of Education. Washington, DC: U.S. Department of Education, Office of Educational Research and Improvement, National Institute on Educational Governance, Finance, Policymaking, and Management.

National Assessment Governing Board. (n.d.). *What do students know? 1996 NAEP science results for 4th, 8th, & 12th graders* [Online]. Available: www.nagb.org/pubs/students/nation.html [1999, May 19].

National Association of Secondary School Principals. (1985). *An agenda for excellence at the middle level.* Reston, VA: Author.

National Association for Sport and Physical Education. (1992). *Guidelines for middle school physical education.* Reston, VA: AAHPERD Publications.

National Association for Sport and Physical Education. (1995). *Moving into the future: National standards for physical education.* St. Louis: C. V. Mosby.

National Association of State Directors of Teacher Education and Certification. (1994). *NASDTEC outcome-based standards and portfolio assessment: Outcome-based teacher education standards for the elementary, middle and high school levels.* Mashpee, MA: Author.

National Center for Education Statistics. (1998a, February 24). *Riley urges students to take tougher courses: Challenges schools and states to raise academic, testing and teaching standards in math and science* (Press Release) [Online]. Available: www.nces.ed.gov/pressrelease/timss298.html [1999, May 18].

National Center for Education Statistics. (1998b). *Toward better teaching: Professional development in 1993–94* (NCES 98-230). Washington, DC: U.S. Department of Education.

National Center for Education Statistics. (1999, September). *Service-learning and community service in K–12 public schools* (NCES 1999-043). Washington, DC: U.S. Department of Education.

National City Middle School. *Schoolwide profile, preface, Spring 1997.* National City, CA.

National Commission on Teaching & America's Future. (1996). *What matters most: Teaching for America's future.* New York: Author.

National Commission on Teaching & America's Future. (1997). *Fact sheet 1997.* New York: Author.

National Education Goals Panel. (1993). *Promises to keep: Creating high standards for American students: Report on the review of education standards from the goals 3 and 4 technical planning group to the National Education Goals Panel.* Washington, DC: Author.

National Institute of Mental Health. (n.d.). *Adolescent depression* [Online]. Available: www.nimh.nih.gov/depression/newhope/adolscnt.htm [1999, June 4].

National Middle School Association. (1995). *This we believe: Developmentally responsive middle level schools.* Columbus, OH: Author.

National Middle School Association. (1997). *National Middle School Association/National Council for the Accreditation of Teacher Education—Approved curriculum guidelines handbook.* Columbus, OH: Author.

National Middle School Association. (Pre-publication, January 1999). *NMSA research summary #16: What are appropriate assessment practices for middle school students?* Columbus, OH: Author.

National Middle School Association. (in press). *The professional preparation of middle level teachers: A position paper of the National Middle School Association.* Columbus, OH: Author.

National Staff Development Council. (1994). *Standards for staff development: Middle level edition.* Oxford, OH: Author.

Neill, M., & FairTest Staff. (1997). *Testing our children: A report card on state assessment systems.* Cambridge, MA: The National Center for Fair and Open Testing.

Newmann, F. M. (1993). Beyond common sense in educational restructuring: The issues of content and linkage. *Educational Researcher, 22*(2), 4–22.

Newmann, F. M., & Associates. (1996). *Authentic achievement: Restructuring schools for intellectual quality*. San Francisco: Jossey-Bass.

Newmann, F. M., Lopez, G., & Bryk, A. S. (1998, October). *The quality of intellectual work in Chicago schools: A baseline report*. Prepared for the Chicago Annenberg Research Project.

Newmann, F. M., Marks, H., & Gamoran, A. (1995). Authentic pedagogy: Standards that boost student performance. *Issues in Restructuring Schools, 8*, 1–11.

Newmann, F. M., Secada, W. G., & Wehlage, G. G. (1995). *A guide to authentic instruction and assessment: Vision, standards, and scoring*. Madison, WI: Wisconsin Center for Education Research.

Newmann, F. M., & Wehlage, G. G. (1995). *Successful school restructuring: A report to the public and educators by the Center on Organization and Restructuring of Schools*. Madison, WI: University of Wisconsin, Center on Organization and Restructuring of Schools, School of Education, Wisconsin Center for Education Research.

North Central Regional Educational Laboratory. (1997). *Finding time for professional Development* [Online]. Available: www.ncrel.org/sdrs/areas/issues/educatrs/profdevl/pd300.htm [1998, March 25].

Nunnery, J. A. (1998). Reform ideology and the locus of development problem in educational restructuring: Enduring lessons from studies of educational innovation. *Education and Urban Society, 30*(3), 277–295.

Oakes, J. (1985). *Keeping track: How schools structure inequality*. New Haven, CT: Yale University Press.

Oakes, J. (1990). *Multiplying inequalities: The effects of race, social class, and tracking on opportunities to learn math and science*. Santa Monica, CA: RAND.

Oakes, J. (1992). Foreword. In A. Wheelock, *Crossing the tracks: How "untracking" can save America's schools* (pp. ix–xv). New York: The New Press.

Oakes, J. (1995). More than meets the eye: Links between tracking and the culture of schools. In H. Pool & J. A. Page (Eds.), *Beyond tracking: Finding success in inclusive schools* (pp. 59–68). Bloomington, IN: Phi Delta Kappa Educational Foundation.

Oakes, J., Gamoran, A., & Page, R. N. (1992). Curriculum differentiation: Opportunities, outcomes, and meanings. In P. W. Jackson (Ed.), *Handbook of research on curriculum* (pp. 570–608). New York: Macmillan.

Oakes, J., Quartz, K. H., Ryan, S., & Lipton, M. (2000). *Becoming Good American Schools: The Struggle for Civic Virtue in Education Reform*. San Francisco: Jossey-Bass.

Odden, A., & Busch, C. (1998). *Financing schools for high performance: Strategies for improving the use of educational resources*. San Francisco: Jossey-Bass.

Odden, A., & Hill, P. (1997, February). *District roles in decentralization: Creating and managing a decentralized education system*. Paper prepared for the New American Schools Development Corporation.

Olson, L. (2000, January 13). Finding and keeping competent teachers. *Education Week, XIX*(18), 12–18.

Olson, L., & Jerald, C. D. (1998, January 8). The achievement gap. In V. B. Edwards (Ed.), Quality Counts '98. The urban challenge: Public education in the 50 states [Special issue]. *Education Week, XVII*, 10–13. [Published in Collaboration with Pew Charitable Trusts].

Opuni, K. A. (1998, November 20). *Project GRAD program evaluation report, executive summary*. Houston, TX: Houston Independent School District.

Page, R. N. (1991). *Lower track classrooms: A curricular and cultural perspective*. New York: Teachers College Press.

Parrish, T. B., & Hikido, C. S. (1998). *Inequalities in public school district revenues* (NCES 98-210). Project Officer, William J. Fowler. Washington, DC: U.S. Department of Education, National Center for Education Statistics.

Partee, G. (1996, April 22). *Reengaging families and communities in the education of young adolescents: A guide for middle grade school reform*. Unpublished paper commissioned by Carnegie Corporation of New York.

Pate, P. E., Homestead, E. R., & McGinnis, K. L. (1997). *Making integrated curriculum work: Teachers, students, and the quest for coherent curriculum.* New York: Teachers College Press.

Paulu, N. (n.d.). *Helping your students with homework: A guide for teachers.* Washington, DC: U.S. Department of Education, Office of Educational Research and Improvement.

Pounder, D. G. (1998). *Restructuring schools for collaboration: Promises and pitfalls.* Albany: State University of New York Press.

Powell, R. R., & Faircloth, C. V. (1997). Current issues and research in middle level curriculum: On conversations, semantics, and roots. In J. L. Irvin (Ed.), *What current research says to the middle level practitioner.* Columbus, OH: National Middle School Association.

President's Student Service Challenge Web Site [Online]. Available: www.student-service-awards.org [1999, June 29].

Price, R. H., Gioci, M., Penner, W., & Trautlein, B. (1993). Webs of influence: School and community programs that enhance adolescent health and education. In R. Takanishi (Ed.), *Adolescence in the 1990s: Risk and opportunity* (pp. 29–63). New York: Teachers College Press.

Ray, S. (1999). Quoted in *An interdisciplinary tiff* [Online]. Available: www.middleweb.com/INCASEIndisTift.html [1999, July 16].

Reese, C. M., Miller, K. E., Mazzeo, J., & Dossey, J. A. (1997). *NAEP 1996 mathematics report card for the nation and the states.* Washington, DC: U.S. Department of Education, Office of Educational Research and Improvement, National Center for Education Statistics.

Renyi, J. (1996). *Teachers take charge of their learning: Transforming professional development for student success.* Washington DC: National Foundation for the Improvement for Education.

Resnick, M. D., Bearman, P. S., Blum, R. W., Bauman, K. E., Harris, K. M., Jones, J., Tabor, J., Beuhring, T., Sieving, R. E., Shew, M., Ireland, M., Bearinger, L. H., Udry, J. R. (1997). Protecting adolescents from harm: Findings from the National Longitudinal Study on Adolescent Health. *Journal of the American Medical Association, 278,* 823–832.

Riera, M. (1995). *Uncommon sense for parents with teenagers.* Berkeley, CA: Celestial Arts.

Rogers, T. M. (1992, October). To give or not to give—Homework. *NASSP Bulletin, 76,* 13–15.

Rotberg, I. C., Futrell, M. H., & Lieberman, J. L. (1998). National board certification: Increasing participation and assessing impacts. *Phi Delta Kappan, 79,* 462–466.

Ruenzel, D. (1998, September 16). War of attrition. *Education Week, 18*(2), 32–37.

Rugen, L. (1998, Fall). Building informed and reflective practice. *Center for Collaborative Education NEWS, 1–3,* 6, 11.

Ryan, S., Guiton G., & Gong, J. (1996, September). *The implementation of* Turning Points: *Clarence Darrow Middle School case report.* Technical Report #D2-96/UCLA/RDSC/TP. UCLA Graduate School of Education and Information Studies, Research for Democratic School Communities.

Salinas, K. C., Clark, L. A., Simon, B. S., & Van Voorhis, F. (1998). *Promising partnership practices 1998.* Baltimore: Johns Hopkins University, National Network of Partnership Schools.

Sanders, M. G., & Epstein, J. L. (1998, August). *School-family-community partnerships in middle and high schools: From theory to practice* [Online]. Available: www.csos.jhu.edu/crespar/CRESPAR%20Reports/report22entire.htm [1999, June 14].

Santa, C. M. (1995). Students lead their own parent conferences. *Teaching Pre K-8, 25*(7), 92, 94.

Saphier, J., & Gower, R. (1997). *The skillful teacher: Building your teaching skills* (5th ed.). Acton, MA: Research for Better Teaching.

Sarason, S. B. (1990). *The predictable failure of educational reform: Can we change course before it's too late?* San Francisco: Jossey-Bass.

Scales, P. C. (1992). *Windows of opportunity: Improving middle grades teacher preparation.* Chapel Hill: University of North Carolina, Center for Early Adolescence.

Scales, P. C. (1996). *Boxed in and bored: How middle schools continue to fail young adolescents—And what good middle schools do right.* Minneapolis: Search Institute.

Scales, P. C. (1999). Increasing service-learning's impact on middle school students. *Middle School Journal, 30*(5), 40–44.

Scales, P. C., & McEwin, C. K. (1994). *Growing pains: The making of America's middle school teachers.* Columbus, OH: National Middle School Association.

Scales, P. C., & McEwin, C. K. (1996). The effects of comprehensive middle level teacher preparation programs. *Research in Middle Level Education Quarterly, 19*(2), 1–21.

Schiamberg, L. B., & Chun, C. (1986). *The influence of family on educational and occupational achievement.* Paper presented at the annual meeting of the American Association for the Advancement of Science, Philadelphia.

Schine, J. (1998, May). *Parent and community involvement in the education of young adolescents.* Berkeley, CA: MPR Associates.

Schmidt, W. H., McKnight, C. C., & Raizen, S. (1997). *A splintered vision: An investigation of U.S. science and mathematics education.* Dordrecht/Boston/London: Kluwer Academic Publishers.

Schmoker, M., & Marzano, R. J. (1999). Realizing the promise of standards-based education. *Educational Leadership, 56*(6), 17–21.

Schofield, J. W. (1995). Promoting positive intergroup relations in school settings. In W. D. Hawley & A. W. Jackson (Eds.), *Toward a common destiny: Improving race and ethnic relations in America* (pp. 257–289). San Francisco: Jossey-Bass.

Schumacher, D. H. (1995). Five levels of curriculum integration defined, refined, and described. *Research in Middle Level Education, 18*(3), 73–94.

Schurr, S. (1996, September/October). Balancing acts: Student-centered and subject-centered instruction. *Schools in the Middle, 6*(1), 11–15.

Senge, P. M. (1990). *The fifth discipline: The art and practice of the learning organization.* New York: Doubleday.

Senge, P. M., Kleiner, A., Roberts, C., Ross, B. R., & Smith, B. J. (1994). *The fifth discipline fieldbook: Strategies and tools for building a learning organization.* New York: Doubleday.

Serna, I., & Guiton, G. (1996, September). *The implementation of* Turning Points: *Jimmy Carter Middle School case report.* Technical Report #C1-96/UCLA/RDSC/TP. UCLA Graduate School of Education and Information Studies, Research for Democratic School Communities.

Shapiro, S., & Klemp, R. (1996). The interdisciplinary team organization: Promoting teacher efficacy and collaboration. *Michigan Middle School Journal, 20*(2), 26–32.

Shields, P. M., & Knapp, M. S. (1997). The promise and limits of school-based reform: A national snapshot. *Phi Delta Kappan, 79,* 288–294.

Shinnyo-En Foundation, Northeast Foundation for Children, Kensington Avenue Elementary School. (1999). *Do social skills enable academic skills?* Greenfield, MA: Northeast Foundation for Children. [Available: www.responsiveclassroom.org/consult_4.htm in pdf format]

Showers, B., Joyce, B., & Bennett, B. (1987, November). Synthesis of research on staff development: A framework for future study and a state-of-the-art analysis. *Educational Leadership, 45*(3), 77–87.

Showers, B., Joyce, B., Scanlon, M., & Schnaubelt, C. (1998). A second chance to learn to read. *Educational Leadership, 55*(6), 27–30.

Silver, E., & Lane, S. (1995). Can instructional reform in urban middle schools help students narrow the mathematics performance gap? *Research in Middle Level Education, 18*(2), 49–70.

Sims, R. R., & Sims, S. J. (Eds.). (1995). *The importance of learning styles: Understanding the implications for learning, course design, and education.* Westport, CT: Greenwood Press.

Slavin, R. E. (1995). Enhancing intergroup relations in schools: Cooperative learning and other strategies. In W. D. Hawley & A. W. Jackson (Eds.), *Toward a common destiny: Improving race and ethnic relations in America* (pp. 291–314). San Francisco: Jossey-Bass.

Slavin, R. E. (1999). *Technical proposal: Design, development, and testing of comprehensive school reform models.* Baltimore: Success for All Foundation.

Slavin, R. E., & Fashola, O. S. (1998). *Show me the evidence! Proven and promising programs for America's schools.* Thousand Oaks, CA: Corwin Press.

Snow, C. E., Barnes, W. S., Chandler, J., Goodman, I. F., & Hemphill, L. (1991). *Unfulfilled expectations: Home and school influences on literacy.* Cambridge, MA: Harvard University Press.

Snyder, T., & Wirt, J. (1998). *The condition of education, 1998.* Washington, DC: U.S. Department of Education, National Center for Education Statistics.

Sparks, D. (1994, March 3). *Professional development for high student achievement.* Speech at the Middle Grade School State Policy Initiative conference, Providence, RI.

Sparks, D. (1997, September). A new vision for staff development. *Principal,* 21–23.

Sparks, D. (1998, September). Teachers must be staff development leaders. *Results,* 2.

Squires, S. (1996, March 5). Are all those tests really necessary? *The Washington Post,* p. Z7.

Steinberg, L., Brown, B. B., & Dornbusch, S. M. (1996). *Beyond the classroom, Why school reform has failed and what parents need to do.* New York: Simon & Schuster.

Stevenson, D. L., & Baker, D. P. (1987). The family-school relation and the child's school performance. *Child Development, 58,* 1348–1357.

Stowell, L., & McDaniel, J. (1997). The changing face of assessment. In J. L. Irvin (Ed.), *What current research says to the middle level practitioner* (pp. 137–150). Columbus, OH: National Middle School Association.

Stringfield, S. (1995). Attempting to enhance students' learning through innovative programs: The case for schools evolving into high reliability organizations. *School Effectiveness and School Improvement, 6*(1), 1–30. (Swets & Zeitlinger, Lisse, The Netherlands.)

Success for All Foundation. (1998). *A proven schoolwide program for the elementary grades: Success for All* [Brochure]. Baltimore, MD: Author.

Summers, A. A., & Johnson, A. W. (1995). Doubts about decentralized decisions: Research questions positive correlation between site-based management and student outcomes. *The School Administrator, 52*(3), 24–32.

Tatum, B. D. (1997). *"Why are all the black kids sitting together in the cafeteria?": And other conversations about race.* New York: Basic Books.

Texas Education Agency. (1999). *Moving toward interdisciplinary curriculum: Trainer's manual for a guidebook, middle school edition.* Austin, TX: Author.

Thomas, D. (1997). "It's not like we have good models to follow. We're learning as we're doing it." A case study of the dolphin team. In T. S. Dickinson & T. O. Erb (Eds.), *We gain more than we give: Teaming in middle schools* (pp. 93–117). Columbus, OH: National Middle School Association.

Thompson, J. D. (1967). *Organizations in action: Social science bases of administrative theory.* New York: McGraw-Hill.

Tierney, R. J., Soter, A., O'Flahavan, J. F., & McGinley, W. (1989). The effects of reading and writing upon thinking critically. *Reading Research Quarterly, 24*(2), 134–173.

Tomlinson, C. A. (1995). *How to differentiate instruction in mixed-ability classrooms.* Alexandria, VA: Association for Supervision and Curriculum Development.

Tomlinson, C. A. (1998). For integration and differentiation choose concepts over topics. *Middle School Journal, 30*(2), 3–8.

Tomlinson, C. A. (1999). *The differentiated classroom: Responding to the needs of all learners.* Alexandria, VA: Association for Supervision and Curriculum Development.

Tucker, M. S., & Codding, J. B. (1998). *Standards for our schools: How to set them, measure them, and reach them.* San Francisco: Jossey-Bass.

Tyack, D., & Cuban, L. (1995). *Tinkering toward utopia.* Cambridge, MA: Harvard University Press.

Tye, K. A. (1985). *The junior high school in search of a mission.* Lanham, MD: University Press of America.

Tyson, H. (1999). Kappan Special Report—A load off the teachers' backs: Coordinated school health programs. *Phi Delta Kappan, 80,* K1–K8.

U.S. Department of Education. (1995). *Building bridges: The mission and principles of professional development.* Washington, DC: Author.

U.S. Department of Education, National Center for Education Statistics, Office of Educational Research and Improvement. (1999, September). *Service-learning and community service in K-12 public schools* (NCES 1999-043). Washington, DC: Author.

U.S. Department of Education, Office of Educational Research and Improvement. (1999, June 3—last update). *21st century community learning centers* [Online]. Available: www.ed.gov/offices/OERI/21stCCLC/ [1999, July 19].

U.S. Department of Health and Human Services, Office of the Assistant Secretary for Planning and Evaluation. (n.d.). *Trends in the well-being of America's children & youth 1998.* Washington, DC: Author.

U.S. General Accounting Office. (1997, May 29). Abstracts of GAO reports and testimony FY97. *Welfare reform: Implications of increased work participation for child care HEHS-97-75* [Online]. Available: www.gao.gov/AIndexFY97/abstracts/he97075.htm [1999, July19].

Urdan, T., & Klein, S. (1998, May 7–8). *Early adolescence: A review of the literature.* Paper prepared for the U.S. Department of Education, Office of Educational Research and Improvement.

Useem, E. L., Barends, R., & Lindermayer, K. (1999). *The preparation of middle grades teachers in an era of high stakes and high standards: Philadelphia's predicament.* Philadelphia: Philadelphia Education Fund.

Useem, E. L., Christman, J. B., Gold, E., & Simon, E. (1997). Reforming alone: Barriers to organizational learning in urban school change initiatives. *Journal of Education of Students Placed At Risk, 2*(1), 55–78.

Valdés, G. (1998). The world outside and inside schools: Language and immigrant children. *Educational Researcher, 27*(6), 4–18.

Valentine, J. W., Clark, D. D., Irvin, J. L., Keefe, J. W., & Melton, G. (1993). *Leadership in middle level education: A national survey of middle level leaders and schools* (Vol. 1). Reston, VA: National Association of Secondary School Principals.

Valentine, J. W., & Whitaker, T. (1997). Organizational trends and practices in middle level schools. In J. L. Irvin (Ed.), *What current research says to the middle level practitioner* (pp. 277–283). Columbus, OH: National Middle School Association.

Valentine, J. W., Trimble, S., & Whitaker, T. (1997). The middle level principalship. In J. L. Irvin (Ed.)., *What current research says to the middle level practitioner* (pp. 337–347). Columbus, OH: National Middle School Association.

Valentine, J. W., & Mogar, D. (1992). Middle level certification: An encouraging evolution. *Middle School Journal, 24*(2), 36–43.

Wagner, T. (1998). Change as collaborative inquiry: A "Constructivist" methodology for reinventing schools. *Phi Delta Kappan, 79,* 512–517.

Walker, R., Palumbo, J., Nelson, J., & Artwell, B. (1998, September). *What it takes to be a successful middle-grades principal.* Education Development Center, Inc., Newton, MA. Unpublished paper commissioned by Carnegie Corporation of New York for the Turning Points 2000 book project.

Watson, M., Battistich, V., & Solomon, D. (1997). Enhancing students' social and ethical development in schools: An intervention program and its effects. *International Journal of Educational Research, 27,* 571–586.

Wehlage, G., Newmann, F., & Secada, W. (1996). Standards for authentic achievement and pedagogy. In F. M. Newmann & Associates (Eds.), *Authentic achievement: Restructuring schools for intellectual quality* (pp. 21–48). San Francisco: Jossey-Bass.

Wells, A., & Serna, I. (1996). The politics of culture: Understanding local political resistance to detracking in racially mixed schools. *Harvard Educational Review, 66,* 93–118.

Wenglinsky, H. (1998). *Policy information report: Does it compute? The relationship between educational technology and student achievement in mathematics.* Princeton, NJ: Policy Information Center, Research Division, Educational Testing Service.

West, M. (1998). Quality in schools: Developing a model for school improvement. In A. Hargreaves, A. Lieberman, M. Fullan, & D. Hopkins (Eds.), *International handbook of educational change* (pp. 768–789). Dordrecht, The Netherlands: Kluwer Academic Publishers.

Wheelock, A. (1992). *Crossing the tracks: How "untracking" can save America's schools.* New York: The New Press.

Wheelock, A. (1998). *Safe to be smart: Building a culture for standards-based reform in the middle grades.* Columbus, OH: National Middle School Association.

White, S. (1999). *The NAEP 1998 reading report card: National and state highlights* (NCES 1999-479). Washington, DC: U.S. Department of Education, Office of Educational Research and Improvement, National Center for Education Statistics.

Wiggins, G. (1998). *Educative assessment: Designing assessments to inform and improve student performance.* San Francisco: Jossey-Bass.

Wiggins, G., & McTighe, J. (1998). *Understanding by design.* Alexandria, VA: Association for Supervision and Curriculum Development.

Wiley, J. A., Robinson, J., Cheng, Y., Piazza, T., Stork, L., & Pladsen, K. (1991). *Study of children's activity patterns: Final report.* Sacramento, CA: Research Division, California Air Resources Board.

Witkin, H., & Goodenough, D. R. (1981). *Cognitive styles: Essence and origins.* New York: International Universities Press, Inc. (Available from Consulting Psychologists Press, Inc., 577 College Ave., Palo Alto, CA 94306).

Wohlstetter, P., & Griffin, N. C. (1997, September). First lessons: Charter schools as learning communities. *CPRE Policy Briefs* (RB-22), 1–9.

Wohlstetter, P., & Odden, A. (1992). Rethinking school-based management policy and research. *Educational Administration Quarterly, 28*(4), 529–549.

Wolk, R. A. (1998, November 4). Strategies for fixing failing public schools. *Education Week,* pp. 43–47. (Special Paid Section by Pew Forum on Education Reform)

Zemelman, S., Daniels, H., & Hyde, A. (1998). *Best practice: New standards for teaching and learning in America's schools.* Portsmouth, NH: Heinemann.

Zill, N., Nord, C. W., & Loomis, L. S. (1995, September 11). *Adolescent time use, risky behavior, and outcomes: An analysis of national data.* Contract #HHS-100-92-0005, Children and Youth Data Analysis Projects. Rockville, MD: Westat, Inc.

Index

ABOUT THE AUTHORS

Anthony Jackson is a director of The Walt Disney Company's Disney Learning Partnership. Jackson directs the Creative Learning Communities grant program, the cornerstone of Disney Learning Partnership's program to support collaborative, schoolwide learning initiatives. Before joining The Walt Disney Company in October 1998, he had been a program officer for Carnegie Corporation of New York, director of education for the Carnegie Council on Adolescent Development, and a senior staff member of the Select Committee on Children, Youth and Families in the United States House of Representatives. Jackson is the primary author of Carnegie Corporation's landmark 1989 report, *Turning Points: Preparing American Youth for the 21st Century.* He is the editor of two books, *Toward a Common Destiny: Improving Race and Ethnic Relations in America* (1995) and *Black Families and the Medium of Television* (1982), and the author of numerous articles on education and related issues.

Gayle A. Davis is a faculty research associate at the University of Maryland at College Park, where she manages projects within the Institute for the Study of Exceptional Children and Youth. She is currently chair of the National Middle School Association's Research Committee, and she also serves on the National Forum To Accelerate Middle Grades Reform and the Association Council for the American Educational Research Association's Special Interest Group on Research in Middle Level Education. Before joining the University of Maryland staff, she was on the technical assistance team for the Middle Grade School State Policy Initiative (MGSSPI) for nearly eight years, first as project associate, then senior associate, and finally as national director. A graduate of the University of North Carolina at Chapel Hill (B.A. and Ph.D.), she has also been a middle grades teacher, a project coordinator for the Center for Early Adolescence, and a consultant for various middle grades reform efforts.

ABOUT THE TURNING POINTS NATIONAL NETWORK

In 1999, Carnegie Corporation of New York asked the Center for Collaborative Education (CCE) in Boston to develop the Turning Points principles into a more complete model for middle grades school reform. Today, Turning Points is a comprehensive middle grades school reform design that helps educators across the nation transform their classrooms and schools.

The Turning Points reform model enables middle grades schools to create caring and challenging learning communities that meet the needs of young adolescents as they reach the "turning point" between childhood and adulthood. Based on a decade of research and experience, this comprehensive school reform model focuses on data-based inquiry and teacher collaboration to improve student learning. Turning Points staff work closely with teachers and administrators to improve learning, teaching, and assessment and to create the school culture, structures, and supports that enable students to learn and achieve at high levels. A Turning Points middle grades school challenges young adolescents with engaging and worthwhile work, while supporting them with close-knit relationships.

For more information about the Turning Points middle grades school reform model and the National Turning Points Network, please contact:

The Center for Collaborative Education
1135 Tremont Street
Boston, Massachusetts 02120
(617) 421–0134